THE AUSTERITY OLYMPICS

When the Games Came to London in 1948

Janie Hampton

Foreword by Sebastian Coe

WINDSOR
PARAGON

First published 2008
by Aurum Press Ltd
This Large Print edition published 2012
by AudioGO Ltd
by arrangement with
Aurum Press Limited

Hardcover   ISBN: 978 1 445 84297 4
Softcover   ISBN: 978 1 445 84298 1

British Library Cataloguing in Publication Data available

Printed and bound in Great Britain by
MPG Books Group Limited

THE AUSTERITY OLYMPICS

CONTENTS

FOREWORD

by Sebastian Coe

That London managed to stage the 1948 Olympic Games so soon after the Second World War is remarkable enough. The fact that the London Games ran like clockwork and produced important legacies for world sport, the international community and the Olympic Movement is another story, a story that has remained largely untold—until now.

Janie Hampton's *The Austerity Olympics* details the unprecedented challenges and risks involved in staging the Games in the aftermath of the world war. It tells the story of the administrators and athletes who beat the odds to organise and perform at the biggest sporting event ever staged. The Games involved over 4,000 men and women from 59 countries, many competing for the first time, across 136 events.

By tracking down many of the survivors at the heart of Games planning, services, and competition, by speaking with spectators and inter-national visitors, and by combing through libraries and archives around the world, Hampton vividly brings alive the cast of characters and circumstances that shaped the 1948 Games.

In a bomb-shattered landscape still with rationing of food, clothing and petrol, London's challenge was unlike that of any other Olympic host city. But austerity did not mean misery or unhappiness—it meant 'Make Do' and ingenuity as well. It is now clear that much was riding on the success of the London Games which represented a new start for both Britain and the Olympic Movement. The Games had not been held since Hitler's controversial Berlin Olympics twelve years earlier, and it was vital that they reflected the Olympic ideals of equality and fair play, and were staged without political or racial propaganda.

'We want to see the best men win, no matter where they come from or who they represent,' said Sir Arthur J. Elvin, Chairman of the old Wembley Stadium, which served as the Olympic stadium centrepiece. Off the field, the race against time to prepare for the Games was as compelling as the competition on the track. Work to upgrade the greyhound track to an international sports stadium was completed in under two months.

Hampton's book conveys the unique power of the Olympic Games to change lives and bring people and countries closer—on and off the sporting field. Most of the US team, for example, travelled together by ship to London, enabling black and white Americans, racially segregated at home, to mix for the first time. 'I shook hands with my first black American on board ship,' remembered rifle shooter Arthur Jackson. 'It was part of the process of eliminating segregation. We were eating and socialising on a white ship.'

*   *   *

The Austerity Olympics also points to several far-reaching social, sporting and commercial legacies that have helped to shape the foundations of modern sport. These include the roles of sponsor companies, volunteers and television coverage, which all featured in 1948 and are now essential for the success of major sporting events.

The 1948 Olympic Games also helped to increase sporting opportunities for women and change attitudes toward disability and sport. The first organised sporting competition involving war-injured patients was held in the grounds of Stoke Mandeville hospital in 1948 to coincide with the London Olympic Games opening ceremony. This provided the inspiration for the Paralympic Games, which has since developed into the world's foremost competition and celebration for elite athletes with disabilities.

Following in the footsteps of the 1948 Games organisers takes on new significance for me and the team at 'London 2012'. The venues, projects and programmes planned for the London 2012 Games include the creation of one of Europe's biggest new sports and community parks, along with thousands of new jobs, homes, skills training and opportunities and other social, economic and environmental benefits.

Appropriately, the new Olympic Park project will regenerate some of the capital's most disadvantaged communities, located in east London, which suffered devastating bomb damage during the Second World War.

While the story of the 1948 Games may have taken many years to reveal itself, the arrival of Hampton's new book is perfectly timed to help celebrate the 60th anniversary of these historically important but under-recognised Games.

I am confident this book will motivate us further in our efforts at 'London 2012' to maximise the power of the Olympic and Paralympic Games to inspire change and reconnect young people with the inspirational power of sport, so vividly captured in the following pages of this book.

SEBASTIAN COE
Chairman, London Organising Committee for the 2012 Olympic Games and Paralympic Games

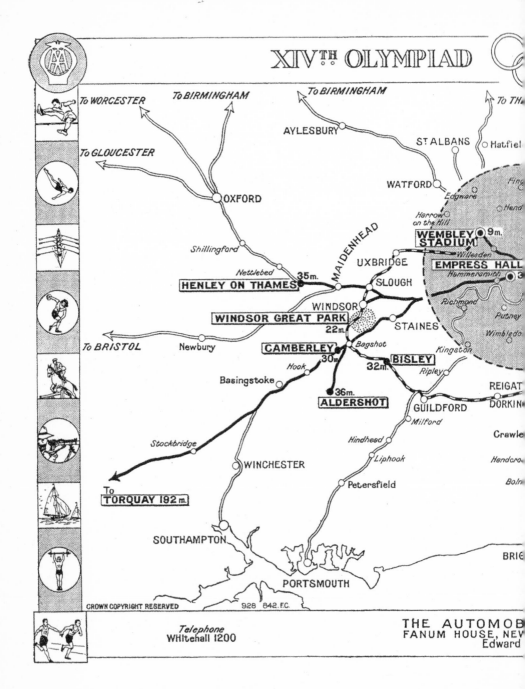

XIVᵀᴴ OLYMPIAD

To WORCESTER
To BIRMINGHAM
To BIRMINGHAM
To TH

AYLESBURY
ST ALBANS
Hatfiel

To GLOUCESTER
WATFORD
Edgware
Fing

OXFORD
Harrow on the Hill
Hend

WEMBLEY STADIUM ●9m.
Willesden

Shillingford
MAIDENHEAD
UXBRIDGE
EMPRESS HALL
Hammersmith ●3

Nettlebed
HENLEY ON THAMES ●35m.
SLOUGH
Richmond
Putney

WINDSOR
WINDSOR GREAT PARK
22m.
STAINES
Wimbledo

To BRISTOL
Newbury
CAMBERLEY
30m.
Bagshot
Kingston

Hook
BISLEY
32m.
Ripley

Basingstoke
ALDERSHOT 36m.
GUILDFORD
REIGAT
DORKIN

Milford
Crawle

Stockbridge
Hindhead
Hendcro

Liphook
Boln

To
TORQUAY 192 m.
WINCHESTER
Petersfield

SOUTHAMPTON
BRIG

PORTSMOUTH

CROWN COPYRIGHT RESERVED   928 842.F.C.

Telephone
WHitehall 1200

THE AUTOMOB
FANUM HOUSE, NEW
Edward

LONDON, 1948

HARWICH

COLCHESTER

CHELMSFORD

Edmonton

HARRINGAY ARENA

Finsbury Pk.

Brentwood

Stratford

River Thames

CADILLY CIRCUS

New Cross

Dartford

ROCHESTER

Lewisham

Farningham

6m.
HERNE HILL

stham

Crystal Palace

Wrotham

CANTERBURY

Westerham

MAIDSTONE

Godstone

HILL

Ashford

DOVER

East Grinstead

FOLKESTONE

Wych Cross

LEWES

NEWHAVEN

LEGEND

Olympic Torch Route ....
Venues shewn thus ... ● **CAMBERLEY**
30 m.
The figures against the venues indicate the distance from Piccadilly Circus.

N

ASSOCIATION
NTRY ST., LONDON, W.I.
ecretary

Telegrams
Fanum Telex London.

INTRODUCTION

Along with thousands of others I stood expectantly in Trafalgar Square on 6 July 2005. We were there to watch the announcement, by live link from Singapore, about the 2012 Olympics. When it came, the euphoria was instant. The Games would be . . . in . . . London. Everyone threw up their arms and shouted with joy. Standing next to me was an old lady, quite still. She turned and said, 'Isn't it wonderful news? I went to watch the Olympics in 1948. I saw the swimming at the Empire Pool. I just had to be here today. But it'll be very different from the last time.'

'Will it? How?' I asked.

'Oh, it was our first celebration after the war, and we were still on rations. We all pulled together. We knew how to make a silk purse out of a sow's ear in those days.' I wanted to know more, but she was gone, leaving me intrigued.

A few days later I phoned a friend. 'I've been reading *The Times* and the *Illustrated London News* from 1948. There's an extraordinary story here. Not like any other Olympic Games, before or since.'

'You'd better write a book about it,' he said.

So I did.

*   *   *

From 29 July to 14 August 1948, 4,000 athletes from all over the world gathered in London for the fourteenth Olympic Games. The fortnight was all

1

about sport, but the meeting of fifty-nine nations brought into focus a great many global tensions.

The founder of the modern Olympics, Baron Pierre de Coubertin, had a vision that by bringing nations together for sport, world peace would ensue. But despite hopes that 1945 would usher in an era of peace, conflicts rumbled on. In June 1948 the Soviet army imposed a road and rail blockade of Berlin. The first Arab–Israeli conflict had begun over the creation of the State of Israel, and there was civil war in Greece. The phrase 'Cold War' had been coined and Czechoslovakia vanished behind the Iron Curtain. Fears about Soviet intentions led the Foreign Secretary Ernest Bevin to accept American atomic bombers at air bases in Britain.

The social and economic condition of post-war Britain was enough to make any planner of an Olympic extravaganza give up in despair. Fighting the war had put enormous pressure upon the health and welfare of every citizen. The winter of early 1947 was exceptionally bad. Food, clothing and petrol were still rationed, unemployment was high and housing was in very short supply. The wartime imperative to pull together had gone and the grumblers and backbiters enjoyed a heyday. Nonetheless, there were signs of regeneration among the ruined buildings and the bombsites. In 1947 the birth rate was the highest for twenty-six years. In 1948 Princess Elizabeth announced her first pregnancy and that summer everyone began to benefit from the new National Health Service.

'It was so obvious to me that the Olympics would be held in London,' said Dennis Hamley, then aged twelve, the son of a Buckinghamshire Post Office engineer. 'Where else could it be? After all, we had won a world war.' In fact London had been chosen, long before the war, for the 1944 Games, which, along with the 1940 Games, had been cancelled.

The organisers invited over seventy nations, though they decided against Germany and Japan. The Soviet Union was a more recent embarrassment, given the Berlin blockade. It had in fact never joined the Olympic movement but still tried to send a team of weightlifters. Burma, Ceylon, Guatemala and Venezuela were represented for the first time. India and Pakistan, divided in August 1947, sent separate teams.

The London Olympic Organising Committee, chaired by the charismatic Lord Burghley, consisted of a dozen male members of the British Establishment, all of whom possessed a title or high military rank. In less than two years they set up the Games like a military operation and persuaded the government that tourists would bring in much-needed foreign currency. On a tiny budget, they discussed every penny and no detail escaped their notice: competitors could be provided with bed linen but should bring their own towels.

It was a 'Make Do and Mend' society, in which demob suits and uniforms still prevailed and blankets were turned into overcoats. The athletes themselves had either to buy or to make their own kit. Audrey Williamson, a sprinter who won a silver medal for Britain, described the shorts she fashioned in the regulation style: 'They were more like big baggy knickers.' Finland was asked to donate the timber for the basketball floor, and Switzerland the gymnastic equipment. Corporate sponsorship was encouraged at new levels and included Coca-Cola, Craven 'A' cigarettes, Guinness and Brylcreem. Coopers' outfitters provided every British male competitor with a free pair of Y-front underpants.

Accommodating the competitors and their coaches posed a huge problem when thousands of British families were still in temporary homes, so RAF camps, schools and colleges were converted into hostels. One legacy of the war was the Ministry of Supply, which could easily provide beds, mattresses, cups and plates. Pre-war arenas and sports centres were refurbished: greyhounds gave way to athletes at Wembley Stadium, swimming replaced the ice-skating rink at the Empire Pool, a weed-strewn velodrome in south London was smartened up for the cycling, and competitors were ferried between them in old London buses.

At first the press poured scorn on the whole idea. The Olympics were considered a waste of public money and editors were convinced they would be a disaster. However, once they started, newsmen from all over the world wanted to be in on the action. The women's swimming events were a particularly popular opportunity to woo readers with photographs of scantily clad competitors.

At the Opening Ceremony in Wembley Stadium it was so hot that many athletes passed out and *Picture Post* commented, 'The brave old show of scarlet and brass that Britain excels in is so dressy, that it has more childhood charm than warlike pomp.' Three days later the new cinder track was flooded by rain and men in Admiralty oilskins had to pierce it with garden forks to disperse the puddles and encourage it to drain.

In researching this story, I spoke to Chinese footballers who barely spoke English. I conducted over a hundred interviews with British and foreign competitors, with the organisers, and with Girl Guides, telephone operators and spectators. Many of them brought out their photo albums and annotated programmes, and modelled their berets and blazers for me. My oldest interviewee was Harry Walker, aged 101, who told me about commentating on the swimming for the BBC. Most were teenagers and young adults in 1948 and they still retained their excitement about mixing with so many nationalities. They were also keen to impress upon me the small but important technical advances made in 1948, such as starting-blocks for sprinters, the 'photo-finish' camera and aluminium diving boards.

In an attic in Loughborough I found boxes of unsorted letters and programmes collected by Mr Sydney T. Hirst, the president of the Southern Counties Amateur Swimming Association and Chief Timekeeper for 1948. Much of the British Olympic Association archive in Wandsworth had been lost in a flood and what was left from 1948 was a random selection of committee minutes. While Wembley Stadium was being rebuilt recently, their archives were moved into a warehouse in south London. Among the reports and letters from the chairman Sir Arthur Elvin, I also found bundles of unsold programmes and tickets, untouched since 1948. I scoured local and national newspapers, which revealed not only the exploits of the competitors, but also the lives around them. I had no idea that there were still

5

prisoners of war in Britain that year, until I saw in the *Wembley News* a photograph of German PoWs building the Olympic Way up to Wembley Stadium. The road is still there. The Public Record Office at Kew holds Cabinet and Foreign Office files, most of them classified until 1996, which reveal that the government had been discussing the Olympics even before the war ended. Churchill himself had sent memos to diplomats about his concerns, and the answers were very surprising.

There is far more to an Olympic Games than medal winners, their times and their records. This is not principally a book about sporting achievements. If you want facts and figures then David Wallechinsky's *The Complete Book of the Olympics* cannot be bettered. The stories of the men and women who lost their events interested me as much as those who won. I wanted to know how they got to London, where they stayed, what they ate, and how they felt about it. This book is also about the people who made it happen, their lordships on the Organising Committee and the schoolboys who ran messages and handed out cups of tea. It features eye-witness accounts by spectators up for the day from the provinces and the journalists and BBC commentators whose job was to turn out the stories.

These were different times from our own. 'Drugs?' exclaimed Joseph Birrell, a hurdler from Barrow-in-Furness. 'We had drugs in 1948. We ate Horlicks tablets by the handful! With no sweets available, they were a real treat.' There was innocence in the athletes' tales of a rarely glimpsed steak and chips and unaccustomed days off work. But they were not naïve: they had lived through the Blitz and fought in North Africa, France and Italy. A weightlifter had been a prisoner of war in a Japanese death camp in Burma. When repatriated in 1945, he weighed less than five stone, yet he recovered to captain the British weightlifting team. Many had been at the Berlin Games and all were acutely conscious of friends and rivals who had perished in the war.

There were other reminders of how times have changed. Sixty years ago, few people objected when women were barred from most sports. The Games took place during Ramadan, but no official awareness was shown in requiring Muslims to train and compete while fasting. Many of the quotations I have used come from contemporary diaries, official reports and newspapers. To modern readers some may seem classist or racist. At a time when people stayed in their own spheres, 'My dear turbaned friends' was a way of saying, 'We weren't at all used to meeting foreigners, but actually we found they were exciting and new.' Possibly never before in London had so many creeds, classes and races come together on an equal footing. For African-Americans, South Africans and British Afro-Caribbeans in particular, racial tensions could be temporarily suspended.

Compared to the modern science of nutrition, the diet of Olympians in 1948 was somewhat haphazard. The British team all talked about the difficulty of training on the basic ration of 2,600 calories per day. Once selected, their intake was increased by a half to the same ration as a coal miner and they also received food parcels from Canada and Australia. But tinned peaches and chocolate powder were hardly adequate training food. The visiting teams brought their own supplies and often an exotic 'pot luck' supper ensued. From Argentina came green tea and spaghetti, Ceylon brought coconuts, and China oiled bamboo shoots. Civil servants were somewhat horrified by the quantity of fresh fruit and beef-steak that arrived daily from California. Government nutritionists were employed to study the 'peculiar dietary habits' of the visiting athletes and discovered that for breakfast, the Australians had a pint of milk, two boiled eggs and a chop, and the Mexicans ate chillies and tripe.

The 1948 Games produced an unforgettable clutch of sporting heroes. The Czechoslovakian Emil Zátopek trained for distance running in his army boots, reputedly carrying his fiancée on his back. When he ran, his tongue hung out, his face screwed up and he wheezed as if about to expire. He was a friendly, talkative person. 'After all those dark days, the bombing, the killing, the starvation, the revival of the Olympics was as if the sun had come out,' he told a British competitor. 'Suddenly there were no frontiers, no more barriers, just the people meeting together.'

Some of the most memorable were the women competitors. Dorothy Tyler, aged eighty-seven, came in from a game of golf to talk to me about a career spanning four Olympics. She had been a high jumper in the 1936 Berlin Games, at the age of sixteen, and in the war she served as driver for the Dambuster pilots. In 1948, married with two sons, she was still Britain's best. 'I'd have won a gold medal if only my bra strap hadn't snapped,' she laughed. The glamorous French concert pianist Micheline Ostermeyer donned sunglasses to win gold in the shot put. Having thrown a discus for the first time only a month earlier, she went on to win that too. The undoubted star of the whole Games was Fanny Blankers-Koen from the Netherlands. As a thirty-year-old mother of two, she was considered too old to run and the *Daily Graphic* revealed: 'She darns socks with artistry. Her greatest love next to racing is housework.' To everyone's delight, she won four gold medals in athletics. On her return to Amsterdam she was presented with a bottle of advocaat by a well-wisher and a bicycle by her neighbours—'So you don't have to run so much.'

The Olympians I spoke to did not boast, but every one, whether in Britain, Singapore, Iran or New Zealand, lit up at the memory of that fortnight. There was something about overcoming adversity that made it worthwhile. Each had struggled to be selected, and their teams had then struggled to raise the money and equipment to compete; and when they got to London, they discovered that the organisers had struggled to host them.

This was the last Olympic Games at which artists competed for medals in sculpture, architecture, etchings, poetry and musical composition. British, Swiss and Danish judges had to choose between poems written in French, Finnish and Afrikaans. Thousands paid to view the entries at the Victoria and Albert Museum in Kensington.

As I delved into that fortnight, I realised that what was at stake was not simply the pride of a handful of athletes, but the Olympic tradition itself, which had been tainted at the previous Olympics by Hitler's arrogance, racism and dirty tricks. What was it about the British national character that was peculiarly suited to reinstating the Olympic virtues of amateurism and fair play? Everyone who attended agreed that Britain made a huge success of staging the Games, raising hopes and lifting morale after everything that had been endured during the long years of war.

It was touch and go at times, though. In 1948 the British definition of 'amateur' was still a matter of social class. Amateurs could only be drawn from the ranks of gentlemen, because they possessed private incomes, needed no financial support and were not open to bribes. Inevitably, it led to absurdities. The oarsman Bert Bushnell had to become a marine engineer because if he had remained a boat hand he would have been classified as a professional oarsman. Frank Turner was a gymnast working as a film extra who would have been excluded from the Games had he performed a single somersault. Other countries were not so fussy, and the Hungarians and Yugoslavs achieved ascendancy by drafting their competitors into the army where they could train all day while being paid as soldiers.

When it was all over, the sailing dinghies, flags and basketballs were sold off. Although the Argentine Olympic Committee's cheque for £280 bounced, much to everybody's surprise, the outlay of £730,000—around £20 million in today's money—generated income which not only covered the costs but produced a profit of £29,000. The London committee was rather annoyed to discover that they had to pay income tax on this. By the end, opinion was unanimous in its approval. 'The dismal Jimmies who prophesied a failure have been put to rout,' said Sir Arthur Elvin, the chairman of Wembley Stadium. Ingemar Garpe of Vasteras in Sweden commented, 'You have really done your best. Wherever, in my bad English, I spoke to someone and asked them a question, I was always given ready advice. In Sweden we think we have the best public—but yours seems to be almost as good.'

In an affluent, multi-cultural Britain where seven years are needed to organise a multi-billion-pound Olympics in 2012, it is fitting to reflect on these 'Austerity Olympics', in which so much was achieved, in so little time, with so little money. Thanks to the lady in Trafalgar Square, I discovered that the 1948 Games were an extraordinary occasion, a true celebration of victory after dark times and one of the most inexpensive and unpretentious Olympiads of the twentieth century. The traditional four-year cycle has not been interrupted since, and only when they return to London in 2012 will we find out how different it will be.

Janie Hampton, Oxford

Money in 1948

Before decimalisation of sterling in 1971, £1 was divided into shillings and pence: 12 pence to the shilling, 20 shillings to the pound. A guinea was one pound and one shilling.

There are several ways of calculating what 1948 prices would be in today's money. Measured by the Retail Price Index, £1 in 1948 would be worth roughly £25 in today's money. In terms of average earnings, £1 in 1948 would be worth about £77 now—so for an average earner, a two-shilling ticket at Wembley Stadium would be equivalent to £7.70 from their pay packet today. Large building projects now cost about 100 times their 1948 value.

Shillings and pence were written as '3s 6d' for example, or often '3/6d'—colloquially 'three and six'.

1

THE TORCHBEARERS

On the morning of 17 July 1948, a Greek Girl Guide from the town of Pyrgos in the Peloponnese put on a home-made robe and sandals and joined her older brother and some of his friends in the ancient stadium at Olympia. Using the rays of the noonday sun and twigs from an olive branch, she kindled the Olympic flame. She had been asked to carry out this honour only the night before, when it became apparent that civil disturbances made it too dangerous for the girl originally chosen to travel from Athens. Accompanied by her young friends and the mayor of Olympia, she carried the flame across the river Altis to the spot where the heart of Baron Pierre de Coubertin was buried, and then passed the torch to Corporal Dimitrelis of the Greek army. Two thousand years earlier, hostilities between the Greek city states had traditionally ceased for the period of the Games, and as a symbol of the present government's commitment to peace, Dimitrelis laid down his weapon, took off his uniform and boots, and set off with the torch, barefoot and bare-chested.

Since 1944, Greece had been ravaged by civil war. The Communist-dominated National Liberation Front, which controlled large areas of the north, had no intention of honouring the Olympic agreement and declared it would disrupt the torch relay. So, instead of travelling to Athens and through Yugoslavia, the flame was carried west to the port of Katakolon and thence aboard the Greek destroyer *Hastings* to Corfu, from where the British frigate HMS *Whitesand Bay* carried it across the Adriatic. During the 22-hour crossing to the Italian port of Bari, the flame was kept alive with butane gas. Once it had landed on Italian soil, a British athletics coach, Sandy Duncan, followed with a reserve flame and spare torches in the official Olympic car, donated by Rolls-Royce and geared down to run at 8mph.

Italy too had its political problems, and for safety's sake, the torchbearers were soldiers, accompanied by military motorbikes. Running over the Simplon Pass into Switzerland, the relay paused in Lausanne to visit the grave of de Coubertin, who had died in 1937, his last wish being that his heart should be taken for burial at Olympia. Normal regulations were waived at the frontiers as the relay continued on through France, Luxembourg and Belgium, visiting towns still recovering from the devastation endured during the war. The torchbearers, escorted by past Olympic champions, roller-skaters and cyclists, were greeted by the mayors and local notables and were cheered on by large crowds: at night, their arrival was marked by fireworks. In Brussels, a ceremony was held at the Tomb of the Unknown Soldier and on the evening of Tuesday 27 July, the torch finally arrived in Calais and was taken on board the British destroyer HMS *Bicester*. After waiting in the English Channel overnight, it arrived in Dover at breakfast time, nine days after leaving Olympia.

That morning, Petty Officer Barnes, who at thirty-five years was reasonably youthful-looking—

14

not bald and not too fat—carried the flame from the ship on to British soil. He ran down the Prince of Wales Pier and through a crowd of 50,000 people lining the seafront. A fifth-form schoolgirl called Janet Turner was one of them: 'A few minutes past eight, there was excitement in Dover. Chief Petty Officer Barnes met the destroyer and when he had taken only a few steps with the Flame, it was blown out for the first time in its 2,000-mile journey across Europe. It was relit from a second torch carried from Greece in case of emergency.' In fact, there was a sleight of hand involving a cigarette lighter as the torch was handed to the Lord Lieutenant of Kent, who passed it to the Mayor, who presented it to the next runner.

*   *   *

In the ancient Olympics, there had been torch relays spreading out from Olympia to tell the people that the Games were starting. In the modern Olympics, it was not until the 1936 Games in Berlin that Carl Diem, a member of the International Olympic Committee (IOC) and chief organiser of the Berlin Games, introduced the torch relay from Greece to the Olympic venue. From a flame kindled in Olympia, a cauldron was lit in the Berlin stadium which burnt for the duration of the competition. The Nazis were already fond of torch rallies and Diem's idea suited Hitler's purposes in staging the Games: the torchbearers would demonstrate to the world the beauty and strength of German youth and affirm the supposed genetic bond between the German fatherland and ancient Greece. Despite the unpleasant associations with Nazi propaganda, the London committee decided that the torch relay was a 'tradition' and as such worth keeping.

In 1936, the Germans had used stainless steel torches with magnesium candles and had changed runners every three minutes—an expensive business. To reduce costs, the Department of Scientific and Industrial Research in London designed a torch with solid fuel that would burn for at least twenty minutes. It contained hexamine wax with added naphthalene to make a luminous flame. Eight of these tablets were sprung in the stem of the torch and each rose up to replace the previous one as it burned out. In order to survive rain, they were encased in nitro-cellulose and trials were run during gales and downpours. 'The fuel has been specially devised,' wrote Denzil Batchelor, a sports journalist, 'to survive typhoon or whirlwind or anything in between which the whimsy English weather may see fit to put upon us.' Once the technical prototype was perfected, the architect Ralph Lavers designed an aluminium torch that was 'cheap to make, of pleasing appearance and a good example of British craftsmanship.' Nearly 2,000 torches were manufactured by EMI, High Duty Alloys, Metal Box, Wessex Aircraft Engineering, Pro-Medico and Cascelloids Limited: enough for a two-mile run each, with a few spares. The firms all worked overtime and charged only costs. The final torch was hand-made of stainless steel and then the cast was destroyed to protect international copyright, which covered the Olympic ring motif. Each runner was allowed to keep his torch as a memento.

Rather than taking the most direct route from Dover to London, the torch was carried through the towns of Kent, Surrey, Berkshire and Buckinghamshire, where each runner represented a different local athletics club. The relay continued through the night of 28 July, accompanied by RAC and AA patrol officers and dozens of local cyclists. At Charing in Kent, 3,000 people mobbed the torchbearer at 1.30 a.m. At Slough, the bearer was Charles McIllvenny, a member of Stoke Poges Physical Recreation Club. 'My father was in hospital and afterwards I took the torch in. He was so thrilled that I had actually carried it. The torch was passed round the ward for everyone to hold. They all felt better.' *Punch* commented, 'A Wembley correspondent has noticed a sudden plague of moths in the district. The local theory is that they have been following in the wake of the Olympic Torch.'

Seventeen-year-old R.S. Ellis of Wembley County Grammar School contributed his account to the school magazine. 'One February afternoon I was asked if I would carry the Olympic flame on its journey from Greece to Wembley. It seemed a comforting way off and I agreed.' Early in July the torchbearers were summoned to Alperton sports ground, near Wembley, to practise running with the torch. 'The route featured most of the well-known public houses between Uxbridge and Wembley, and one or two of the more sober-minded individuals seemed a little uncertain of the exact path, so it was decided to walk over the entire route the following Sunday. All we learned was that there is nowhere to get a cup of tea on a

17

Sunday afternoon in the four miles between Uxbridge and Wembley.' Despite assurances, Ellis was worried:

... a typical London downpour might go a long way to reverse the result of laboratory tests. But July 29th dawned clear and bright with every promise, later fully realised, of being a 'scorcher'. I had, up to that point, pursued an ostrich-like policy of not thinking about the business at all, but the sand was completely blown away by the newspaper reports of that Thursday morning. First the Flame had gone out on two occasions; then one runner was reported to have been mobbed by enthusiastic crowds and unable to continue; but worst of all was the story of a Kent butcher who had practised religiously for three weeks with a four-pound hammer to develop his arm muscles. This was the last straw. As I trudged along to Uxbridge station I felt miserably certain that I would never be able to carry the torch for two yards, let alone two miles.

When the great day came, the manager of the Bell Punch Company in Uxbridge had allotted a room in his bus-ticket-machine factory for the runners to change into their kit of plain singlet, shorts and white plimsolls. Ellis recounted:

This was zero hour and much forced gaiety was in evidence. I suddenly remembered that I didn't know how to light one of these torches, and with that essentially British brand of courage, I felt it would be foolish to ask.

Luckily I was saved by an old-fashioned custom—the directions were printed on a label. The torch bearers and escorts were carried in a coach to their 'take-over' positions. It was about 2 p.m. and already huge crowds lined the route ready to give the flame a cheer on its way to Wembley. I was amazed at the extent to which this ceremony had captured the public imagination. There were hundreds of people along the road and by the time the coach reached the Hop Bine in North Wembley it was thousands. The crowd surged around, displaying such a keen interest in the torch, which I tried to hide in my sweater, that I was afraid they would dismantle it there and then. However, a number of policemen, suitably big and broad, took the situation in hand and we instinctively made our way to the doorway of the Hop Bine. We looked around with a 'What shall we do next?' air, for there was at least half an hour to wait. Then the landlord of the Hop Bine invited us in—this was succour indeed! We were offered a drink and with much regret but some prudence I ordered a soda water. There were numerous interruptions by autograph hunters. In years to come the respective owners will wonder what the dickens R.S. Ellis is doing next to Winston Churchill. Just after 3 p.m. the torch-bearer arrived and a great wave of cheering went up. In the general excitement I forgot to wonder whether my torch would light, or even how I was going to get through the crowd which was now completely blocking the road. I only remember shaking the runner by the hand and making some fatuous remark, then with the torch alight I was off into the path cleared for me by six motor-cycle police.

Ellis was carrying the penultimate and 1,687th torch, in a relay that had travelled 3,160 kilometres across eight countries and two seas.

It was a natural reaction to the waiting I suppose that made me dash off like a March hare, but I soon got a warning toot from the official car following to slow down. The pavements were lined with cheering people, a wonderful experience which made me forget about the weight of the torch, or indeed the heat of the sun, which was blazing down in equatorial style. Past Preston Manor County School and up Brook Avenue it was fine. But at the top of Olympic Way there seemed to be no way through at all, though the motorcycle escort made sure we never actually stopped. The going was very hard notwithstanding, and in the dip of Olympic Way we lost the slight oncoming breeze which had helped to keep us cool and got instead the full blast of the motor cycle exhausts and the dust churned up from the newly surfaced road.

The new road was lined with flags from all the competing nations, beneath which were people still hoping to get inside the stadium. 'I was definitely earning my living by the sweat of my brow but the end was in sight, and with a final roar the motor cycles cleared the last few yards to the tunnel entrance, and I had arrived. And then the supreme anti-climax!'

Young Ellis had run so well that he had arrived at the Empire Stadium early. Inside, 80,000 excited spectators were still watching the fifty-nine Olympic teams march in to the accompaniment of the massed Guards Band. The opening ceremony was running like clockwork. At 16.00 the King would announce the Games open, at 16.01 the Olympic flag would be raised, and at 16.05, 7,000 pigeons would be released. The Olympic torch was not scheduled to enter until exactly 16.07. Ellis was ordered to go and wait in the dressing room before anyone saw him.

Here, sweating vigorously, I sat and held the torch, which was by now uncomfortably warm, with an arm which was definitely aching. I talked to the 'mystery' runner who was to kindle the Olympic flame with the easy assurance and nonchalance of one who has performed his task. After some time, the muffled report of guns sounded the signal for the arrival of the flame. The mystery runner and I went out to the entrance to the track and here the last torch was kindled and my part in the proceedings finally finished. Did I wait to see the final flame being lit? I am afraid not. In true cross-country tradition, I dashed back to the dressing room to be first in the bath.

To add to the excitement, the authorities had kept the identity of the final torchbearer secret until this moment. Some people thought it would be the Duke of Edinburgh, who the previous November had married Princess Elizabeth, and

21

who was said to possess the charm and grace of a classical Greek. Most expected to see the balding and bespectacled Sydney Wooderson, the popular English holder of the world record for the mile. The social satirist H.F. Ellis of *Punch* kept up a sardonic commentary throughout the Games, his descriptions sometimes written before the event. He imagined the scene:

And now, as my favourite commentator always says, we catch our first glimpse of the Torch-bearer—a glimmer of white against the dark background of the Tunnel. And a light figure, running easily on the balls of her feet—Yes. Some say the final runner will be Wooderson, others say it will be Stalin. My own guess is that it will be Britannia, draped from head to foot in a linen sheet, to symbolize Export, and perhaps, imaginative touch this—releasing one or two additional pigeons as she goes.

At the stroke of 16.07, all eyes turned to the Competitors Tunnel. An unknown young man in plain white singlet and shorts stood in the sunlight, framed by the darkness. He stood for about five seconds holding the flaming torch high with his right arm before running right round the track. Few people in the crowd had any idea who he was, but with his flowing hair and long, elegant strides, he looked every inch a young Greek god.

Above him the scoreboard displayed this message:

THE IMPORTANT THING IN

THE OLYMPIC GAMES IS NOT

WINNING BUT TAKING PART.

THE ESSENTIAL THING IN

LIFE IS NOT CONQUERING

BUT FIGHTING WELL

2

HOW THE GAMES
CAME TO LONDON

The first recorded Olympic Games were held in Greece in 776 BC. They reputedly then took place every four years until 385 AD, a remarkable duration of 1,161 years. They were eventually abolished by the Christian emperor, Theodosius the Great. Some 1,500 years later, a young French aristocrat, Pierre de Coubertin, abandoned a political career to devote his resources to the introduction of sport into French schools, and in 1892 he proposed a revival of the ancient Olympic Games. De Coubertin believed that the interests of peace could best be served by competitions between nations represented by amateurs. 'I am often asked,' he said, 'whether I consider the Olympic Games help towards international brotherhood. My feeling is that the more you bring people together for something in which they take a special interest, the more it leads to increasing friendship'. De Coubertin wanted the modern Olympic movement 'to contribute to building a peaceful and better world by educating youth through sport, practised without discrimination of any kind.' The Olympic spirit, he said, was one 'which requires mutual understanding' and 'friendship, solidarity and fair play'. As of old, his games were going to be more than an athletic event. '*Olympism* is a philosophy of combining a balanced body, will and mind. Blending sport with culture and education, *Olympism* seeks to create a way of life based on the joy found in effort, the educational value of good example and respect for fundamental ethical principles'.

There was a significant English element to the revival. De Coubertin had drawn inspiration from the Corinthian spirit on display at Rugby and other English public schools. The Victorian ideals of gentlemanly amateurism, fair play and muscular Christianity, typified in Henry Newbold's famous line 'play up and play the game', had struck de Coubertin as a living embodiment of the Olympic tradition. Nor was that tradition limited to the English upper classes. The Shropshire town of Much Wenlock had held its own 'Olympic Games' since a Mr Penny Brookes had initiated them in 1850. Every October, a band led a procession from the Gaskell Arms to the town's racecourse, which was renamed 'The Olympian Fields' for the day. The programme included football, cricket, a blindfold wheelbarrow race and a prize of a pound of tea for the fastest old woman.

De Coubertin realised that an organisation dedicated to staging an international Olympic Games must place the welfare of all ahead of that of a few. He foresaw that nationalist struggles for prestige and advantage would inevitably infect the basic ideals of the Games. However, he also ensured that the first International Olympic Committee was composed of his own friends, though he took care to recruit both aesthetes and athletes, two classes of person then often at loggerheads.

*   *   *

As a result of de Coubertin's efforts, the first Olympic Games of the modern era were held in Athens in 1896. The original stadium at Olympia had been considered, but was deemed to be too far from the capital. There was no accommodation, and anyway the stadium was buried beneath twelve feet of mud. The stadium in Athens was the property of the King, George I, who paid for its restoration. Two recently excavated and magnificent *Hermae* presided at either end, their female protuberances discreetly veiled by wreaths. 'These had the unfortunate habit of slipping and forming a frame for what they were supposed to conceal,' observed George Robertson, a Classics scholar from Oxford who took part. The forty-three events included swimming, athletics, fencing and gymnastics; the rowing, scheduled to take place at sea, had to be cancelled owing to rough weather. The 260 competitors and officials came mainly from Greece, though six Britons participated and the crew of HMS *Howe*, docked in Piraeus, attended as spectators. A Mr L. Elliot took part in the 100-yard dash and rope climbing, and won gold for weightlifting.

George Robertson noted:

The only novel feature for the 19th century athlete was the discus. None of us, except the Greeks, had ever seen a discus before and it would never have occurred to us to imagine the strange object, which did not correspond in material, shape, size or weight to any known discus of the ancient Greeks. And we found that we were supposed to throw it in a manner based on a misunderstanding of the statue of

Myron's *Discobolus*. But there it was: it was more intelligent than the present method of throwing.

Robertson threw the discus, sent daily reports back to *The Field* and competed at lawn tennis, though he confessed to barely knowing the rules. He also went prepared to deliver his own Olympic ode in Aeolic Greek, but the committee would not allow it, having already refused this privilege to many Greeks. However, the King heard about it and requested a recital, afterwards awarding Robertson both a laurel and an olive branch, in compensation for his sporting failures.

Despite de Coubertin's hope that the Olympics would outshine all other sporting events, the sometimes eccentric nature of the early Games meant that they acquired little status among athletics organisations. After Alfred Flatow of Germany won three gold medals and one silver for gymnastics, the governing body of German gymnastics suspended him from international competitions for two years, for 'taking part in an unauthorised event'. The 1900 Games in Paris included a cross-country run, baseball, 'Irish Sports' and 'Bohemian Gymnastics', all of which were soon dropped. The third Games travelled to St Louis, Missouri, and the fourth took place in London in 1908. Events that year were centred on the White City Stadium and included real tennis, tug-of-war, motor-boat racing, rackets and rugby. At Stockholm in 1912, new items such as football, ladies' lawn tennis, cycling, game-shooting, equestrian competitions and yacht racing were added. The fastest man on water was Duke

Kahanamoku of Hawaii on a surfboard. Then there was a break occasioned by the First World War, but the Games resumed in Antwerp in 1920, followed by Paris in 1924, Amsterdam in 1928 and Los Angeles in 1932.

The international standing of the Olympics was increasing, but when in 1936 the Olympics travelled to Berlin, Hitler initially showed little interest in them. However, the attempts by some in the USA to boycott these Games, because of the Nazi treatment of the Jews, had the effect of awakening his interest. Even if the International Olympic Committee claimed to be apolitical, Hitler decided to use the Olympics to demonstrate the Nazis' political strength and the superiority of the Aryan race. He bought the silence of the ailing de Coubertin for 10,000 Reichsmarks, the equivalent today of about £200,000. Hitler enjoyed the support of Avery Brundage, a Chicago building contractor and member of the IOC, who had competed in the 1912 pentathlon. An ambitious and slippery character, Brundage was easily convinced that the Olympic boycott movement was a Jewish plot, orchestrated by the Communists. Although he spoke no German, he saw only a clean and Jew-friendly nation during his visit to Germany in 1935. He also made useful business contacts and was delighted to meet the Führer. The British Olympic Committee fared little better, accepting the Germans' argument that the anti-Semitism question was irrelevant because few Jews were interested in sport. Even Harold Abrahams, a British Jew and medal winner in 1924, believed that a boycott might result in German policy becoming even more dangerous. It was not until the British team got to Berlin that they fully understood how Hitler had planned to make use of the Olympics as propaganda. 'The Games had grown in political importance until the Germans overstepped all bounds of sportsmanship with a vulgar display, calculated to impress visitors not so much with their prowess as with their military efficiency,' wrote John Macadam of the *Daily Express* in 1948.

*　　　*　　　*

After Berlin, the IOC met to consider where the Games should be held in 1940. The choice lay between London, Helsinki and Tokyo, and the committee's discussions reveal just how significant the Olympics were becoming to host cities. Still trying to maintain their apolitical stance, the IOC also took little notice of the deteriorating international situation. The Finns wished to remind the world of their independence from the Soviet Union. In London the construction and hotel industries saw the Olympics as a way of attracting government subsidies to aid their recovery from the Great Depression. Tokyo, the first Far Eastern city to be a candidate, wanted to mark the 2,600th anniversary of the Japanese Empire. With such a high economic advantage at stake, manoeuvring took place at the highest level. The Japanese government agreed to stop selling arms to Ethiopia, if the Germans and Italians would support their bid. Officials in Washington and Ottawa believed a concession to Tokyo might reduce military tensions in the Pacific, and the Canadians stood to supply Tokyo with huge quantities of timber, while American railroad, steamship and airline companies would profit in transporting people westwards. Inducements were also given to individual members of the IOC: William Garland enjoyed a holiday in Japan with his wife in 1937 and Brundage began to amass his huge collection of Far Eastern art with the aid of Japanese friends. Unsurprisingly, Tokyo was selected to host the 1940 Games.

Matters did not rest there. In December 1937, when the international press was expressing outrage at the Japanese invasion of China and the pillage of Nanking, the authorities in Tokyo warned the IOC that 'nobody would trust the committee in the future if it broke the promise it had publicly given.' As in 1936, the IOC proved impervious to reality and reaffirmed the Tokyo Games. However, in July 1938, the Japanese and Soviet armies began an undeclared war in Manchuria and Tokyo announced its own withdrawal from the 1940 Olympiad, hoping instead to be considered in 1944 'when our finances are more secure'. The 1940 Summer Games were consequently awarded to Helsinki. So determined was the IOC to remain above international politics that the Germans were encouraged to prepare for the Winter Games at Garmisch-Partenkirchen two months *after* their army had invaded Poland in September 1939. The Summer Games were not abandoned until May 1940, six months after Finland had been invaded by Soviet forces. A stadium in Helsinki seating 60,000, a velodrome and an airstrip for the new sport of gliding were abandoned.

There was thus no twelfth or thirteenth

Olympiad. After 1936 the Germans retained control of the movement and when the Belgian president of the IOC, Henri Ballet-Latour, died in his sleep in 1942, they insisted upon an ostentatious public funeral in Brussels, at which the coffin bore swastika wreaths from Hitler and Goebbels. However, the Nazis didn't have it all their own way. The IOC presidency went next to a Swedish neutral, Sigfrid Edström, and when Carl Diem tried to move the Olympic archives from Lausanne to Berlin, Lydia Zanchi—who had been de Coubertin's secretary—hid the most important documents in her cellar.

By 1944, it was clear that the IOC could start to plan the fourteenth Olympiad for 1948. Although Helsinki had already built an Olympic stadium, the city was now too war-damaged to host the Games. London remained an option, but Brundage, now the vice-chair of the IOC, lobbied for Los Angeles. 'London, half destroyed by bombs, will have a lot more important things to do than stage an athletics meeting,' he wrote. The London representative, Lord Aberdare, was furious and pointed out that the IOC had already offered them the 1944 Games. London was duly reselected, before the war had ended.

*   *   *

London had not staged a major sporting event since athletics meetings in 1939, and a sober appraisal of its infrastructure would not have convinced anyone as late as 1947 that it could stage the Games in a year's time. Opinion among the city's 3.3 million inhabitants was divided. Some

31

welcomed the Games as a further victory celebration; others worried that they would divert vital resources away from those who most needed them.

In the three years since the bombing of Hiroshima in Japan, an astonishing eighty-five per cent of that city's streets had been rebuilt. But in London, bombsites still scarred every borough and St Paul's Cathedral stood out among the craters which had once been offices and theatres.

During the eight months of the 1940–41 Blitz, 16,000 tons of high explosives had destroyed factories, warehouses, docks and railway stations. Landmarks such as Buckingham Palace, the Bank of England and the National Gallery had been patched up, but forty acres of the City around the Barbican were still a bombsite. Odd buildings stood in empty streets, like single rotten teeth, their inner walls revealing fireplaces, staircases and wallpaper. In midsummer the sites glowed pink with Rosebay Willowherb, also known as Fireweed because of its rapid invasion of fire-damaged land.

Bridges had been rebuilt, gas and water mains repaired, and telephones reconnected, but dozens of ancient churches, many designed by Christopher Wren after the Great Fire of London in 1666, still lay in ruins. In Oxford Street, Selfridge's was still standing, but the John Lewis department store had gone. Behind Oxford Street, the Queen's Hall, home of the Proms concerts, had been destroyed, and the Proms now took place in the acoustically appalling Royal Albert Hall.

The House of Commons was still damaged but it didn't stop members of parliament debating.

Officially, the government reckoned that 700,000 more homes were needed, but other authorities estimated the true figure to be double this; and only one third of urban homes had baths with running water. Among those who had been bombed out, the lucky ones now had 'prefab' bungalows, and most back gardens in London still sported Anderson air-raid shelters, now housing garden tools or chickens.

Britain may have won the war, but many felt morale was actually lower than it had been five years earlier, when people had pulled together to survive. The prolonged conflict had left raw nerves in unexpected places. With shortages in nearly every aspect of public and private life, there was much grumbling that the Games were a scandalous waste of money. Frank Butler, sports editor of the *Daily Express*, told the *Minneapolis Tribune*, 'Our country will not be able to handle the Games: it will take too long to rebuild London. England would be jolly well satisfied never to hold the Games again.' In September 1947 the *Evening Standard* declared, 'The average range of British enthusiasm for the Games stretches from lukewarm to dislike. It is not too late for invitations to be politely withdrawn.'

Even the poet John Pudney felt moved to write a verse for the *Observer*, called 'The Games':

> The Games are all right
> Though they rest upon muscle
> And glorify might.
> The Games are all right,
> Played blithely in spite
> Of doctrinaire rustle.

The Games are all right
As a muscular tussle.

The novelist Angela Thirkell described contemporary upper-class opinion in *Love Among the Ruins* in 1948:

Lady Graham said she thought everything had got a bit beyond the government. 'I must say,' said Martin, 'that it seems very silly to have Olympic Games here. To begin with, we shall be the only real amateurs, and to go on with, our teams will be perfectly under-nourished. Still, if that's what the government wants.'

The Labour government had been elected in 1945 with a large majority, with pledges to create the 'welfare state'. Between 1946 and 1948, Prime Minister Clement Attlee embarked on a programme to nationalise the railways, gas, electricity, coal, steel and the Bank of England, and 3,000 private hospitals as a basis for the new National Health Service. But the war had left Britain virtually bankrupt, which was not helped in 1945 by Attlee and his Foreign Secretary Ernest Bevin secretly investing £100 million in building a British atomic bomb. Then the harsh winter of 1946–47 continued until mid-March, with snow blizzards and atrocious conditions impeding the transport of coal. Exports virtually ceased, whole counties went without electricity and two million people became unemployed. In the overcrowded prisons, officers threatened to strike over their £5 wage for a compulsory 47-hour week. In August 1947, the convertibility crisis almost wiped out the

Treasury's reserves of gold and foreign exchange. Although the government had granted India its independence and withdrawn its forces from Palestine, there was still the huge expense of running foreign bases and the occupied zone in Germany. These economic strains meant that export industries had to take priority over domestic reconstruction, and imports kept to a minimum, with further food rationing. People found themselves eating even fewer calories than in 1945: thirteen ounces of meat, six ounces of butter, eight ounces of sugar, two pints of milk and one egg—per week. Clothing and petrol were also still rationed.

The main reason the British government had agreed to support the Olympics was in order to generate hard currency from ticket sales, tourists in hotels and, hopefully, foreigners buying British goods. 'There are few better ways of making such a net contribution to the balance of payments with so little offset in the form of imported materials,' wrote Attlee's deputy, Herbert Morrison, in August 1947.

With just a year to go before the Games, there remained doubt among some officials over their feasibility. The Director-General of the BBC, Sir William Haley, wrote to the government in confidence, requesting prior warning if there was 'any likelihood of the Games being abandoned or postponed' so that the BBC could make savings in 'both money and manpower'. Harold Wilson, then Secretary for Overseas Trade, reassured him that Attlee was committed to the Games as a source of foreign income. 'The government's main interest is to seize the occasion to develop the tourist trade,' reported H.W.A. Freese-Pennefather, a civil servant in the Foreign Office. 'If we can get our shop window properly arranged in time, arrangements might be made for tourists to see our modern factories, civic centres and law courts.'

The Home Office had enough worries without planning for an invasion by several thousand foreigners. For example, it was still coping with large numbers of deserters from the armed forces. Following a general appeal in 1947, 837 of them gave themselves up for court martial, expecting leniency. Instead they were given six months' hard labour, with the result that, a year later, 19,000 deserters were still on the run. Moreover, out of the 22,000 British children fathered by American GIs prior to D-Day, several hundred still posed a problem for adoption agencies.

*   *   *

The Olympic ideal also faced severe challenges abroad, as wars and simmering tensions continued all over the world. In January 1948 Gandhi was assassinated, leading to further violence between Hindus and Muslims. The Western allies introduced a common currency in the three zones in Germany under their occupation, a first step towards a West German state, and the Soviet Union responded by blocking road and rail access to Berlin. The airlift mounted by the Royal Air Force and US Air Force averted all-out war by flying food and supplies into the city. Germany was felt to be sliding into chaos, and fears about Soviet intentions led Bevin to accept the stationing of American atomic bombers in Britain: the first arrived a week before the Games. That year Arabs and Israelis were at war over the creation of the State of Israel; the French were fighting in Indo-China, the Dutch in Indonesia, and the British were fighting Communist insurgents in Malaya; there was civil war in Greece and Colombia. Czechoslovakia disappeared behind the Iron Curtain after a Communist coup d'état, and Yugoslavia partially emerged from behind it, expelled for 'deviationist heresies'.

It was not all bad news, especially in Britain. At the Winter Olympics in St Moritz, the British team won two bronze medals, for figure skating and skeleton toboggan, despite having scarcely seen a skate or a slope for seven years. In January 1948 Marks and Spencer opened the first self-service shop in Wood Green. By the summer of 1948, employment in Britain had picked up and 200,000 new houses had been built: 70,000 bicycles a year were exported to Holland; 20,000 watches were manufactured each month; and the export of cars to the USA rose from nine in June 1947 to 1,452 a year later. In July 1948 the National Health Service came into effect and people flocked to clinics for free dental treatment, spectacles and hearing aids. It was also a year for domestic improvements: Hoover opened a washing machine factory in Merthyr Tydfil; Scrabble, the word-making game, was patented; and the British film industry produced over 170 films. Bureaucracy was so efficient that C.J. Epril of Pall Mall felt moved to write to the editor of *The Times*: 'One word of praise where it is due. A passport applied for at 3.30 p.m. yesterday was ready for collection at 10 a.m. this morning.'

Attlee had always made it perfectly clear that while he supported the idea of the Games, they would have to be organised, and paid for, independently of the government. Luckily there were experienced people on hand to do the job. The British Olympic Organising Committee consisted of a variety of Establishment figures, many of them titled and wealthy, who were capable of pushing their weight around and willing to work for nothing. They were joined by civil servants seconded to the housing and transport sub-committees. Business began in 1946 in an office above the Army and Navy Stores in Victoria and when the staff reached nearly a hundred, they moved to a house in Mayfair where the accountants worked in the servants' rooms on the top floor.

In the chair was 43-year-old Lord Burghley, formerly a Conservative MP and Governor-General of Bermuda, who had won a gold medal in the 1928 Olympics. Educated at Eton and Cambridge, he owned a pack of fox hounds and had recently divorced his wife, the daughter of a duke. 'On the maiden voyage of the *Queen Mary*, for the gratification of H.G. Wells and Lord Camrose he ran 400 yards after dinner, in evening dress, round the upper deck in 58 seconds,' wrote the *Observer*.

Handsome and articulate, calm and genial, Burghley successfully torpedoed opposition to the Games with charm and persuasion. It was said that he could persuade Molotov, the Soviet statesman, to enter an egg and spoon race with Uncle Joe Stalin as starter. His commitment to the Games was both ideological and practical. He firmly believed that they would contribute, 'however humbly, to the real progresses of mankind. We have a reputation for hospitality, good sportsmanship, tolerance and kindliness, so let us each and every one do our uttermost to show our visitors that this reputation is well founded'. His arguments, however, were financial, and in the wake of the sterling crisis, Burghley convinced the Labour government that foreign visitors to the Games would bring in at least £1 million in hard currency, a sum impossible to prove. Accommodating these visitors was going to present a problem, as the recent introduction of paid holidays meant that British workers would put pressure on hotel rooms in August. Bevin suggested holding the Games in June but the IOC rejected the idea. The Ministry of Agriculture tried to help by advertising for workers to take their holidays on farms: 'Come and help with the harvest. The cost of accommodation is halved, and your rail fare will be refunded.'

The chief administrator of the committee was the Oxford-educated Colonel Evan Austin Hunter OBE who had been secretary of the British Olympic Association since 1925 and organised the Empire Games in 1934. Hunter was an avuncular, genial man who had fought in both world wars, and although not particularly sporting, he was well organised and efficient. Now, at sixty-one, this unpaid post gave him his biggest challenge, which he met with the efficiency of an army officer and the zest of a former athlete.

A third charismatic member of the committee was Sir Arthur Porritt CBE, FRCS, who was appointed director of Olympic medical services.

Porritt was a New Zealander, educated at Oxford and a bronze medal winner in the 100 metres in the 1924 Olympics. A brilliant doctor, in 1948 he was surgeon to the Royal Household and an originator of the National Health Service. 'He was a tall and handsome man,' wrote a contemporary, 'with a ready smile, youthful vivacity, the newly scrubbed appearance of an athlete who has just emerged from the changing-room showers—and a fresh rose, daily, in his buttonhole.'

Britain's most distinguished athlete, Harold Abrahams, then aged forty-nine, was appointed treasurer. His father had migrated to London from Lithuania in 1902 and produced four extraordinary sons. Adolphe, a consultant physician, was knighted in 1939 and served on the Olympic medical committee; Solomon competed for Britain in three Olympics and then became chief justice of Tanganyika; and Lionel was coroner for Huntingdonshire. Harold, the youngest, won a gold medal in the 100 metres sprint at the Paris Olympics in 1924, and held the long jump record for thirty years. After the war he became a barrister, radio commentator and president of the Amateur Athletics Association. 'Abrahams has managed by his force of personality to raise athletics from a minor to a major sport,' reported *The Times*. 'He possesses a fresh resonant voice, while his clear diction and wide vocabulary are models for any British speaker.'

This group of efficient and worldly men now had the challenge of staging the Olympic Games. They had all just spent six years working for the war effort, and now they would put the same skills to use and run the Olympics like a military operation.

3

ORGANISING ON A SHOESTRING

Starting in 1946 and with less than two years in which to prepare, the Organising Committee had to work hard and with considerable ingenuity. It had been done before: after Rome was selected for the 1908 Games, Mount Vesuvius erupted and the Italians were forced to bow out. London was chosen on that occasion and the stadium at White City near Shepherd's Bush in West London was constructed in only ten months. Since the First World War it had fallen into a state of disrepair, and now there was neither time nor money to build a new stadium big enough to hold 75,000 spectators and with sufficient facilities to hold all seventeen Olympic sports. Instead, existing sites had to be identified which had not been destroyed by bombing. The task was enormous, but the committee knuckled down and suitable venues were found, though most had not been repaired in over ten years. Cycling would take place at the Herne Hill Velodrome in south London; basketball at Harringay Arena in North London; shooting at Bisley in Surrey; rowing twenty miles upstream at Henley-on-Thames and yachting 150 miles away in Torbay, Devon. Alexandra Palace and Olympia were rejected as too expensive. Schools within the capital would be used to house athletes, and government buildings to provide offices.

The largest venue needed was for the opening

and closing ceremonies, athletics, football and equestrian events. The impressive Empire Stadium at Wembley, with a football pitch in the middle of a greyhound racing track, was ideal. Back in the 1880s, the Wembley Park Leisure Ground had contained football and cricket pitches and a running track, together with fountains and waterfalls. After the First World War the government planned a British Empire Exhibition and a stadium had been built in just 300 days, using the most modern engineering techniques, with room for 83,000 spectators in a huge bowl surrounding a football pitch, overlooked by two giant towers. The first event to be held there was the FA Cup Final of 1923, when more than 200,000 people attempted to squeeze into the ground. Over 27 million attended the subsequent exhibition with its lakes, gardens and pavilions. During a war-time raid, bombs fell on the pitch and destroyed buildings outside, but the stadium and its corrugated iron roof were unharmed. Over the years, it had acquired iconic status and in 1947 King Farouk of Egypt asked for the plans in order to build a copy outside Cairo.

The chairman and managing director of Wembley Stadium Ltd was Sir Arthur Elvin, also known as 'The Governor of Wembley', who had been responsible for organising sporting events there since before the war. He was a remarkable man who had left school at fourteen and worked as a clerk in a Norwich boot factory. While serving in the Royal Flying Corps on the Western Front, his plane had been shot down and he was made a prisoner of war. 'After getting out of a German prison camp, following the armistice in 1918,' he recalled in the *News of the World*, 'I got a job in charge of labourers dismantling ammunition dumps in France. That is how I learnt the technique and trade of demolition.' At the age of twenty-four, he was earning £4 a week managing a tobacco stall at the Empire Exhibition. As other kiosks around him had gone bust, he had bought the leases and made them work, and when the exhibition had ended he had secured the contract for its demolition. He had not only done this in record time, but had made a £50,000 profit by selling whole buildings off to organisations that could re-erect them elsewhere. One pavilion re-emerged as Bournemouth football club; the West Africa building went to Letchworth and became a jam factory, the Palestine building went to a Glasgow laundry and the Burma pavilion was rebuilt in Australia.

Two years later, the stadium itself, which had cost £506,000 to build, had gone into receivership. Elvin's bid of £125,000 was the highest and when the owner committed suicide, he had found the money in one afternoon, persuading friends in the City to invest £150,000 on condition that he kept £25,000, retained a block of shares and became Managing Director. By the end of 1926, the dog track he had set up was returning a profit and in 1929 Speedway was added. From then on, Wembley Stadium Ltd coped with two million spectators every year, became known as 'The Ascot of Greyhound Racing' and hosted Cup Finals and Rugby Leagues.

'From Cigarette Kiosk to a Stadium of Empire,' declared the *News of the World*, 'Elvin's flair for staging the spectacular, the original and the unique has brought shows from all four corners of the earth.' The sports journalist Denzil Batchelor wrote of Elvin:

There is no flamboyance about him, nothing gaudy or theatrical. His great qualities are his smoothness and his coolness. He is tall, with reddish hair at the back of a high-domed head, a large nose and a smile which is agreeable, but never expansive. He is the soft-footed big business man incarnate, rarely seen in public except on nights when the greyhounds are racing. When he takes up his stand opposite the judge's box, an immaculate unruffled figure with a pluperfect dove-grey Homburg crowning the auburn locks, you would suppose you were looking at any bland, impassive spectator, mildly interested after a day's work. The man and the organisation he has created are ideally suited to the Herculean task of staging the large part of the greatest sporting festival ever staged in Britain.

Elvin was a perfectionist, even sending a memo to the printer when he noticed a missing asterisk in one of the Olympic Athletics programmes.

Choosing the Olympic venues was only the first hurdle to overcome. Wembley Stadium needed converting from a greyhound track into an international venue. The Empire Pool next door, currently an ice rink, needed expensive and complicated repair work to make it fit for swim-ming, and a new approach road was needed to link the stadium to Wembley Park railway station. The estimated cost of the Games was originally

£150,000, with the immediate repairs to the stadium needing £89,000 (£2.2 million in today's money). The government was unable to lend this, but Elvin came to the rescue when he persuaded Wembley Stadium Ltd to put up the money, hoping to recover it from the ticket sales. He made himself responsible for the reconstruction, and also organised transport for competitors, the design and sale of tickets for all venues, and the entertainment of VIPs. Despite all this effort, as a mere businessman he was not invited to join the committee.

The bureaucratic culture created by the war added to the difficulties. An Act of Parliament was required to make structural changes to the stadium. In late autumn 1947, with only nine months to go, Sweden and Finland donated enough timber to replace the rotting seats and floors, but only after a senior intervention did Customs and Excise release it without charging duty. The planks of wood to build the platform for the Olympic flame required a licence from the Board of Trade, as did two Douglas Fir trees donated by the Canadian Swimming Association to make diving boards. A dozen iron girders for the boxing ring required a 'Control of Iron and Steel Order' and valuable time was lost when the Ministry of Works failed to approve the release of materials. Twenty painters were dismissed because there was no paint available and work was suspended on strengthening the Empire Pool because of a shortage of cement. When Switzerland offered to donate gymnastic equipment, duty was only waived when Burghley and Viscount Portal, President of the London committee, put up a guarantee of £10,000 that they would not sell the equipment.

Operating within such a tight budget, the committee were sticklers for economy. When swimming officials submitted a Claridge's bill for a meeting in October 1947, Abrahams was furious. 'The staff at Wembley are working on an austerity basis and with the utmost economy,' he fumed. One hundred basketballs, footballs, boxing gloves and hockey balls were ordered from manufacturers on condition they were sold off at cost after the Games. Wooden kiosks erected outside the stadium were let to Lloyds Bank, the British Overseas Airways Corporation, the BBC's publishing arm and the British Tourist Board for £118 each.

Another source of income was corporate sponsorship, which had been encouraged since the Stockholm Olympics of 1912 when photographic rights were sold. Participating companies included Nescafé, International Combustion Ltd, Gillette Razors, Martel Brandy, Ovaltine, Quaker Oats, Sloane's Liniment, Guinness and Brylcreem. Coca-Cola continued the support which it had begun in 1928. The official souvenir magazine was filled with so many advertisements—for items like Gilbey's gin, Craven 'A' cigarettes, Stein's garters and Aertex underwear—that it is difficult to find the articles. Any company that paid £250 was permitted to use the five-ring Olympic emblem. After the event, only one was found to have infringed these rights by not paying—Tresies Drip Mat Co.

The BBC was asked to pay £1,000 for transmitting the Games on radio and television.

Although television was relatively new, by 1948 radio had fully come into its own. Wireless programmes had begun in 1922, and the Olympics were first broadcast in Britain in 1936. The war had established the scope and excellence of BBC reporting and by 1948, it was broadcasting in forty-three languages to the world via short-wave transmission. Television ownership was increasing dramatically every year. Covering the Olympics was the largest single operation the BBC had ever undertaken. Whereas journalists writing for newspapers could turn up with their notebooks, the BBC needed a year of planning to set up its overseas transmissions. Preparation began in November 1946, using both the experience gained in Berlin in 1936 and plans made for Finland prior to 1940.

Progress on the work at Wembley was painfully slow. In January 1947 Robert Hart, the Director of Building, wrote: 'Not a single man has been sent through the Ministry of Labour and, quite frankly, without this labour we see little hope of achieving the programme of works within the time still remaining.' After two months, only two lavatories had been built, and after six, work came to a standstill because all labour was tied up in building hospitals for the new National Health Service. (The NHS programme also caused a national shortage of scaffolding which held up the construction of the Olympic scoreboard.) One source of labour was still available: not all of the 400,000 German prisoners of war had been repatriated. Some were drafted in to build the new road. They pushed wheelbarrows and operated pneumatic drills to create Olympic Way and a pedestrian subway connecting Wembley Park railway station to the stadium, cutting eight minutes off the walk.

Another problem faced by the organisers was the defeatism of the press. In August 1947, the sports writer Colonel F.A.M. Webster wrote to *The Times*, concerned that not enough was being done to foster interest. He had just been to Finland where he was impressed by the preparations already underway for the 1952 Olympiad. In September the *Evening Standard* described the Games slightingly as 'a Jamboree of weight-lifting and other sports'. This later gave way to doom-mongering. 'The Olympic Games have inspired so great an interest among the people,' Sigfrid Edström remarked at a meeting of the IOC, 'that the press has made a mountain out of the smallest incident'. *London Calling* magazine asked, 'Are the Olympic Games of today worthwhile? Has big business, nationalism, the win at all costs attitude defeated the original Greek conception? Are they, in short, more of a headache than a pleasure to all concerned? Here, clearly, is stuff for another of the BBC focus programmes, those incisive down to the table dissections of topics of current interest.'

The *Manchester Guardian* viewed the prospect with mixed feelings but conceded, 'If we do not stage the Games with quite the splendour and elaborate organisation which the Germans provided in 1936, they will be none the worse for that, nor will they suffer at all if a little of our carefree attitude towards sport creeps in to lighten the excessive ardour of former Olympic Games.'

Once it was clear that the London Olympics would definitely happen, the press began to carp that it was not being done properly. On 8 May 1948, less than three months before the Games began, *The Times*' leader ran: 'By now any other nation would have called in the best stage managers, the best costume designers, the best architects, typographers, and sculptors to help and advise. With only a few weeks left there is little evidence that Britain is grasping this opportunity. The decorations sub-committee has, presumably, a special duty to look after the visual side of the Games, but it includes not a single architect, artist, or professional designer.' A few days later C.J. Janse described in the same newspaper his 'dismay at the absence of any visible signs of preparation for the reception of our guests from overseas.'

The government, meanwhile, was minding its own business. When Denzil Batchelor telephoned the Ministry of Works in early 1948, they could give him no information on their plans for the Olympics. 'The Ministry of Works passed me from one apathetic department to another, and finally admitted that nothing was being planned by anyone. There was to be no pageantry or pomp, there was not even to be a relaxing of the licensing hours so that bewildered foreigners could get a drink at times which the rest of the world considered civilized.' All he could find were plans for flags in Piccadilly Circus and a notice in three languages in Paddington station welcoming overseas visitors to the Games. 'Outside the great stadium, so grim an austerity reigned that the first American visitor I met said dismally that he proposed attending at Wembley every afternoon and commuting to New York to have some fun in the evenings.'

The *Observer*'s William Clark reported overhearing 'a bloke with a transatlantic accent' say, 'The trouble with you British, is that you've no sense of publicity. Look, there are no flags, no advertisements, no excitement. Why, in Los Angeles in 1932 we just lived, breathed, thought and slept Olympics. London has just swallowed the Games, like it swallowed the Blitz. The most festive sign on the Harrow Road rather bleakly announced, "Welcome to the Olympic Games. This road is a danger area." '

In the end, the efforts of the organisers came together. Most of the work to upgrade Wembley Stadium was completed in only two months. Kiosks and souvenir shops appeared, the giant scoreboard was erected and dressing-room 'hutments' were built which, according to Denzil Batchelor, 'would do credit to a Hollywood country club with their arrays of hip-baths, showers, and two great plunge baths, 15 yards by 10 yards.' Signs that previously read 'Toilets—men and women' were repainted as 'Ladies & Gentlemen' and the 'VIP toilets' became the 'Royal Retiring Room', outlined in gold. On 6 July, three weeks before the Games began, Alfred Barnes, the Minister of Transport, opened the Olympic Way in a procession of thirty cars. Hand-painted plywood shields decorated the lamp posts from which hung huge Olympic flags. Tea was served in the new restaurant at the stadium. Joseph Bickley, who had recently been demobbed from the Royal Navy, was working as a chef in the West End. 'Suddenly the posters appeared in the underground stations emblazoned with the Olympic rings and welcoming visitors from foreign

50

shores. Poor old London looked so shabby, what with the blitz damage, bomb sites and the shortages of practically everything.'

Two days before the opening, Tom Driberg MP asked Mr Key, the Minister of Works, if the government could run to floodlighting of principal public buildings, Trafalgar Square and the lake at St James Park. He was rebuffed with the answer, 'I should not feel justified in diverting the labour and materials necessary.'

In addition to the lack of support from the government, it was still not clear how keen the public were, though it was hoped they would develop an appetite for athletics now that the football season was over. Elvin knew that some of his own regulars were more interested in dog races than human ones, and published an apology in the *Wembley News*. 'I would ask patrons to accept my apologies while they are deprived of enjoying their favourite sport for a few weeks by the temporary suspension of Greyhound Race Meetings. During the Games the kennel staff will maintain the usual standards of training to ensure our kennels are fully up to strength on the resumption.'

Within hours of the last dog race, and just two weeks before the Games began, one hundred workmen dug up the greyhound track and replaced it with 800 tons of specially dressed cinders from the hearths of Leicester. The floodlights were removed and, at a cost of £3,320, extra seats were constructed.

Letters between Elvin and the committee show that his businesslike efficiency sometimes led to strained relations with the committee, who tended to be more gentlemanly in their approach to problems. But he knew the importance of putting on a united front. Writing in the *News of the World*, he asked:

Cannot everyone in the world see that even in far-away Moscow, it is better that men should run and jump against each other than blow each other to pieces on the battlefield? The approach is quite different from the 1936 Berlin Games. We want to see the best men win, no matter where they come from or who they represent. The committee want to run this great festival efficiently and in keeping with its tradition and those who think the old country is no longer capable of putting on a show of such magnitude will get a surprise. There has been a good deal of talk about an Austerity Olympiad but this should not be misunderstood. Of course we haven't wasted our money but we have spent wisely and I have no doubt that our technical efficiency and skill in putting on the Games will be as good as anything in their long and honoured history.

The weekend before the opening ceremony was anything but peaceful in the Elvin household, reported the *Wembley News*:

His phone at his home rang all day long with calls from all sorts of people, mostly strangers, who asked where they could get tickets, how they could get to the stadium and why wasn't Wembley Stadium in the telephone directory? Upon turning to the latest directory, he found that Wembley Stadium was not listed as such under the W's, but rather under the E's as Empire Stadium, and it seems that many people do not realise this is its proper name. To overcome the difficulty the BBC has agreed to broadcast the stadium's proper name and telephone number in the one o'clock news on Monday.

4

WHO CAN JOIN IN?

The Olympics had not always been a competition between nations. In 1908, the City of London Police beat the Liverpool Police in the Tug-of-War final. By 1948, there were over sixty nations boasting Olympic committees, all of which were entitled to compete. Given the recent cessation of hostilities, the question of nations the London committee might wish *not* to invite caused considerable diplomatic headaches.

Moreover, since 1945, borders, affiliations and even national identities had changed. When Finland had competed in the 1908 Games, it had been a province of Russia (whom the Finns defeated at football) but since 1920 it had entered as an independent nation. Lithuania, Estonia and Latvia on the other hand all won medals at the Olympics between 1920 and 1936 but in 1940 they had been annexed by the Soviet Union. The Russians had not so far been a success at the Olympics. A team had intended to compete in London in 1908, but they arrived too late: it transpired they were still working on the Julian Calendar which runs thirteen days behind our own. There was a small entry in 1912, which won a bronze medal for sailing. They were not coming to London now. Many people have since assumed that this was because Stalin either believed the Olympics encouraged individualism or feared that his athletes would be seduced by the West. The Soviet magazine *Ogonyok* reckoned that the Games were an Imperialist plot concocted by the USA. In a 1947 article entitled 'The Role of Spam in Sport', the author Sevidzh claimed: 'The Americans are prepared to bear the cost of the London Olympics, and guarantee food and sports equipment to ensure that sportsmen are from "politically reliable" countries. There is no doubt that the Olympic emblem will adorn not only belt clasps and ties, but also tins containing American Spam, in the guise of American pseudo-philanthropy.' In fact, since 1917 the USSR had never seen fit to form an Olympic committee, and without one it could not compete. Since the Allied victory in 1945, it had received every encouragement from the IOC, but following the Berlin blockade in May, attitudes in London towards the Soviet Union had chilled considerably. Despite this, the Soviet Embassy bought eighteen tickets at 10s 6d each for the opening ceremony. They must have liked what they saw because shortly afterwards they declared that an Olympic team was actually on its way. The Foreign Office averted a diplomatic crisis by informing them that it was 'impracticable' to send wrestlers and gymnasts at such a late hour.

Following the precedent set after 1918, Germany

and Japan were not invited, the official reason given being that there was no address to which to write. Both countries in fact still had representatives on the International Olympic Committee, including His Excellency Duke Adolphe Frederik zu Mecklenburg-Schwerin and Count Michimasa Soyeshima, a graduate of Cambridge University. Neither they nor their countries had been expelled because, as the Foreign Office noted in a confidential memo, 'hitherto they had lain doggo and it was not thought desirable to raise the question which might cause unnecessary bother.' The organisers prayed that they would remain doggo, but only weeks before the event the Japanese announced their intention to send a team. This caused a flurry at the Foreign Office where it was felt their presence would cause 'serious public resentment'. As the peace agreement had not yet been signed, Japan was still technically an enemy, and its athletes could not attend any function at which the King was present. Ciphered telegrams flew between Japan and the Foreign Office, and, to save face, the Japanese were reminded that none of their subjects could leave the country under the rules of the Occupation. Germany, in the throes of division between East and West, did not even try to compete. The German IOC member Dr Karl von Halt claimed that as he lived in British-occupied Berlin, he could come as a Briton, but was firmly told that visas were not available.

As ever, the International Olympic Committee refused to countenance political nuances or national feelings. Edström thought both Japan and Germany should attend and took the British refusal to invite them as a personal affront. He wrote to Lord Burghley, 'I am surprised that you take this attitude three years after the war has ended. We men of sport ought to show the way for the diplomats.'

Once they had made their decisions, the British Organising Committee sent out invitations to over seventy countries a year in advance. Although entry forms had to be delivered four weeks before the Games began, only a few national committees managed to do this properly. Most of those that submitted their forms in time had omitted essential information such as the weight of a boxer or the sex of an athlete. Some countries entered events which were no longer on the programme, such as polo. The use of airmail did not help as it encouraged last-minute entries and airline flights were often cancelled. If all the offending teams had been rejected, there would have been only twenty-three nations left to compete. Urgent telegrams were despatched to hurry them along.

Countries such as Burma, Ceylon, Colombia, Guatemala, Lebanon, Panama, Puerto Rico, Syria and Venezuela were represented for the first time. Italy was invited on the strength of having joined the Allies late in the war. India and Pakistan, divided in 1947, were represented separately for the first time. The number of possible entries from the still substantial British Empire was huge. The decision was made that 'any person who is eligible to represent a British Dominion, Colony or Dependency with an Olympic committee should *not* represent Great Britain unless he [*sic*] was either born in the UK or has resided there for 5 years and bona fide intends to make his permanent home in the United Kingdom.' At the last minute, Trinidad and Tobago put together a team of five competitors who were accompanied by a Chef-de-Mission, assistant Chef-de-Mission, athletics coach, cycling official and two officials with unidentified roles. El Salvador, Guatemala, Bolivia, Bulgaria and Paraguay accepted, but did not come. Haiti sent no team but a M. Sylvio Cator was surprised that his request for free accommodation in 'a first-class London hotel' was rejected.

Palestine had already accepted an invitation, and their Olympic team had started training, when it received a telegram in May 1948 stating that its registration had been withdrawn following the creation of Israel. The IOC, who could notice political situations when they chose to, then averted an Arab boycott by ruling that Israel could not compete because it did not yet have an Olympic committee.

Once a country had decided to compete, their next task was to select competitors from the relevant sports associations. Whichever side they had been on, all European teams had lost many of their best athletes in the war. Jewish Hungarian fencers and Dutch gymnasts who had taken part in the 1936 Olympics were among those who had perished in Nazi concentration camps. Many North American athletes had lost their lives or limbs, fighting in the Pacific or Europe.

A question that concerned everyone was that of amateurism, which sometimes also involved consideration of a person's class. In 1896 Edward Battell, a servant at the British Embassy in Athens, had almost been barred from entering because his employment showed he was not a 'gentleman'. He was vindicated when he became one of only three competitors to complete the 87 km cycle race and won the bronze medal. More usually, competitors were debarred if evidence suggested that they earned their living from their sport. The Italian gymnast Alberto Braglia won the gold medal in 1908 and then worked as 'The Human Torpedo' in a circus. He struggled to be accepted for the Italian team in 1912. Exactly what constituted amateurism was not always clear because every sport tended to have its own rules. In 1908 both the Royal Yacht Squadron and the Hockey Club often handed out large prizes and paid professionals to compete alongside amateurs. In 1924, a swimmer called Richmond Eve won a gold medal for Australia and a year later he was declared a professional because he had received expenses for travelling to a diving exhibition. The Irish-Native-American Jim Thorpe won both the decathlon and the pentathlon gold medals in 1912 and was described by the King of Sweden as 'the greatest athlete in the world', but in 1913 his medals were taken back and he was struck from all records. Avery Brundage, who had competed against him in 1912, had reported Thorpe for earning $25 playing baseball. Despite huge support from his fans, Thorpe's reputation was not restored until thirty years after he died in 1953.

In 1937 the IOC decided that swimming coaches were professionals and had to be barred from competition. 'We had an astonishingly strict honorary secretary for over forty years called H.E. Fern CBE JP,' said Harry Walker, a BBC commentator and member of the Amateur

Swimming Association. 'He made it very hard for us. He was so amateur he thought all my BBC fees should go to the ASA. He didn't approve of me at all.'

When it came to football, Matt Busby, the manager of Manchester United who was appointed British Olympic football manager, commented:

If the Olympic Games is a yardstick of quality, then amateur football in Great Britain does not compare very favourably with the amateur game in other countries. Some of their big stars, though they may all have other jobs for the benefit of the casual enquirer, play football the year round—and they are paid money, often big money, to help attend to the necessities of life. Those nations who continue to act according to the book are faced with two alternatives: they must either refuse to compete against such unfair odds, or enter for the Olympics knowing they have no earthly chance of victory. A cleft stick, indeed.

The British policy was to enter, Busby added, 'on the assumption that it is better to have the Union Jack trampled into the turf than not to show the flag at all. Every four years Britain's football-clerks, football-grocers and football-pitmen are exposed to something akin to ridicule.'

Sweden and the rest of Scandinavia sought 'broken time', whereby athletes could be paid wages for time lost in international competitions. Britain, the USA and France were all opposed, arguing that it would lead to 'veiled professionalism' and in 1946 the IOC decided not to consider this until after 1948. As an influential member of the London committee, Harold Abrahams felt there was a need to regain the spirit of amateurism:

> The Berlin Games were such a spectacle that something very vital was missing. I came away having watched a wonderfully organised but rather mechanical and inhuman exhibition. How to combine world-record achievements with the spirit of amateurism is a problem which becomes more and more acute each year. We have a grand opportunity to make the first post-war Olympic meeting the starting point for something really worthwhile.

In 1948 and despite the efforts of the Labour government, this 'spirit of amateurism' was still bedevilled by social class. Bert Bushnell was a sculler who had been educated by the State. In the select world of Henley rowing, he would have been classified as a professional had he been employed in his family's boat business. Amateurs were still gentlemen, and gentlemen had private means: such competitors, it was said, needed no financial support and were therefore not open to bribes or commercial offers. There were Olympic committees in countries such as Hungary and Yugoslavia who circumvented the problem by ensuring that their team were all serving in the army where they could be paid as soldiers and not as sportsmen.

The British Amateur Athletics Association set standards of almost absurd purity. One person who fell foul of their codes was Denis Watts. He was picked for the long jump and hop-step-and-jump, at which he was the AAA champion, only to find that he was classed a 'professional' because he had applied for a job as a sports teacher. Had he delayed his job application until after the Games, he would have been able to compete. The AAA decreed that its professional coaches were not allowed to work directly with Olympic athletes and so they in turn had to train amateur coaches. Frank Turner, captain of the British gymnastics team, related:

If you did a job in any way connected with gym, you were considered a professional. At thirteen I was employed as an extra in a film with Gracie Fields. I had to sit on a beach eating a stick of sugar rock. The director asked me to do a somersault as she walked past. I was about to do this, when luckily somebody warned me that a simple somersault would mean I was a professional gymnast. I was already in the national gym team and would have been banned from all competitions, including the Olympics.

Ferenc Pataki, on the other hand, had also been discovered as a potential gymnast when he too performed acrobatics in a film: but he was whisked into the Hungarian army. However many rules were made to create a level playing field between competitors, some were more equal than others. No expense was spared in training the US athletes, many of whom received college scholarships. Despite his own strict stance on amateurism,

Avery Brundage gave Asa Bushnell, the US Olympic secretary, a blank cheque to cover the team's expenses in London.

*   *   *

After the blatant cheating of the Germans in 1936, when German judges ignored their compatriots flouting the rules, and they won 89 of the 250 medals at their own Games, the London committee felt it was doubly important for the British to show fair play. Members of the British team were selected by their particular sports associations, with a few to spare. To ensure against injury or reduced performance, so many 'possibles' were chosen that often individuals did not know until weeks, or even days, before the event, whether they were actually competing.

To give everyone a chance to train, Billy Butlin, the owner of six holiday camps, invited the British athletics team for a week after Easter at Clacton-on-Sea. For some, this holiday atmosphere held uncomfortable memories. 'It was a bit like being in the Forces again,' wrote the poet John Pudney, who had been in the RAF, in the *News Chronicle*. 'My papers told me which chalet I was in, which table I would occupy for meals, the row it was in, and in which sitting I should participate. Somebody, I thought, is going to make me *do* something: and he is going to be unlucky. All that happened was that I had to be punctual for meals. I soon realised that the camp deliberately catered for many *different* things at the same time.'

The camp had its own amusement park, private beach and L-shaped swimming pool. During the war it had housed first prisoners of war and then an army training base. It had been reopened in 1946 'to the great relief of the general public and the joy of all who had been there'. The Olympic contestants were greeted by Captain Bond, the physical trainer, and Gladys Painter, the first-ever Red Coat, whose motto was 'Our true intent is all for your delight'. After training hard all day, the athletes were entertained in the evening with a beauty contest and learned to sing 'Butlin's Buddies':

> Give yourself a holiday, beside the shining foam.
> Come on, all you scholars, and put away your
>   studies,
> Come and join the happy band
> That's known as Butlin's Buddies.
> Now that summer's come again and life is gay
> And we're all together on our holiday.
> With hip hip hip hip hip—hooray.

5

THEY'RE ON THEIR WAY

The London Games were due to open on 29 July. Early in that month teams began to arrive from all over the world: roughly 800 from North America and 1,000 Spaniards, South Americans and Italians; another 1,000 Scandinavians, 562 Eastern Europeans, 350 from the Middle East and 900 from Britain and the Empire. The Home Office decided to save time at immigration by waiving visas and instead issuing Olympic Identity Cards which were valid as passports into the United Kingdom, for one journey in each direction. They were designed by the Aliens Department to be impossible to counterfeit and yet easy to read.

The team that travelled further than any other and arrived earliest was from New Zealand: it consisted of a manager, three track athletes, a boxer, a cyclist, a weightlifter, a female swimmer and her chaperone. Each had signed an Olympic bond before they set out, promising they would 'win without swank and lose without grousing'. 'For at least two years after my return to New Zealand', it went on, 'I will not to be guilty of any act or omission whereby I may become liable to be declared a professional. I undertake to learn all I can about my branch of sport while abroad and to make this information available to my association on my return.' No one in the team had a personal coach nor had they ever competed internationally. Their Olympic Association accepted no responsibility for injury or illness but they did provide a uniform. The journey from New Zealand to London lay via the Panama Canal and took five weeks. The six men shared a cabin overlooking the cargo deck, which was overrun with cockroaches. 'The boat trip over was sheer hell really,' the weightlifter Maurice Crow remembered. 'We struck it rough in the Atlantic. They were bad storms. The ship was too unsteady to do any weightlifting and I could only do push-ups and sit-ups.' The 16mm film they took shows the deck swaying as Crow climbs up the rigging and holds himself horizontal in mid-air, toes pointing neatly in the 'flag' position. He lifts his compatriot

'Dutch' Holland, who is almost two feet taller, onto his shoulders as if he were a set of weights. Harold Nelson was intending to run for his country in the 10,000 and 5,000 metres and it was vital that he did not lose fitness while at sea. 'We ran round and round the boat, eleven circuits to the mile. It was difficult; you would be jumping over deck chairs and dodging people. Holland, a hurdler, had one hurdle put out on the deck.'

Ngaire Lane was a 22-year-old swimmer and the only female member of the team. She had been away from home only once before.

One of the holds had been turned into cabins with a rather basic bathroom and dining room added. It was not very comfortable! There were six boys and myself. At home I had three sisters, so it was quite a learning curve to be with these young fellows for five weeks. My chaperone, Mrs Mima Ingram, became 'mother' to the team and was a huge factor in our over-all happiness. We soon became like one big family. There was no opportunity to train on the boat. The ship's carpenter built me an oblong box which he lined with canvas. It was filled with sea water every day. It was barely one foot longer than me. I could lie on my back and kick.

The cyclist Nick Carter had rollers built on deck and managed to cycle on the spot. 'That gave me some exercise,' he said. 'I had ropes mounted for stability in case the boat lurched. But it was hard to ride with the side to side motion of the boat. I couldn't ride at all if the roll was too great.'

In contrast, the Americans sailed from New York in some style, the women in first class and the men in second. The athletes from Hawaii had brought their ukuleles and serenaded the team across the Atlantic. 'SS *America* was a large boat,' said the hurdler Craig Dixon. 'We took ten days on the high sea and it was a marvellous experience. The first couple of days down in the dining room, all the bread rolls went very quickly. We didn't realise we could order anything we wanted.'

'It was the first time I had crossed the Atlantic,' said the sprinter Mel Patton. 'The camaraderie was unbelievable. For a Californian it was very difficult to train because we weren't accustomed to running on boards on the deck. The organisers tried to restrict us by setting curfews but we just ignored them.' Avery Brundage was not with them: he made a later passage in the state rooms of the *Queen Elizabeth*. This was probably a good thing, for in 1936 he had dismissed a female swimmer, Eleanor Holm, for enjoying herself too much in the bar.

Always racially segregated at home, black and white members of the team now mixed for the first time. 'I shook hands with my first black American on board ship,' remembered the rifleman Arthur Jackson. 'We were eating and socialising together on a white ship.' The French magazine *Point de Vue* showed a photo of 'Le chocolat' Harrison Dillard embracing R.B. Cochran. 'This photograph provoked a scandal in the United States,' ran the caption, 'where it is not customary for whites and blacks to fraternise. But in the joy of winning their event, they paid no attention to racist doctrine.'

Vicki Draves was a 24-year-old diving star. She

had been born in California to an English mother and a Filipino father. 'In the San Francisco schools there were many different races. It was a melting pot. My twin sister and I learned to swim and dive at the nickel baths.' Vicki was barred from the local diving club because of her Filipino father, forcing her coach to set up a special club for her and substitute her mother's maiden name, Taylor, for her Filipino name, Manalo. 'I didn't feel great about it because there was this distinction. But if that was the only way I could start, I would have to accept it. The kids did not care what my race was.'

The African-American sprinter Mal Whitfield recalled, 'I was so hepped up about going to London for the Olympics that even though I hated water I didn't care how I got there. I had an English teacher in the States and when we docked at Southampton there was a big sign, "Welcome Mr Whitfield". What a welcome, such warmth!' Other visitors from the USA were not so welcome. Greeting a flight from New York, a London airport official heard a hat-box say 'Help'. The luggage was checked and the *Daily Mirror* reported that Mrs Janet Patry of New York was 'immensely surprised' when her pet budgerigar was found there. 'I don't know how it got in,' she said. The bird was flown back to the US.

The Games took place at a crucial moment for British attitudes to immigration. In May 1948, the SS *Empire Windrush*, a decommissioned German troopship en route from Australia to England, stopped to pick up migrant workers in Trinidad and Jamaica. When news reached London that this boat was on its way, the prospect of 500 black men arriving to take British jobs was trumpeted by the press, and Parliament debated whether they should be refused entry. It was pointed out that they all possessed British passports and many had fought in the war. The country was seriously short of labour and over 100,000 Poles had been employed as labourers with no fuss from anyone. When the *Windrush* docked a month later, half the passengers found work straightaway in London Transport and the National Health Service. The other half were housed in Clapham South bomb shelter, a mile from Brixton Labour Exchange. As the men found work, the area became home to London's Caribbean community. Despite a warm welcome from a local church and the Clapham Communist Party, the West Indians met with the racism then endemic in Britain. Indeed, while the Games were in progress, a riot took place in Liverpool between a white mob and African seamen which ended in the arrest of thirty-five black men and one white. Claims of police brutality were ignored and most of the defendants were found guilty of disorderly behaviour. But British law did not condone racism or religious prejudice. The *Evening News* reported that, 'Bertram Dukepile of Shepherd's Bush was bound over for a year today and fined £50 under an Act of 1360 following complaints of a "persistent course of Jew baiting". Dukepile had made two inflammatory speeches and was a disturber of the peace likely to persevere in such conduct.'

The competitors who were billeted in homes were treated as part of the family. One group was the three women of the first-ever Jamaican team. Fifteen-year-old Jennifer Welson of Wembley reported:

68

Mavis the hurdler, Carmen the high jumper and Kathleen the all-rounder came to stay with us for an enjoyable six weeks. Coming from a sugar-producing island they had a sweet tooth and introduced a new dish into our home of boiled rice, grated coconut and red beans. They found the heat unbearable because it lacked their cool breeze. They were genuinely surprised when people went to work in the rain looking happy. They were delighted with the zoo and Kew Gardens, and thrilled to hear Big Ben. We were only sorry to see them return home.

The Bermudan women's team stayed in the home of Denise Verrinder, a fifth-former at Wembley School:

There was Phyllis Edness, a dark-haired girl of 18, who was a natural runner, Phyllis Lightbourn of English descent who had trained for the long-jump, and their chaperone, the team manager's wife, Mrs Heywood. They were thrilled by the speakers in Hyde Park trying to put the world to rights, and by the excitement of meeting the royal family at Buckingham Palace. They also remarked on the cheapness and quality of our utility clothing and the inexpensiveness of food. They used their water very economically; their baths were only a few inches deep. And when it rained, they exclaimed what a pleasant sound it was to hear the rain running down the gutters. They had a very friendly way and acknowledged everyone in the street. When they came into our garden they said 'Gee, apples growing on trees!'

Denise used her food coupons to bake Phyllis Lightbourn a cake on her birthday.

Mr G. Wilson of Borough Road, Hounslow, took in two Indians: Gurnham Singh, a high jumper, and Bonta Singh, a wrestler, who used signs to communicate. Mr Wilson was proud to introduce 'his turbanned friends' to the mayor. Mr Wright of Wembley School commented:

We were most fortunate in having British colonials as our guests. The flags of Bermuda, Ceylon, Jamaica, Trinidad and Malta fluttered gaily around the Olympic flag. One day Duncan White of Ceylon beat the Olympic hurdles record in the semi final, to the delight of everyone. Arthur Wint of Jamaica won the 400 metre final in grand style. Rodney Wilkies, our little negro from Trinidad, came in second in the world weightlifting championship and returned home to the school with a smile which persisted to the very end of his stay with us. Tuesday August 10th was also a red letter day when Mr Arthur Creech Jones, the Colonial Secretary, came to take lunch with us.

The Scottish footballer Angus Carmichael remembered, 'It was the first time that many of us had ever seen black people. One day a black American accidentally bumped into one of our team, a rather cocky cockney. "Watch it, Sambo!"

70

he said. The man turned, rose to his greatest height and said quietly, "I have a handle to my name." Later I realised it was the great sprinter, Harrison Dillard.'

Like the Americans, the Argentinean team was also large, comprising 200 men, five women and a dozen horses. They brought their own blacksmith, iron for shoeing, food for the horses, and maté tea and spaghetti for the grooms, who were all army conscripts.

The New Zealanders arrived in June. 'When we got to Britain we were still suffering from seasickness,' said Crow. 'We took a month to get our land legs back. The sight of bomb-damaged London was a shock: street after street, full of stinking water holes. There were damaged buildings and roads all around, vacant lots everywhere. London was a sad place, but I was impressed by the way the British were putting up with so much.'

Raising the money for transport, accommodation and training, not to mention surmounting foreign exchange regulations, proved difficult for many of the small countries. Xavier Frick was the manager of two decathletes, who were the whole Liechtenstein entry. 'A Count von Bendern told us that his wife could put a certain sum of money at our disposal. We therefore did not have either to buy black-market pounds nor pay over the odds for legal tender. The amount more or less covered our outgoings while we were in England.'

The Swiss team travelled by train via Paris and Calais, meeting up with the two decathletes from Liechtenstein. Exploring before the Games opened, Xavier Frick found London an enormous city:

Uxbridge is a whole hour's train ride from the centre, which had suffered severe rocket damage during the war. We went to see the badly bombed St Paul's Cathedral. However, we ended up in an office full of women. It was a huge surprise for them to see so suddenly in their office three Olympic participants in their uniforms. Even though the British are very pro sport, they seemed strangely more interested in the cricket match against Australia than in the Olympic Games. At least half of the inhabitants of London have no idea there was an Olympic Games.

One of the last arrivals came from even closer to home: the Irish team of seventy-two competitors and forty-four officials who left Dublin only five days before the opening ceremony. The Irish government had no funds to support their Olympic Council, who had to borrow the money for the boat and rail fares, and survive the long journey on sandwiches.

As soon as the Irish team arrived, a row broke out when the British noticed that some of the Irish entries had been born in Northern Ireland. J.F. Chisholm, their manager, pointed out that under Irish law since 1935, any citizens of Northern Ireland were also considered members of the Irish Free State, if they wanted. Opinion was divided. The International Rowing Federation allowed an oarsman from Belfast to join the seven Dubliners in the Irish boat and the Northern boxer Ken

Martin managed to compete for Ireland, but two swimmers did not.

*   *   *

The London committee had placed its faith in revenue from tickets as the chief source of its income, and attracting advance sales was an essential part of its strategy. However, only Ireland, Portugal and Iceland had paid up by the deadline for reduced prices and in December 1947 the amount received was less than £6,000. The United States had ordered a massive £98,000 worth of tickets, Sweden £26,000 and other countries £44,000, but none had actually sent a penny. Three weeks before the Games opened, the Hungarians threatened to pull out after the Foreign Office announced that while the team would get ID cards, their supporters would not be granted visas. Their Embassy returned all their tickets, which were worth £1,500, and this galvanised the diplomats into finding a compromise.

The media were once again not helping matters. In mid-July news reached the press that the US Olympic Committee had sold only 10 per cent of their tickets and the papers proceeded to declare the Games a flop. Then word spread that tickets had actually sold out. They hadn't, but the rumour slowed sales even further. By 19 July, £450,000 had been taken, only half what was needed to cover costs. Desperate to 'preserve an aspect of success', the committee issued a statement saying, 'The present demand for tickets, although not heavy, is steady.' Availability to the British public picked up on 28 July, when the Americans realised they had over-estimated and finally paid £18,000 and returned the rest.

Ticket prices varied from two shillings for hockey to one guinea for rowing at Henley. Tickets for fencing were six shillings while for the equestrian event a two-shilling ticket simply gave one entry to Aldershot where there were no seats. Boxing and swimming at the Empire Pool were sold out before they began. Wembley Stadium contained 83,732 possible places, made up of seats, benches and standing on the terraces. Despite attempts to prevent a black market, the inevitable touts gathered round the stadium. The *Wembley News* reported that Mr William Baker of Wood Green was arrested outside the Empire Pool after a fight with a uniformed official who had tried to stop him touting tickets. 'I am satisfied that Baker is one of the "spiv" type of ticket touts,' proclaimed the local Justice of the Peace. Robert Munday of Holloway, a peddler, pleaded guilty to stealing a briefcase on Olympic Way containing Olympic souvenirs belonging to another peddler. 'The rightful owner of the case had laid it by some railings as he served two customers,' reported the *Wembley News*. 'Pleading guilty, Munday said he had been badly wounded at El Alamein and had himself recently lost a case of goods at Petticoat Lane. He was bound over for two years.'

Some of the touts were foreigners trying to raise money for their keep. Peter Antill, a pupil at Wembley County School, observed: 'It was rather remarkable to see the many different nations represented by the people selling tickets outside the stadium. A Chinaman was selling swimming tickets at four shillings and sixpence, which was less than cost price. There was one grey-haired old man who refused to be hurried but had tickets for everything even if he did make a hundred per cent profit on some. One man sold two tickets for the morning swimming session at twelve o'clock.'

Even the officials were hawking tickets, reported the *Evening News*:

The Wembley Olympic box office authorities have had to call in extra commissionaires to prevent ticket-touting. Wembley say that this selling of tickets is upsetting the box office and the arrangements for seating in the stadium. They threatened prosecution for anyone who is found trying to sell tickets to the queue. Among those who were discovered selling tickets today and ordered to stop were competitors and officials of the Games. In many cases the foreign competitors were selling tickets because they had run short of sterling and this was the only way they knew to obtain some. Among those warned off were French and Finnish officials wearing their national blazers and badges. One of the Frenchmen said, 'Our country allowed us only nine pounds each to spend here and now we are almost broke. I foresaw this and bought a hundred pounds worth of tickets. Now I am trying to sell them to get some money. It is the only way we can live here. We are like beggars, it is a terrible shame. One of our coaches has got £400 worth of boxing tickets.' Nearby stood a tall bronzed Finnish athlete holding a book of tickets in his hand and smiling with embarrassment. 'You buy a ticket from me,' he pleaded. 'I have no money left.'

Sales for the opening ceremony were so slow that 3/6d standing tickets were issued free to schoolchildren, students, nurses and Girl Guides. Two complimentary tickets were given to each member of the International and National Olympic Committees and to every one of the fifty-seven embassies in London, on the understanding that this did not constitute any kind of inducement by the government. Panama, which was fielding one runner, requested nine diplomatic places. The Mayor of Wembley, H.S. Sirkett, was annoyed that he had not been invited to meet the King and Queen. With his usual dextrous tact, Sir Arthur Elvin sent him a pair of complimentary season tickets 'in a favourable position near the Royal Box'. Seizing his opportunity, Mayor Sirkett asked for two more for his sons.

A special section in the stadium was reserved for the 1,500 athletes so they could watch each other's events. However, they were not entitled to complimentary tickets outside their own venues, which meant that the swimmers could watch the boxers at the Empire Pool, but, unless they were prepared to pay for it, neither swimmers, boxers, cyclists, hockey players nor gymnasts could go to see the football. At the stadium, footballer Angus Carmichael had a marvellous time. 'Wembley was a unique place; nowhere else could have been better. There was always a lovely friendly atmosphere among the spectators and the competitors. It felt such a privilege after the war to be able to mix with so many different people in a relaxed way.'

A joke went the rounds about three men who were disappointed to learn there were no more seats to be had. Undaunted, the first picked up a manhole cover, and went up to an attendant. 'The name is Smith,' he said. 'Discus thrower.' He was admitted. The second found a long sewer pipe and carried it to the gate. 'The name is Brown,' he said. 'Pole vaulter.' He, too, was admitted. Not to be outdone, the third fellow found a roll of barbed wire. 'The name is Jones,' he said. 'Fencing.'

6

SETTLING IN

The Games brought to London some 4,000 athletes, together with their managers and coaches, all of whom had to be housed at minimal cost. Clearly London could not afford to construct an Olympic Village of the kind built for the 1932 Los Angeles Games, with bungalows, a hospital, a library and canteens. Nor could the Brits hope to compete with the Germans, who in 1936 had erected a village with 150 cottages around four new stadiums, swimming pools and a polo field. The committee discussed housing the visitors in ships but the demand on the merchant navy was such that no vessel could be allowed to remain inactive on the Thames for a fortnight. A Mr W. Hackett of Edgware proposed that 'each household should host two athletes for this welcome invasion, a boon to both hosts and visitors.' A civil servant even suggested using prisoner-of-war camps: 'Provided the camps are a good standard and the barbed wire removed, I see no objection to their use.'

Eventually over thirty sites were identified as 'reasonable (but not extravagant) Housing Centres', including RAF camps, schools, colleges and nurses' hostels. Neither government offices nor schools were paid any rent. The eighteen Middlesex County Council schools agreed to start their summer holidays one week early, which left a few hours in which to convert classrooms into dormitories. The organisers decided that although the sports arenas were scattered around London, each nation should be accommodated together, in order to cater for different languages and diets. At Torbay and Henley, campsites and hotels were used. The equestrian and pentathlon competitors at Aldershot stayed at the Royal Military Academy at Sandhurst, while the grooms slept in barracks near their horses.

The Ministry of Works had plenty of experience in furnishing wartime hostels at short notice. They equipped thirty housing centres with 33,000 yards of curtaining, 34,000 sheets, 13,000 small chairs, 36,000 pieces of crockery and 4,000 wardrobes. Typewriters, billiard tables and pianos were borrowed; bains-marie bought for the French kitchen and 'Special Scandinavian vapour baths' installed. Bedding was provided but competitors were asked to bring their own towels, though some were available to hire. 'As was expected,' noted the official report, 'these were in great demand.'

Nearly two thousand men were housed in Richmond Park in the original wooden huts built in 1938 to accommodate army recruits. During the war, the camp had become a military convalescent home and afterwards a barracks for women of the Auxiliary Territorial Service. Kingston Council had hoped to use it for local homeless families but was refused permission. When journalists visited the site in June 1948 they discovered underground air-raid shelters festering with garbage, stagnant water and mosquitoes. But by the time the 1,600 male competitors arrived, together with their managers, everything was spick and span with fresh creosote and green painted doors. The transformation, which cost £35,000 (about £500 per man, nowadays), was described by the *Surrey Comet*:

Comfort but few luxuries. Final touches are now being given to the 20-acre Olympic Games Centre in Richmond Park. The main work on this 'austerity-plus' home for visiting athletes has now been completed by a staff of 400 men from the Ministry of Works. First impressions always count and the designers have fashioned a broad sweeping driveway in the woods surrounding the old guardroom, now the reception centre. Interpreters will be on hand to smooth language difficulties and every effort has been made to provide a pleasant 'home from home' while ingenuity has been shown in economy and reuse of materials.

Officers' quarters have been converted into shops selling cigarettes and newspapers, shoe repairs, a laundry, and a branch of the National Provincial Bank. In the Barracks rooms each cubicle has well-polished linoleum and sprung iron beds with horse hair

79

mattresses, with ivory-coloured quilts, and blue-painted wooden tallboys. It looks comfortable and yet bears the stamp of austerity. No charges could be levelled against money being spent on exorbitant luxury.

No allowance had been made for the size of competitors, and one bed collapsed under an Argentinean wrestler. The *Comet* reported that 'There was not enough room for two men to get out of bed at the same time.' It continued:

Australians visiting the 'homeland' for the first time, Indians, South Americans and Mexicans all have a common appreciation of the helpfulness and friendship shown by Kingstonians. Laurie Birkes, featherweight boxer from Brisbane, said that he liked the town, although the stores were not so large as those in Sidney [*sic*]. Prices, complained Australian R. Magee, weightlifter from Sidney, are 'solid' compared with those in Australia, particularly socks and shirts. 'People very good; town very good,' said the Argentine boxing trainer, who won the heavyweight title in 1928. He was in the gymnasium, where his team were training in the rings, dark bodies weaving an intricate pattern against the white walls. Outside on a grass track surrounding a flowerbed, Uruguayans were practising for the flat races, watched by Paraguayans and Argentineans. A couple were drinking maté from calabashes. 'A very fine place, so tranquil,' said their trainer, and he expressively spread his hands out to encompass the rolling greenery of Richmond Park. Augustine Garcia, the Mexican basket-ball coach, had bought a sweater and woollen socks and found purchase tax had made them expensive. 'Everybody is so nice, so kind,' he said. 'The people,' said R. Bhatti from Bengal, 'are obliging and friendly. We are impressed by their good manners and behaviour. The policeman is a very gentle man, always'. Samu Chatterjee from Calcutta, who is in the Indian water polo team, declared, 'I have seen many places in London, but I think your moving staircase is the most marvellous.' [Bentall's department store in Kingston had installed escalators in the 1930s.] Six elderly men in a corner of the camp have done no work since they arrived. They are all retired from the London Fire Brigade. So far, no one has even dropped a lighted match.

Tim Lowry, aged fifteen, lived nearby:

Somehow we heard they were recruiting messenger boys and about half a dozen of us were taken on. You had to provide your own bicycle and received no pay, but got three meals a day. Most of the competing nations brought their own food, so we ate well and were able to take home all sorts of goodies to swell the bare larder. I spent virtually the whole summer holiday there. Some of the competitors were very slow in going home and so the camp stayed open long after the Games were over. On Sundays, children queued up for autographs.

Dennis Newton, aged fourteen, attended King's College Grammar School in Wimbledon:

It was coming up for the school holidays and I saw an ad in the local paper that messenger boys were wanted up at Richmond army camp. My dad told me to apply. I expect he thought it would be safer for me than what we normally did in the holidays, which was collecting bits of bombs. I cycled to the camp every day. We were two boys on duty at a time, waiting in the reception office to run errands—parcels, telegrams, letters—for the athletes. Few of them spoke English, and there weren't any phones for them. The athletes lived in long wooden huts and ate in the canteen cookhouses. Nobody minded, it was normal.

The messenger boys were taken by bus to the opening ceremony at Wembley. Newton remembered: 'That was a grand day out. Another boy got me a poster of a discus thrower in front of Big Ben.'

Collip's Gentleman Outfitters in nearby Kingston-upon-Thames did well from the visitors. 'The shop was run by my dad, Frederick,' said Newton. 'None of the athletes had raincoats, and Collip's soon sold out of the newfangled "Pac-a-macs". Cotton Y-fronts sold well too.' Visiting athletes must have spotted this novel item of underwear in the changing rooms, for each British team member had been given one free pair.

The New Zealand team were among sixteen other countries based at Richmond. 'The first few days we stayed at the Crofton Hotel,' wrote their team captain, Harold Nelson. 'When the village at Richmond Park was ready, we shifted in. We were amazed that there were no fences. The deer appeared quite tame, the squirrels chased each other round the branches. It was hard to believe that they had survived, in view of the shortage of meat during the war.'

On arrival the New Zealanders were taken to the asphalt parade ground and lined up in front of a flagpole. Maurice Crow was not impressed. 'At the flag-raising ceremony no New Zealand flag was on hand, so Lord Burghley and his retinue hoisted the Australian flag instead. Obviously we did not sing "Advance Australia Fair".' The Australian team had actually been having a raw deal. They arrived when the London dockers were on strike for more pay and despite an army presence, their luggage was pilfered on the wharf and they lost all their tracksuits. A telegram was sent to Australia and thirty new ones were despatched by plane.

Coin-operated phones were installed. 'We cannot risk competitors making long-distance trunk calls and not paying their bills,' said the organisers. Each housing centre endeavoured to provide a bank, a cinema, laundry, barber, newsagent, tailor and boot repair shop. All this, in dormitories of four to six men and three meals a day, cost each competitor 25 shillings a night. The scheme was run like a military operation, without any choice. If people didn't like it, they were free to look for a hotel at their own expense. Apart from one group of Scandinavians who took one look at Richmond and booked into a hotel, the teams from Australia, New Zealand, Asia and

South America all hoisted their national flags and got on with training in the park. 'The next team to arrive were from Afghanistan,' wrote Nelson. 'They would fill the bath up to the top, wash themselves outside of the bath, sluice themselves down and when they were clean, get into the bath. We pointed out that the showers were for cleaning themselves with and the water drained away, but no, they persisted with their ritual.'

The Kingston Chamber of Commerce wanted to take athletes on sight-seeing tours, but the Ministry of Fuel refused to issue extra petrol coupons for 'non-essential travel'. The New Zealanders, looked after by their High Commissioner, clearly got preferential treatment. 'Horlicks Ltd sent two Daimler cars to take us on a scenic drive to Windsor Castle,' wrote Harold Nelson. 'We passed the beautiful spot where King John signed the Magna Carta in 1215. We were shown through the Castle and saw paintings by Rubens and Rembrandt. We had lunch in the Director's boardroom. Doug Harris had picked up his chicken wishbone & used it as a monocle. He liked to take off the aristocracy. Well he dropped it and someone stood on it and broke it. He made such a fuss that the technician took it off to the Laboratory and wired the pieces together. What's more, two days later Doug received a brand new gold monocle in the mail with the compliments of Horlicks.'

Merely employing enough catering staff was a headache, given the nationwide shortage of manpower, so 1,000 students were recruited by the National Union of Students. At the largest centre of all, the RAF camp in Uxbridge, seven miles west of Wembley, over 300 students were employed to wash dishes and clean floors. The Camp Commandant, Captain A.E. Smith, a gunner who had won medals in both wars, was pleased. 'They are doing a grand job of work. The standard of workmanship is high and we are very pleased with them. They come from universities all over the country and a few are foreign students. One, a Norwegian, hitch hiked to the camp from Newcastle.'

To save the cost of their transport and ensure they turned up to work on time, the students slept in tents on site. James Pilditch, an art student at Reading University, spent his summer looking after more than 1,500 Americans, Britons and others at the Uxbridge camp. Each street in the nearby town was invited to adopt a different nation and provide flowers from their gardens to decorate the dormitories.

'The glamorously entitled Olympic Village at Uxbridge,' wrote Pilditch, looking back nearly fifty years, 'had been the headquarters of Fighter Command who won the Battle of Britain in 1940. During the day, student workers like me wore khaki denim overalls. But one young man from Oxford refused to conform. He always wore a blazer, with the added affectation of an upturned collar.'

The official report claimed: 'All gates were manned by police officials who scrutinised the passes of all.' But Pilditch's version was rather different:

My first job, manning the gate, didn't last long. We put a brick on the pedal which controlled

85

the turnstile, so that anyone could walk through. That was unpopular with the officials. But rather than fire us, the commandant gave me the task of working out a roster for staff involved. It worked quite well for me. The camp had a hospitality lounge, where important visitors were received. I made sure my job was to man it overnight. After a free dinner I went on duty at 9.30 and stayed awake until midnight. Then I slept in a bedroom off it, in case there were phone calls, but who would phone a bar in the middle of the night? At 8 a.m. I was off for the day. Officially I had been on duty for ten and a half hours—most of it asleep. Such devotion entitled me to two and a half hours' overtime pay, free breakfast, and a free bus down the road to Wembley. There I saw not only the grand opening ceremony but most of the field and track events too. After splendid days, I bussed back to Uxbridge for more free meals and undisturbed evenings.

Harry Koskie, the British swimming coach, complained:

Although comfortably housed we were unfortunate in living in a part of the camp which was terribly noisy at night. Despite a 10.30 p.m. curfew it was frequently impossible to get to sleep until the early hours of the morning; although I constantly protested. What is more, whilst I appreciate it is customary to segregate the sexes, I nevertheless greatly deplored an arrangement which separated our team by seventeen miles.

This undoubtedly affected the spirit and made it impossible to supervise the final training.

The British runner Bill Nankeville didn't sleep too well either. 'I shared a room with Tom Richards, the marathon runner. He was a psychiatric nurse in Tooting Bec and told me gruesome stories about his patients which gave me terrible nightmares.'

'The North American competitors introduced British men to new forms of personal hygiene such as talcum powder and deodorants,' said the footballer Angus Carmichael. 'I borrowed a Canadian's after-shave for the opening ceremony.' He was amused by the signs outside the sleeping quarters: 'NO NOISE—COMPETITORS IN ....
ASLEEP'. The gap was filled in every night with the most important event of the next day: '100 m final' or '400 m relay'.

'There were no parties—just training and early to bed,' remembered the Scottish sprinter Alastair McCorquodale. No alcohol was available but the malt drink company Horlicks set up stalls supplying competitors with free hot drinks. 'Drugs?' said Joseph Birrell, the hurdler. 'We had drugs in 1948. We ate Horlicks tablets by the handful. With no sweets they were a real treat.' A free supply of Multi-Vite tablets was also available: 'Mainly,' the medical committee admitted, 'as a psychological stimulant'.

The British hockey player Neil White said:

Boredom was a problem. But as long as one could watch and study the great athletes at work, life was fascinating. The American

87

training was rigid and strict and their chief coach put them through their paces in the most rigorous fashion. 'You've come here to win gold medals, not to sign autographs', he yelled at Mel Patton. Each athlete could pace themselves to finer than a second, and Patton could more or less tell his time over 200 metres to a fifth of a second. The jumpers, divers and gymnasts all seemed to be double-jointed and it made some of us feel old.

Indeed most of the British team were older than the Americans.

'I noticed that when the US athletes arrived they took a quick lunch and then went training,' remembered James Pilditch. 'The British team ate, and then sprawled on the grass to sunbathe.' He also commented:

While the Olympians were getting on fine, unpleasant memories of the second world war were still fresh in the minds of some. One night the Korean team wandered out to the pub in Uxbridge. A habitué of the local mistook them for Japanese, whose cruelty in the war was widely known. The local man provoked an argument. Unfortunately, he picked on the Korean wrestlers and boxers. English bodies flew through the pub door and littered the pavement outside. Quick police work prevented a scandal. The Koreans were escorted back to the camp, and the press never got to hear about it.

A few days before the Games started, the New

Zealand and Australian teams were moved from Richmond to Willesden Technical College, a modern three-storey brick quadrangle set in spacious grounds about three miles east of Wembley. 'It was just empty classrooms with desks moved out and beds moved in,' wrote Harold Nelson. 'The nearest toilet and wash basins were down four flights of stairs and the showers were as far away from our corner as they could possibly be. The Australians were not very impressed at having to leave Richmond Park because it was the Italians who took their place. We had been fighting them a few years before.'

'The Olympic Flag,' reported the *Surrey Comet*, 'which has flown at the camp since it opened seven weeks ago, was taken from the main flagstaff on Thursday night, by the Australians who were annoyed at leaving the camp. Another flag is to be sent down from London and in future it will be hauled down at sunset.'

'The hurtful thing about it for us Returned Servicemen,' said Maurice Crow, 'was that we were moved out for the Italian, Argentinean and Portuguese teams. This did nothing towards promoting good feeling when we met in the competitions. Our team was put on the third floor in draughty rooms, with cold showers on the ground floor.' However, they made the best of it:

Food rationing in England made what we had in New Zealand look like a banquet. The Australians had meat, we had butter, honey and condensed milk and the Irish had eggs. So we pooled it and ate reasonably. We got on very well together and made a lot of friends.

89

We had a big party at the college the night the Australian high jumper John Winter won the gold medal! Some crazy Irishman tossed a Roman marble figurine out of a three-storey window to crash into pieces on the pavement below.

The Irish team manager, Chisholm, felt that despite Willesden's bright and airy dormitories, and recreation rooms equipped with television and radio, 'The charge of 25 shillings per head was excessive. There were too many beds and no padlocks for the lockers.'

Inspector Jones of Willesden Green police station was consulted about the problem of schoolchildren seeking autographs. 'We have some excellent fencing, recently erected round the grounds,' a school official told the *Willesden Chronicle*. 'But no gates! The children are a bigger problem than the girls who come to gaze at the competitors.'

Down the road, Wembley County School was getting ready to house over a hundred athletes. The Senior Master, Mr Henry Wright, wrote:

The day after the school broke up for the summer holidays, the Ministry of Works started transforming it into a residential hotel. The Art Room, furnished with occasional tables, sixty easy chairs, a radio and a piano, was the competitors' lounge. Class Six, similarly furnished, was the staff and visitors' lounge. The Geography Room became the indoor sports room complete with table tennis, dart board and card tables. The prettiest room of all was the Dining Room, with tasteful folk-weave curtains at the windows, white cloths and vases of flowers on the tables, and coloured coco-nut matting. A full size boxing ring, wrestling mats and weight-lifting platforms were installed in the gym. In front of the school, seven flag poles had been grouped in an impressive semi-circle.

Lloyd Valberg, a 26-year-old fireman and high jumper from Singapore, was the first to arrive at the school. As the only athlete representing his country, he was told to organise his own flag-raising ceremony. Singapore had no flag of its own and so he hoisted the Union Flag, alone, and in tears. 'I felt miserable and lonely. Nobody took any notice of me. I got switched from one room to another and got browned off being constantly among strangers. I was ready to catch the next boat home when the Ceylonese team arrived and became my friends.' Six days later, he was invited to compete in the AAA championships at White City. Although still homesick, Valberg had a great sense of humour and became quite a hit in athletics circles. He was made an honorary member of the London Athletic Club and when a journalist asked him when Singapore would hold the Olympic Games, Valberg replied, 'When Nelson gets back his eye.'

*　　　*　　　*

Fewer than 10 per cent of the competitors in 1948 were women. The sexes were strictly segregated, and when the Hungarians demanded to be housed

91

together, the organisers ruled that 'no variation could be made that men's and women's housing should be entirely separate.' The women and their chaperones were housed in three centres. Half stayed at Southlands College in Wimbledon, where the twenty-four American women complained the mattresses were too hard. 'It was like a boarding school,' remembered the US diver, Vicki Draves, who shared her room with Juno Stover, another diver. 'They would send us off with lunches in paper boxes—there was no café for us at the pool.' The boxes contained a cheese sandwich, an apple and a boiled egg, to last until supper time. Women's Voluntary Service drivers took them to and from Wembley Pool for practices in fifty half-timbered station wagons. Many visitors assumed that their green uniforms were military.

Like their male compatriots, the New Zealanders Ngaire Lane and her chaperone Mima were shocked that England was still on fairly stringent rations:

For us, the ration was very short on meat and dairy products. We had brought food parcels with us which helped a little. Southlands was a lovely place with beautiful lawns and trees about. Unfortunately we were soon uplifted, for reasons we never found out, to the Domestic Science Training College at Eccleston Square, just behind Victoria station. We found this college dark and cramped, and missed the open air of Wimbledon. Being so far from the venues I did not see many of the other events except on the television. That proved just wonderful for all of us. The

92

Australian girl swimmers were in a big room next to mine and there was always lively company and happy noise in our area. Micheline Ostermeyer, the French discus thrower, was there, practising the piano.

'On arrival at Eccleston Square,' said the British high jumper Bertha Crowther, 'we received a bronze medallion souvenir, a free sponge, sweet coupons, a beret to complete our uniform and tickets for a daily pint of milk. When we required it, Muriel Taylor, the team masseur, brought us back to health and strength with her cheerful service.'

'It was a very old mansion,' remembered the French swimmer Monique Berlioux, 'with five small, uncomfortable beds to a room. Not very tidy or pleasant, with a leaking gas pipe behind the bed. There were very few things for women.'

The British fencer Mary Glen Haig worked as an administrator at King's College Hospital:

The college was hard by the bus station and it had no double glazing, so was not at all quiet. I shared a room with Guiter Minton and Betty Carnegie Arbuthnott, both fencers. Guiter was very nervous about the competition the next day and she worried so much she might have forgotten something that she rose in the middle of the night and got fully dressed in her fencing kit. All was well but we were wide awake while she was doing this.

The British women's swimming team slept on the eighth floor at Eccleston Square and the lift

93

was broken. 'Apart from the annoying inconvenience', said the Amateur Swimming Association's official report, 'it was decidedly against the swimmers' interests to be continuously climbing so many flights of stairs. Such exercise might have been acceptable to certain other athletes and it is a pity a little more foresight was not used in the allocation of accommodation.'

*   *   *

The problem of moving the competitors and their managers from the ports to their accommodation was borne by the London organising committee. Most of the competitors brought much more luggage than had been anticipated and extra lorries were needed. Some also brought crates of food, horses, sculptures and even yachts with them, rather than risk sending them separately as freight. On the busiest day, 23 July, when a thousand competitors were on the road, 'the mislaying of only one package was reported,' the committee proudly announced. 'This was a small suitcase placed on the wrong coach and delivered to Richmond Park instead of Uxbridge. It was re-delivered the same day.' The four principal railway companies, newly nationalised as British Railways, agreed to halve their fares, and Thomas Cook persuaded railway companies in Europe to do the same.

Moving the competitors around London was another important problem to be tackled by Lord Burghley and his colleagues. The transport sub-committee had calculated the cost at £70,000, which was twice the amount they had been allowed. Then in January 1948 the London Passenger Transport Board was nationalised and it agreed that all competitors could travel free on London's buses, trams and Underground, on production of their special ID cards.

There was already a shortage of buses for regular London commuters, but London Transport agreed to hire out some of their double-deckers and twenty smaller buses 'of an obsolete type, their condition well below standard.' At first, buses were sent in advance to the aerodromes and docks, but so few passengers arrived on time that five students were then despatched around the country to report imminent arrivals by phone. Even so, not all journeys went to plan. One early evening, 'Wembley Transport Control' were told that the aircraft containing the Hungarian team was circling above Northolt airport and sent a bus at once. Two hours later Northolt announced that the aircraft had been redirected to Blackbush in Surrey and the Aldershot Traction Company went to meet them. At 10 p.m., Manston Aerodrome, eighty miles away in Kent, phoned to say that some Hungarians had arrived. Now, the East Kent Road Car Company in Herne Bay was alerted, and by 12.30 a.m. the Hungarians were in Hendon School where, half an hour later, they sat down to eat, six hours after first sighting their housing centre from the air.

Once installed at their housing centres, the teams had to be taken daily to any one of sixty-seven training centres or thirty Olympic venues. The police had insisted that all Olympic bus routes should be approved by them in advance, so two men had spent six weeks working out over 750 possible routes covering 400 square miles of London. A central Transport Control had been established at Wembley, in a local Roman Catholic church hall, and here a dozen men worked for eighteen hours a day. Their equipment was a line of telephones and three blackboards, representing Today, Tomorrow, and the Day after Tomorrow. As requests came in they were chalked up in columns and wiped off as each job was completed.

Some sports presented unusual problems. The organisers had assumed that the cyclists would get themselves to the velodrome at Herne Hill on their machines. But the competitors wanted to put their bikes on a bus, which the bus drivers refused to allow. The committee thought of hiring lorries to follow the buses, but the cyclists did not trust the lorry drivers with their precious cargo. The solution was to remove the seats from one side of a bus, allowing the riders both to travel in comfort and keep an eye on their bikes.

The French team manager was dismayed that his team's equipment took so long to arrive from Paris. While their freight train had taken only two days to travel to London, the transport company recommended by the British Olympic Committee took a further two days to deliver the crates containing the athletics, swimming and wrestling costumes. 'We telephoned many times to the French Consul in London to find out if our wagons had been detained in Dover or Dieppe,' wrote their manager in his report to the French Olympic Committee . 'It seemed that we were not the only Olympic delegation whose wagons had gone astray.' The manager concluded that the British should never have taken on the Olympics if they couldn't build an Olympic village, or give the French their own kitchen and dining rooms.

Ngaire Lane's memories are cheerful: 'We were ferried back and forth to Wembley by a big red double-decker bus, with everyone singing their different countries' songs.' But for those in charge, it was not so easy. 'Generally, teams were bad time keepers,' the committee reported. 'A much too optimistic view was taken of our ability to move vehicles between districts of London, especially those areas unfamiliar to the drivers.' Halfway through the fortnight, the bus crews were changed and routes had to be learned all over again. One double-decker bus went the wrong way and smashed into a low bridge. An eight-seater vehicle was badly damaged in Windsor Park when an excited trainer tried to drive it away. Two buses were driven away by competitors: the culprit in London spent a night in a cell, and was released without charge, while the Henley joy-riders got away with it and were never traced.

7

WHAT IS THERE TO EAT?

In the Ancient World, athletes ate dried figs, boiled grain and cheese; they drank only small quantities of water and were forbidden sex; and slaves flogged them with branches to accustom them to pain. The athletes at London in 1948 were also discouraged from drinking water and having sex, and their diet was not much more interesting.

The food rationing introduced during the war was still in place and just before the Games, on 21 July, meat allocations were reduced still further. An adult was permitted one shilling's worth of meat, canned or fresh, per week. The Ministry of Food warned the public: 'OVER 70s BEWARE! Don't throw your tea coupons away!' Semolina, 'soy-ghetti' and dried peas were easier to obtain. The government was also keen to inform the nation that, despite rumours, the British were now drinking 10 per cent *more* milk than in 1938; everyone was eating a third more fish; and only half of the food consumed was imported. Not everyone was convinced by government policy. 'The maximum retail price of rice has been fixed by the Food Ministry at 9d a pound. Should any rice become available the price will of course be subject to alteration,' chuckled *Punch*.

A year before the Olympics, the Minister of Food, John Strachey MP, announced in Parliament that foreign visitors could bring in the legal 25lb of food allowance but British competitors would be given no extra rations. 'Like anyone else, our own athletes can go to a restaurant as often as they wish,' he said. Dr Magnus Pyke, a nutritionist with the Ministry of Food who later became an eccentric television science pundit, disagreed. He recommended that British competitors should receive Category A Rations, as fit for heavy industry workers such as dockers and coal miners, which contained 3,900 calories, compared to the daily 2,600 calories allowed to everyone else in Britain. This covered basic food stuffs, but fresh eggs, butter and sweets were still scarce.

Although everyone agreed that athletes required

more food than ordinary people, the *British Medical Journal* admitted that little was known about their nutritional needs. 'A generally high standard of performance on the part of British athletes must make obsolete the belief that large quantities of meat provide the best foundation for athletic prowess.'

'Nobody knew anything about diet,' said the runner Sylvia Cheeseman recently. 'It was very hard to get hold of meat, though there was unrationed whale meat. It was horrible but I was so intent on getting my protein that I ate it.'

'About six weeks before the Olympics, our rations were increased,' remembered the cyclist Robert Maitland. 'We had six ounces of meat a day, one pound of potatoes, half an ounce of bacon, two ounces of sugar, one of preserves, one of cheese, one third of tea, one tenth of dried eggs, two pints of milk, one pound of bread, and once a week, half a pound of sweets or chocolates.' Due to an unprecedented fruit harvest, greengage, bramble and rhubarb jam came off rationing.

There was some argument about feeding the Olympic support staff who stayed in the housing centres. It was felt by the organisers that 'the exiguous nature of nutrition to which we in Britain have now been reduced will be profitably demonstrated by the restriction to nothing more than the civilian ration for officials, and athletes after their races.' They were reminded that although this might show how abstemious the British were, it would be impossible to administrate, as most people would simply share their food equally. So the idea was dropped, and all the visitors received industrial rations. The

99

Minister of Food, John Strachey, estimated that the required increase in food would amount to less than 1 per cent of national consumption. To pay for it, the government allocated extra barley to the Scotch Whisky Association, already Britain's largest dollar earner, who increased their exports to the USA to 10 million gallons.

Many of the British athletes received food parcels from anonymous donors both from Britain and around the world. The sprinter Alastair McCorquodale's wife Rosemary was expecting their first baby. 'Lady Nancy Astor saved our lives—she sent over food hampers from Cliveden.' The footballer Jimmy McColl recalled, 'We received parcels of food from New Zealand— mainly tinned fruits and other niceties!' 'We got vitamin chocolate,' remembered the gymnast Frank Turner. 'It wasn't very pleasant to eat but we thought it was good for us. The parcels had unusual things like sugar, and dried milk. Anyway, my mum gave me half her rations.' 'We got parcels from Canada with tinned ham and maple syrup, which was very exciting,' said the runner Doug Wilson. 'I'm not sure what good it did our bodies, but it was certainly a morale booster.'

Neil White, a hockey player, remembered:

It is a wonder our athletes did not just grow fat on those wonderful food parcels. There was real international sympathy for the British, as we were looked upon as the saviours of civilisation. We stayed at Uxbridge for three weeks to train, under strict management. We had to take our ration books with us, but we ate lashings of bacon and eggs, waffles and

100

maple syrup, fruit juices and rolls and butter, the like of which the ordinary Brit had not seen for years. My favourite supper was steak and chips with fried eggs and mushrooms followed by a plateful of ice cream.

Angus Carmichael found that he was served extra large helpings in London restaurants when he wore his Olympic blazer. 'It was quite embarrassing, with food rationing on for everybody else. They would pile up your plate with extra food, saying "Eat up. We need to build up the British team." '

'Always eat wholemeal wheat,' advised Harry Koskie, the British swimming coach. 'Fruit rather than boiled pudding. As much sugar as you can get; fresh uncooked greens. As much meat as is procurable. (Oh! for some nice juicy steaks!) Eat plenty of cooked beetroot, potatoes cooked in their skins, home-made cakes and at least one halibut oil capsule per day.'

'We had no dietary advice about vitamins or proteins,' remembered the swimmer Don Bland. 'Nor was there even any mention of fluid intake. My special race mix was three or four glasses of water, each with six teaspoons of sugar.'

The canteens in the housing centres were highly organised. 'Meals are served at fixed times and members of the team must keep to these hours,' stated the rules. 'Members of the team unable to eat during this meal period may request a packed meal the previous day. No cash allowance can be claimed for meals not taken.' Wherever possible, nations with similar diets were housed together. Veeraswamy's Indian restaurant in Swallow Street

101

in the West End provided the catering at Pinner County School for the 100 Indians and Burmese; and Ley On's Chop Suey from Wardour Street in Soho fed the team of thirty Chinese competitors at Willesden County School.

The government set up a scientific committee to study the physiological and nutritional problems occurring in the training and performance of Olympic athletes. Magnus Pyke and two Ministry of Health dieticians, Miss Chalmers and Miss Beveridge, focused on 'more interesting types of athletes' with 'peculiar dietary habits'. They discovered that an Australian athlete's breakfast consisted of a pint of milk, two boiled eggs and a chop or steak and the Mexican team of eighty-two men, based at Preston Manor School, had beans and chillies. 'We enjoy it so much,' said one. 'Everybody here is so kind, so nice.' Exact replicas of their meals were taken away in Kilner jars for analysis. For lunch the Mexicans ate liver or tripe, and more beans and chillies for supper—a total of 6,000 calories per man. The nutritionists noted that they wasted a lot of their food but were still overweight for their age and height. Their diet was also deficient in vitamins, despite the fact that Major Mario Solorzaro, the Mexican doctor, treated several cases of acute bronchial infection with injections of vitamin C.

The commercial restaurants that provided catering were given a budget of 25 shillings per day per competitor for three meals. Some were so efficient that they only charged 17 shillings. They were allowed to run cafeterias serving teas and snacks for profit, and those that installed ice cream soda fountains did very well, even on rainy days.

102

The visitors were keen to sample English specialities. 'I tasted my first cider at the Hop Bine Tavern in North Wembley,' said Maurice Crow, 'though the official drink was Horlicks. We must have drunk gallons of the stuff. The English fish and chips were a lifesaver. We were given tins of a drink called Aktavite by a New Zealand company, but after drinking it, we renamed it "Aktashite".'

Language sometimes created a problem. One evening two Turkish wrestlers decided to treat themselves to a meal at the Ritz. The only words they understood on the menu were 'large' and 'small'. Feeling in need of a sustaining meal, they pointed to 'Large'. Their meal took a long time coming and by the time it arrived they were famished. The waiters whipped the lids off huge silver dishes with a great flourish, and revealed their order: a lobster each, surrounded by a forest of lettuce.

Some teams brought their own chefs who were given a refrigerator, a small gas cooker and English cooks to supervise. Most teams also brought food, wine and spirits, for which no import duty was charged, provided only team members consumed them. These supplies were carefully transported by the War Office from the docks to the housing centres. Denmark sent 160,000 eggs; another 5,000 eggs came from Ireland and 20,000 bottles of mineral water from Czechoslovakia. China sent oiled bamboo shoots, preserved eggs, dried shrimps and green tea. Hungary sent poppy seeds, paprika and 20,000 lemons. Ceylon brought coconuts and spices. The Dutch farmers and ship owners sent 100,000kg of fruit and vegetables, 7,000 eggs, 900 ginger cakes, 100kg of cheese and

250kg of sugar. Mexico sent liver, kidneys and tripe. However, during an unofficial strike by the London dockers in June, their ton of butter went rancid. The New Zealand team brought tea, butter, sugar, honey, dates, mutton dripping, toilet soap and condensed milk to share with other competitors.

The British Trawler Association donated 40,000lb of fresh fish, which they sent daily to Billingsgate fish market. The Herring Board sent kippers and Iceland sent mutton. Australia and Switzerland specified that their food was also for the British team, though as the British were billeted with the Americans, they already ate very well. The Americans went overboard with 15,000 bars of chocolate, 5,000 steaks and daily flights from Los Angeles to RAF Uxbridge carrying enriched white flour and fruit. The civil servants considered this to be 'an extravagant disregard for geography and expense'. By chance, bread rationing was lifted the week before the Games started but there were still restrictions on the quality of the bread made. Special permission was granted by the Ministry of Food to use the high-quality flour donated by the USA to make decent bread for all the competitors.

Over 300 tons of food were imported altogether, feeding over 5,000 people for a month. Somehow, like the Biblical loaves and fishes, 80 tons of food were left over afterwards and these were donated to London hospitals.

Although the organisers hoped that visitors would be sympathetic to what Britain had been through during the last eight years, they forgot to tell the Americans what was expected of them.

'The food wasn't too good because it was English-style, which was quite greasy,' remembered the runner Clifford Bourland. 'And you could only order one meal in a restaurant. I was often so hungry I had to go to a second restaurant to get enough to eat.' A compatriot was heard in a canteen saying, 'I don't mind eating horse steaks but I do object to having the saddle put in too.'

When the Americans demanded more chicken and fresh oranges for their 'stomach trouble' brought on by English food, the committee replied, 'It would be impossible to justify treating the Americans exceptionally, especially as they share housing with other nations. One orange per competitor could be found, though this would mean depriving British children of them. The same applies for poultry.'

A few Americans did witness the harsh reality of life in Britain. The hurdler Craig Dixon made friends with an English boy who took him home for supper. 'One little potato and one piece of boiled beef was all they could get. It seemed that we had been eating like kings at Uxbridge.'

'OLYMPIC VISITORS ARE STARVING,' reported the *Wembley News*:

Olympic overseas visitors billeted in private houses in Wembley have protested strongly about the lack of meal facilities. 'We wandered round and round Wembley almost semi-starved,' complained a group of them standing at a coffee stall. An Overseas Visitors Bureau official stated today, 'They should have asked for hotels if they wanted meals all day. It is not our fault if they asked for bed and breakfast and then could not get into the cafés.' Reuter reports from Paris that French athletes attributed some of their failures at the Games to insufficient food. The French newspaper *L'Intransigeant* quoted an athlete complaining that her diet consisted of 'cucumbers, tomatoes, beetroots and meat only at noon on Sundays'.

Napoleon Bonaparte is reputed to have said of his countrymen, 'The French complain of everything, and always.' The French team's manager was stung by criticism in the French press, which ran a story under the sardonic headline 'Business as usual: 1,700kg of meat is the only meal for our starving athletes'. His unpublished report on the 'séjour de la délégation française aux Jeux Olympiques de Londres' runs to fourteen typed pages, twelve of them about the catering. To ensure that the team of 285 men and women were well fed, two freight trains were readied to depart from Paris for Uxbridge railway station, a week before the Games. A freezer technician advised that if the refrigerated wagon left on 22 July, the meat and fresh provisions would remain edible in English fridges until 14 August. The journey normally took two days, but to be on the safe side, enough ice was provided to last three. After the wagon had been filled, it was discovered that an export licence was required from the French Office of Exchange. 'Their financial department was on strike,' wrote the report's author. 'When the picket line was approached, the strikers dismissed our pleas with, "Les Jeux Olympiques, nous nous moquons!" [We couldn't care less about the Olympic Games!] We will not report the strong and energetic language that followed.'

Five days later the wagon left for London, and then took a further four days to reach Uxbridge. The manager was not sure whether to blame the French railway company or the British one. 'The enquiry was too laborious. Whoever it was, it did not diminish the consequence of the lateness.'

When the food supplies arrived, they had to wait a further seventy-two hours for the arrival of the export licence before the train could be opened. They were then horrified to discover that although 'the English asked us to bring chefs to prepare our food in keeping with our taste,' the kitchens were not properly equipped and there were only three cooking pots to share between twelve nations: 'Two for Westerners and one for Easterners from Egypt, Turkey and Korea.' Worse still, there was not even a proper restaurant, but 'the system of "cafeteria" so loved by the English, which involved queuing up with a plate in the hand to be served. Something like a soup kitchen.'

After the long delay in hot weather, the meat was now only just edible. 'The English refrigeration inspector told us that unless we consumed our meat on the day of delivery, it would be illegal. We had 1,700kg!' The French attaché in London, Paul Grall, came to the rescue and found a pickle factory that would take the meat that day and can it—an illustration of how desperate Britain was for fresh meat. Monsieur Grall then persuaded the Ministry of Food to replace it with fresh English meat, of whatever quality could be found. This worked out at 6kg of meat per French athlete for two weeks, considerably more than the ration a British athlete could expect in a month.

Mary Glen Haig remembered the French team's catering at Eccleston Square:

> I had to take my rations with me from the hospital kitchen. I received an extra quarter pound of meat the month before the Games. One night, after a rather small supper, the wonderful smell of steak and chips assailed our nostrils and reminded us that we were still very hungry! We stole out of our rooms and began a sniffer-dog exercise down to the basement and along some passages. We found ourselves in the French women's quarters where they were in line to receive their meal. We rushed back and fetched a plate each and then, without saying a word, lined up for their food. The steak and chips made an excellent meal and sleep that night was dream-free.

Even more annoying to the French than the fate of their food was the long wait endured for their wine. A special wagon had been sent on a month in advance so that the wine would have time to settle. 'But we had so many complications from the English customs, even though the freight papers clearly carried the name Mouton-Rothschild, and the wine was only for drinking.' The British customs officials could not believe that quite so much wine, of such a high quality, could be needed by the French athletes and so they had impounded it until duty was paid. This took a further eight days to sort out, and meanwhile more bottles of *premier cru classé* Bordeaux from Pauillac were air-freighted from Paris. The Mouton-Rothschild was released without duty being paid, just in time to celebrate the end of the Games.

8

THE OPENING CEREMONY

The Opening Ceremony, on Thursday 29 July, fell just before the bank holiday weekend. School was out and many workers were on their annual week's holiday. Not everyone was on their way to Wembley. Down the road at Lord's cricket ground, the Australian cricket team, captained by Don Bradman, was earning its nickname 'The Invincibles' by beating England yet again. (They were the first test match side to play an entire tour of over thirty matches without losing one.)

However, over 80,000 spectators surged down Olympic Way that afternoon past a one-man band wearing a top hat and a large drum on his back. Retired policemen lined the approach roads, British Legion veterans attended the car parks and Boy Scouts and army cadets ran messages.

'Fate was kind in providing a glorious day,' reported the *Wembley News*. 'The scene, with most men in their shirt sleeves and the women in flimsy summer frocks, reminded one more of an American sports arena than the usual prosaic British assembly.' At 93 degrees Fahrenheit (34 centigrade), it was the hottest day in London since 1911. It was so hot that the previous day three army cadets had died of heatstroke while on route marches. Men removed their jackets and ties and shaded their heads with folded newspapers and knotted handkerchiefs; the women rolled down their seamed stockings and raised their umbrellas as parasols. Even so, strong men swooned and old ladies collapsed on the concrete stands. The crowd listened patiently to the massed drums and pipes of His Majesty's Brigade of Guards band as they marched about the arena in their red woollen uniforms and bearskin hats.

Seating was on wooden benches, which could be made more comfortable with hired cushions. There was no barrier to stop spectators invading the track, only a low wooden wall which children sat on. Many had brought packed lunches and thermos flasks, for only a few had enough coupons to eat in the cafés. Nobody expected the service to be good. 'New table dishes are made of clear glass,' reported *Punch*. 'We understand that at one Wembley restaurant, diners can see the darns on the table-cloth through the soup.' There was a long queue at the stall selling mineral water, and the Stop-Me-and-Buy-One Wall's ice cream tricycle was very popular.

'We shared our first ever bottle of Coca-Cola,' noted Malcolm Tappin, a schoolboy. 'It was imported to satisfy the Americans. We were not too keen and did not buy any more, especially as it cost one shilling a bottle. Ice cream was available in tubs. If you were fortunate you might get a little wooden spatula; otherwise you shaped the cardboard lid and scooped it out with that.'

A.J. Kemp, a sixth-former at Wembley Grammar School, got a job in the bar situated behind the

Royal Box:

Some customers understood no English at all, nor my version of French. There was one Swede who wanted a Jin-ess. 'Well,' I said, 'we don't seem to have that. How about a gin and French or a gin and Italian?' No, he definitely wanted a Jin-ess. He marched up and down the counter and seized a bottle, muttering 'Jin-ness'. So I served him with a Guinness. Then a Mexican in full traditional costume of red and blue and a large flowing cloak strode up and enquired whether we sold marsh-eaze. Thinking this was a Mexican drink I said, 'Only lights, browns, Pilsners, Bass, lagers, splits and shorts.' 'Nor, nor,' he said, gesticulating wildly. 'Marsh-eaze, marsh-eaze, furr my cee-gar!'

'The stadium was thronged with supporters of all colours and speaking many tongues,' wrote the *Wembley News*. 'Over the east wall was the giant scoreboard with the peristyle containing the Olympic flame holder below it. On the twin towers of the stadium flew the Union Jack and the Olympic flag, while all round the wall fluttered the flags of the competing nations.'
Even the London correspondent of the *Manchester Guardian* was impressed:

The ballyhoo can be nauseating and it can be absurd too when it reveals the chemical composition of the Olympic flame, but one found the cynicism dissipating. The scene had a lightness and delicacy that one has never before witnessed in England. Not a dark

111

garment was to be seen. The stands were like a gigantic hanging garden of mixed stocks whose colours were pastel blue and pink. Not a man wore his coat and many knotted their handkerchiefs around their heads. Even the drab concrete of the stadium walls was mellowed by the sunshine.

The committee kept a tight hold on souvenirs and only their official magazine was on sale in the arenas, price five shillings. McCorquodale's printers requested permission to include the Royal Coat of Arms on the cover. They were informed that although the King would open the Games, 'The Olympic Games are international, and not of national importance or in any way connected to the Royal House.' McCorquodale's also printed the daily shilling programmes, in exactly the same layout used in pre-war Olympics. Results would be telephoned through for inclusion the next day and each sport had a different coloured cover. Plenty of space was provided for spectators to fill in results and add their comments, thus making each programme a unique souvenir.

'It was a happy crowd in shirtsleeves or light print dresses that made the tiny group of VIPs sweating and fumbling in morning dress appear like unlucky burnt offerings on the altar of fame,' wrote William Clark in the *Observer*. In the Royal Box were five European princes, His Highness Raja Bhalida Singh of Patiala and His Royal Highness Ghazi Shaw Wali Khan of Afghanistan. The British royal family received warm applause, especially seventeen-year-old Princess Margaret, who had recently recovered from measles. The

112

Prime Minister, Clement Attlee, was the only politician. King George VI, then fifty-one years old, looked thin and weak in full uniform but he walked firmly onto the track accompanied by Viscount Portal, the president of the British Olympic Committee. He greeted the IOC president, Sigfrid Edström, and was presented to members of the international committee who wore black silk top hats, tail coats and carnation buttonholes as if they were at Ascot races. They were elderly, titled men like Count Clarence von Rosen of Sweden who had been on the IOC since 1900. Others were sportsmen like Almond Massard, French Olympic fencing champion in 1920, Thomas Fearnley of Norway, captain of his country's tennis team in 1912, and Baron De Trannoy of Belgium, an equestrian contestant in 1912. There were notable absences: the representatives of Czechoslovakia, Estonia, Hungary, Poland, Latvia and Austria all disappeared between 1939 and 1946.

However traditional and dignified the scene, several of the serving members of the IOC were of doubtful character. Churchill, who had been prime minister when London was selected to host the Games, believed that the Olympics played a part in diplomacy. In May 1945, just before losing the election, he had telegraphed the British embassies for opinions on the IOC 'old guard'. Government files, classified for fifty years, now reveal that Churchill did not share the IOC's trusting belief in rigid neutrality with regard to the Games. For him, the character of the people involved, and their recent behaviour, could not be ignored.

British diplomats informed Churchill that the

Marquis Melchoir de Polignac of France was 'definitely not suitable' and pointed out that 'he and his wife have been imprisoned for collaboration'. The same was true of the Bulgarian, Belgian and Norwegian members. General Giorgio Vaccaro of Italy had supported the Fascists; General Svet Djoukitch of Yugoslavia was 'certainly non grata'; and of the Netherlands delegate, the Foreign Office 'would be astonished if Colonel Scharroo was ever allowed to take any role again.' He had done nothing to protect the Jewish women who had competed for the Netherlands as gymnasts in Berlin, all but one of whom had perished with their children in Nazi gas chambers. The Egyptian was considered to be 'a very bad man who should be dropped'. The Polish delegate was 'not suitable, a rabid extremist and anti-communist'. With the exception of the Bulgarian collaborator Stephan Tchaprachiken, who had committed suicide at the end of the war, all these men were still on the International Olympic Committee. Continuing his enthusiasm for the Berlin Games in 1936, the IOC's vice-chair Avery Brundage had sent food parcels to those Nazis who had been imprisoned after the Nuremberg trials. Back in 1945 it had not occurred to Churchill to enquire into the character of a US citizen.

Churchill's research may have been communicated to the IOC, but if so, it did not affect their decisions. Whatever their affiliations, all these men shook hands with the King.

There was, however, at least one honourable exception. Lieutenant-Colonel Charles Pahud de Mortanges had won equestrian Olympic medals in

1928, 1932 and again in 1936. When Germany invaded the Netherlands in 1940 he joined the Free Dutch army and was captured and tortured by the Gestapo but managed to escape in 1942.

The King regained his seat and then it was the turn of the competitors. On that morning a fleet of 220 buses had collected them and they had already been assembled for over two hours. By now, the temperature was 94 degrees and where they waited there was little shade and no refreshments. 'When we got to Wembley the only place to change into our uniform and silk stockings was in the back of a lorry,' said the Scots swimmer Helen Gordon. 'There were over a dozen of us girls in there, in the sweltering heat. Berets had to be worn one inch above the eye and tilted. We were reminded, "Berets will not be removed." '

The high jumper Dorothy Tyler recalled:

We were all standing around for hours. It got hotter and hotter. We could hear the spectators cheering but we didn't know what was going on in there. There hadn't been any rehearsal or anything. The British team found some shade under some trees and nearby there was a factory. Someone discovered that if you stood on tip-toes you could see inside and they had a television in there. So we watched the procession on the telly through the window, even though it was only a few hundreds yards away. That was the first time I'd ever seen a television.

While they waited, they mingled with the other teams. The British rower Michael Lapage

115

remembered, 'A smartly dressed Pakistani in national costume came over and greeted me with a smile. Surprise, surprise, it was Paul Raschid, a friend from university, in the boxing event.'

At exactly three o'clock the Guards Band struck up 'The March of the Gladiators' and the 3,714 men and 385 women, 100 more than in 1936 and a new Olympic record, began to file in. The Greek team, descendants of the founders of the Ancient Games, headed the parade, and the rest came in alphabetical order. Iraq and Iran, never the best of friends, had to march in line. Britain, as the host, entered last. A member of each team carried their national flag while a Boy Scout carried a name board. Not all of these were spelled correctly: 'Uruguay' had an extra U; and Liechtenstein was spelled Leichenstien.

In *Punch*, H.F. Ellis mused:

Sitting here at the Empire Stadium Wembley, it is a beautiful English afternoon, with the sun shining gaily down on the flags of the nations. My word those Afghans look fit. One assumes the entrants march past in alphabetical order, and not in the order in which their envelopes were opened. If so, these hefty-looking Belgians must either be rowing men who have caught the sun or unusually pale Bolivian wrestlers. Good luck to them in any case. Would those be from Chile, do you think? Look, there, with the snow on their boots. The two hundred and twenty-one competitors passing us now must be from the United States. Their forty-four coaches and managers and the twenty-nine doctors, nurses and small fry they brought with them follow close behind. Would those be Uruguayan yachtswomen fraternizing with javelin throwers from Venezuela? Hand me the programme, dear.

John Glenister was a fifteen-year-old Scout from Harrow and remembered the day well:

We were told to turn up at Wembley Stadium but we had no idea what our duties would be. It was an exceptionally hot day, but I was sustained by my favourite picnic lunch—sandwiches of Heinz sandwich spread and a chocolate biscuit. Being already six foot tall, I was picked to mark the saluting base, holding the Union Jack aloft. I was stationed on the trackside by the royal box. We had to stand there for ages before the ceremony began, fully exposed to the glare of the sun. I decided it would be wise to sit down. The Scout next to me remained standing, and he fainted. As the athletes marched past my flag, they did an 'eyes right' to acknowledge King George VI and then an 'eyes front' as they passed another tall Scout posted beyond the royal box. It felt as if they were all looking at me!

The athletes had been told not to salute as they entered because the Olympic salute, with the right arm raised and slightly outward, was very similar to the Nazi one.

The *Wembley News* commented on this too:

When the teams passed the Royal Box, the Colombian banner bearer introduced a novel note by changing from a normal march to the goose step as he approached. There was surprise too at the number of old men in the Austrian team; the Indian representative who marched round carrying a zip bag in one hand; the zest with which the Finns came on parade; and the verve of the Hungarian girls. It was amazing, the number of athletes who were able to recognise shouts from personal friends among the dense crowd and to wave individual greetings to them.

The South African team was led in by a fifteen-year-old Boy Scout called Peter Hammond. 'As S is low down in the alphabet, we waited for a long time in a bomb site outside the stadium, sitting on a pile of rubble with these strangers. There were about thirty men, mainly boxers and wrestlers, and one woman: Daphne Robb, an athlete. Daphne gave me an orange—my first since before the war.' The South Africans were all white. Only three months earlier, the Afrikaans-speaking Nationalist Party had taken power and introduced racial apartheid policies. Ron Eland, a South African weightlifter, was competing for Britain because of the colour of his skin.

The eleven athletes from Britain's oldest colony, Bermuda, were the first mixed-race team from Bermuda to compete at the Olympics. Phyllis Lightbourn remembered, 'We were wearing white sharkskin suits and white pith helmets, we needed them that day, it was so hot! In Bermuda not everyone was happy that a mixed-race team was representing the country for the first time. Segregation did not end there until 1968.'

'The men from Iran wore white naval caps and marched in with a suggestion of a goose-step,' noted the *Manchester Guardian*. 'Though it was nothing to the old original version of it shown by the Colombians.'

The Irish team were still experiencing problems. Only their boxer, fencers and rowers were taking part in the opening ceremony, because there was not enough money to buy uniforms for the rest of the team. Furthermore, their manager J.F. Chisholm was trying to insist that his team was called 'Ireland', not Eire, and would march between Iraq and Italy, and not between Egypt and Finland. 'The staff officer stated that if we persisted, we would not be allowed in the Parade and I enquired who would stop us?' wrote Chisholm afterwards, in his country's official report. 'He got somewhat nonplussed and remarked that it looked as if this affair would develop into an International Incident. Colonel Johnstone, the Chief Marshall, said that the people of England knew us as Eire, and he always addressed his letters to his brother-in-law over there to Eire.' Chisholm eventually backed down, but later wrote to the organising committee: 'I strongly protest. The name of the state is ÉIRE in Gaelic, or in the English language, IRELAND. Under the IOC rules, Spain is not called España.'

Korea was one of the nations that had not competed before. The country had been occupied by the Japanese for thirty-five years and Koreans had competed in 1936 under that flag. In 1945, Korea regained independence and in 1947 joined the IOC. The president of the Korean committee had brought with him a pair of stuffed pheasants as a present for King George. The team wore double-breasted suits, Oxford bags with turn-ups, brogues and homburg hats and the one woman, the discus thrower Pong Sik Pak, wore a traditional silk costume.

One of the smallest teams was from Malta, the Mediterranean island with a British naval base that had survived a three-year siege by the Germans. 'Malta was still nursing the severe wounds she had received during the war,' wrote the Maltese sports writer Lewis Portelli in 1960. 'But if Britain set an example, then we would follow.' Full of enthusiasm, and delighted to be officially recognised by the IOC, the Maltese decided to send a football team but found there was no money. 'When the footballers were given up as lost,' wrote Portelli, 'Nestor Jacono, who had proved himself to be one of Malta's outstanding runners, was recommended. Nobody had seen much of Jacono during the war but soon after, he started serious training and registered great speeds.' Jacono's friend, F.X. Zammit Cutajar, was appointed Malta's team manager, and said: 'At the Opening Ceremony I felt a curious sensation on entering when 80,000 spectators rose up and applauded our meagre team which consisted of one athlete. Whilst we marched around the stadium we heard shouts of "Brave Malta".' Nestor Jacono himself, a dapper young man sporting a white cap and a thin moustache, remembered, 'It was a magnificent spectacle of brilliant colour on a glorious afternoon: the fresh green grass carpet of the arena; the blazing scarlet patch of the massed bands with their bearskins, and a huge chorus robed in white. For the full circuit of the track the people roared their greetings with deafening cheers, for the two men from the George Cross island, marching in a sea of space between Luxembourg and Mexico.'

The team from New Zealand felt rather ashamed of their uniforms. 'It was a poor quality wool with the edges held together with white bias binding and it soon got very shabby,' wrote Harold Nelson. His compatriot Ngaire Lane had similar feelings:

In my case, it was a mid-grey flannel, nicely cut skirt, and a black blazer with the national emblem on the pocket. I had a grey velour hat – not terribly stylish by any stretch of the imagination and very drab in appearance. I had to provide my own cream blouses. We had a black wool flannel track suit with a huge silver fern and NZ on the front and back. It was very warm. The Australian girls, by contrast, had a most attractive uniform: cream frocks in a very fine woollen material with the Olympic rings and the Australian coat of arms embroidered up by the collar; a really natty little small-brimmed straw hat which suited all the girls; green blazers with gold trim and tan shoes to complete it. They looked very smart and I envied them their bright and stylish appearance.

'As each contingent marched in through the east gate, the brilliance of the afternoon was accentuated,' reported the *Wembley News*. It went on:

121

The green blazers and white tarboosh of the Afghanistan representatives; the equestrian team in the Argentine contingent in white uniforms, the rest of their team in blue. The South Africans in green blazers, white flannels and white trilbies, the Danes in vivid red and white outfits, and the Peruvians in light blue blazers. The Indians wore pale blue blazers and similarly coloured turbans while the Pakistan members had identical outfits in pale green. The women looked beautiful and the picture of athletic grace. All had New Look skirts or dresses, under coloured blazers. Almost at the end of the parade came the United States in navy blazers, white flannels and white trilbies.

The US women were reckoned to be the smartest, in white berets, white pleated skirts, and elegant white high heels. The US team also looked the most relaxed and confident, chatting among themselves and chewing gum.

'The British team was the last to go in,' remembered Malcolm Dalrymple, a javelin thrower. 'So while we waited outside, a Guards drill sergeant made us all practise marching six abreast. I reckon only the British team really got it. But then most of us had been marching around for six years.'

Huge cheers naturally greeted the home team when the 400 British athletes and coaches entered six abreast. The clothes rationing in force specified that a man could buy one pair of shoes a year, a shirt every twenty months, a waistcoat every five years, and an overcoat every seven years. In

122

practice, most men still wore uniform or their demob suits. The Olympic officials had used their coupons to buy a black blazer with badge for £3 10s 5d, white trousers for £4 15s, a tie for 5s 6d and the Olympic badge for 2s 10d. The competitors were given a free uniform. As well as their two pairs of Y-fronts from Coopers, the men got 'a nice outfit from Simpson's in Piccadilly,' according to the footballer Jimmy McColl. 'That was very grand.' At the last moment, it had been decided that the team should wear berets, and they had careful instructions on how to wear them—with the band level round the head, one inch above eyebrows, and the badge over the left eye. There wasn't the time or money to make metal badges, so Women's Institutes had embroidered them instead.

Not all the British competitors were so thrilled with their uniform. 'We got an ill-fitting black blazer with a pair of white bags,' commented the oarsman Bert Bushnell. 'It was after the war and I think all the tailors had been shot. They must have been cut out with a knife and fork. The Olympic tie was so short it stopped halfway down your chest.'

The British women competitors had been instructed to take their ration books to Bourne & Hollingsworth, the outfitters for domestic servants in Oxford Street. Their uniform consisted of a blue serge collarless blazer with Union Flag badge on the pocket, a white beret and a white cotton frock with buttons up the front. 'The sort of thing we used to call a kitchen dress, that you might give to your cook,' said the fencer Mary Glen Haig. 'We had to buy our own white leather shoes, which were expensive, and provide our own socks which used up two coupons,' remembered the high jumper Dorothy Tyler. The women were instructed to wear their uniforms at all official events. 'My Olympic uniform was the smartest thing I owned,' said the long jumper Lorna Lee-Price. 'I even wore it to my sister's wedding.'

The fencer J. Emrys Lloyd, the oldest member of the team, was the man chosen to carry the Union Flag. Minutes before he was due to enter he discovered that his beret, upon which he had been carefully sitting, had disappeared. He thus became the only hatless flag bearer in the parade, but this problem had paled into insignificance when he realised that he had no flag.

Colonel Evan Hunter of the organising committee had driven to Wembley with Roger Bannister, a nineteen-year-old medical student who had turned down an invitation to run for the Olympic team and had instead volunteered as Hunter's assistant. In his autobiography, Bannister recalled:

We had been told that a car carrying the flags of all the nations was to drive along the line of assembled teams just before they marched into the stadium. In this way there would be no danger of any team mislaying its flag. As we were leaving RAF Uxbridge, my eyes caught sight of an old Union Jack which we had used at the camp flag-raising ceremonies. We kept it rolled up in a corner of the office. I suggested we should take it with us 'just in case'. On arrival at Wembley the car park was crowded and we left it to the driver to find a place.

Hunter and I made our way to the assembled teams, where the flags had just been handed out and, oh dear, a mistake had been made. There was no flag for the British team. There was less than twenty minutes to go before the British team, parading last as host nation, would enter the stadium.

Hunter commandeered a jeep and an army sergeant and ordered Bannister to find the flag.

We tore off towards the car park on the other side of the stadium and drove furiously through the crowds which still packed the approaches. I kept my hand on the hooter so that it sounded continuously. We reached the car park. There were thousands of cars and to find ours in time seemed impossible. Everyone stared as we rushed like madmen up and down the lines. It took us ten minutes to find ours. It was locked and I hadn't got the keys. So I smashed the back window with a stone, while the sergeant restrained a policeman who wanted to arrest me. I rushed back to the jeep and we set off for the other side of the stadium. But it was soon hemmed in on all sides by last-minute arrivals. Hooting was useless. Time was perilously short. I jumped out of the jeep and, using the flag pole as a battering ram, with the spike foremost, I charged through the crowd. I reached Emrys Lloyd moments before he marched into the stadium.

'I suppose everyone attending the Olympic

Games as a competitor is a little nervous and slightly awed by the occasion,' recalled the long-distance walker Harold Whitlock. 'One is very proud of selection, and determined, having got this far, to do one's best and to fight to the bitter end to honour one's country. Travelling to the Olympics is a mixture of relief that one is on the way, and terror, that one should let the side down.'

Peter Elliot was a diver from London, and remembered hanging around for hours before going in to the stadium:

I didn't really think much of it—we were already hot and tired before we even started competing. We were given a horrible beret, I looked like a French onion seller. Beside me was the wrestler Ken Richmond, all six foot four inches of him. They called out the name of Great Britain and I looked up. There were tears running down Ken's cheeks. As we marched in there was this amazing roar, like seven hundred lions, and I started crying too. At that moment I realised how amazing it all was. Ken and I wept our way round the stadium. I couldn't see a thing. I was looking for my parents and I couldn't see them and this giant beside me was sobbing his heart out. It was the emotion after the war, the emotion of any Olympics. It is a competition against the world, you represent your whole nation.

Dorothy Tyler had marched at Olympics before. 'Berlin 1936 was rather chilly, but this time it was frightfully hot, though at least everyone was much more relaxed. Watching that telly in the factory didn't prepare us for the reality. As we got inside, something funny happened. It was so big, with so many people, making so much noise cheering, that it seemed to come and go in waves, the sound and the sight.'

'Nearly four hours after our arrival in the waiting area,' said the oarsman Michael Lapage, 'we were at last called into the stadium. Eighty thousand pairs of eyes surrounded us—just like the Book of Hebrews says, "So great a cloud of witnesses". And in the Royal Box, a solitary figure standing steadily at the salute, George VI, already failing in health.'

'Men, women and children were cheering, chanting and waving flags,' recalled Roger Bannister. 'They had all survived six hard years of war and here, at last, was an opportunity to celebrate not just Britain's victory over the Nazis, but also Britain's survival.'

'As we marched in, I felt my tummy lurch inside,' remembered Boy Scout Geoffrey West. 'I just wanted to cry with pride. The next time I felt like that was when my son was born.'

Prime Minister Clement Attlee had been summoned away and returned just in time to see the British team enter. He glanced at his watch— the Foreign Secretary Ernest Bevin was about to make a statement on the Berlin crisis in the House of Commons.

The march of the competitors had been dovetailed precisely into an hour, and at four o'clock, Lord Burghley invited the King to declare the Games of the XIV Olympiad open. As Patron of the British Olympic Association, the King had already sent a message to his team: 'Although I shall follow all the contests with the keenest interest, I am confident that, whatever may be their result, the British Team will be second to none in consideration to our honoured guests.' Now he simply announced, 'I proclaim open the Olympic Games of London celebrating the fourteenth Olympiad of the modern era.'

The gymnast Frank Turner was proud that his wife and four-week-old son were up there in the grandstand, not far from the royal box. 'As soon as the King announced the Games open, my baby howled into the silence.' In the next moment, however, Baby Turner's contribution was overwhelmed by the trumpeters, in glorious red and gold uniforms with velvet hats, white breeches and shiny black boots, who sounded a fanfare. Above the stadium the huge, white Olympic flag was hauled up the masthead and broke open on the breeze. This very flag, made of satin and embroidered with five interconnected rings signifying the five continents, had first appeared in 1920 at the Antwerp Games and was then passed to each Olympic city. It was assumed to have been lost during the war until allied forces discovered it in the safe of the Berlin Municipality in 1945.

The schoolboy John Glenister was watching from his post immediately below the royal box. 'Immediately behind me was a long line of wicker baskets, each one attended by a Scout. I was suddenly nearly knocked over by a tremendous gust of wind. The next moment I was engulfed in pigeons, all flapping past me. They were conveying the message to the whole world that the Games were open.' The 350 baskets had arrived in London that morning by train from pigeon racing clubs all over Britain, as well as six European countries. They were competing for a special cup. 'We were pleased to see a good contingent from our French friends,' reported *The Racing Pigeon* a week later. 'Belgium also sent a selection. Not a vast number, but of superior quality. Luxembourg too. The release was simultaneous and the birds covered the arena like an umbrella when they were let go at 4.02 p.m. British Summer Time.'

'The flash of wings was like a snowstorm on that brilliant summer afternoon and as the pigeons swooshed round, seven thousand shadows on the grass added to the thrill of the moment,' declared the *Wembley News*.

H.F. Ellis commented less reverently, in *Punch*, 'The scarcely less numerous wireless commentators have been hard at work jotting down suitable epithets for this very moment for weeks past. You may have seen them with their notebooks in Trafalgar Square.' The British team had been warned to keep their berets on. The US team in their white felt hats were also prepared, but Angus Carmichael noticed one American holding his hat in his hand. 'The crown was stuffed with dollar bills. I asked him why he needed so much money, and he told me that the American team were running a sweepstake. The winner would be the first hat to be blessed by one of the pigeons.'

The 7,000 birds rose from their baskets and flew three times around the stadium. Outside on the stadium forecourt, the Royal Artillery fired a 21-gun salute. The blast from the blank charges broke the headlamp glass of a nearby car and the pigeons were scattered by the biggest bird-scarer they had ever heard.

As the gunfire died away, all eyes turned to the east tunnel where a tall young man appeared. He paused and held the blazing Olympic torch aloft, a gesture which earned probably the mightiest round of applause so far. Then, with an effortless style, he ran round the track.

The identity of the mystery torchbearer was a surprise, for, contrary to popular expectations, this was neither the record-holding runner Sydney Wooderson nor the glamorous Duke of Edinburgh. Indeed, nobody had heard of John Mark, a 22-year-old medical student from Surbiton who had been president of Cambridge University Athletic Club. Standing six foot two inches tall and with fair hair, Mark was strikingly handsome and had been chosen by the committee to personify Youth and Vitality. Like all the other torchbearers, he wore a plain singlet and shorts, with no insignia. 'As soon as we stopped dodging the pigeon mess, everyone broke ranks and ran to the edge to watch the final torch bearer,' said Frank Turner. 'He looked the part—a real athlete.'

Not everyone was happy with the choice, some feeling that his looks too closely resembled the 'Aryan ideal', and that a shorter, darker or older athlete would have been more tactfully suited to the post-war mood. Bill Nankeville was in full agreement with Matt Busby, standing next to him, whose opinion was: 'It was an awful snobbish thing to do, to choose that handsome young chap. Our greatest miler, Sydney Wooderson, had fought well in the war, and should have done it.' Wooderson, nicknamed 'The Mighty Atom', had run the fastest ever mile in 1937. He had only just retired, but his

130

appearance—bald, bespectacled, with Brylcreemed hair and skinny white legs, was decidedly not the epitome of youth and sport.

John Mark's torch contained extra magnesium so that it would shine out in even the brightest sunlight, and this last torch was larger and heavier than those carried across Europe, though Mark only had to run with it once round the stadium. Strict security had been maintained while he trained for his ordeal at the BBC Sports Ground in Motspur Park, near Kingston-on-Thames. 'We are very proud and honoured that our son was chosen to carry the torch at Wembley,' his mother told the press once she had been released from her vow of secrecy.

Robert Robinson, a US basketball player, was impressed. 'With his lovely long, slow, running action he circled the track amidst the cheers of the crowds, ran up the ramp, stood for one second and lit the flame above his head. Everybody went crazy. They were all so glad to be doing something normal again. They weren't braving the next bomb.'

'I had the feeling,' wrote Roger Bannister, 'that we were witnessing sacred rites being performed in an open-air cathedral.'

'After long years of almost unending national and international strain and stress,' Harold Abrahams felt, 'here was the light of a flame which crossed a continent without hindrance, caused frontiers to disappear, gathered unprecedented crowds, and lit the path to a brighter future for the youth of the world.'

*   *   *

Now attention switched back to the band. Despite wearing a full ceremonial uniform of bearskin and tunic, not a single musician had passed out in the heat. Now they joined the Wembley Philharmonic Orchestra and the massed choral societies of the BBC, City of Westminster, Harrow town and the National Provincial Bank, all dressed in white. The recently appointed director of the Proms, Sir Malcolm Sargent, held the conductor's baton. His biographer Charles Reid wrote that it was to be

> . . . music of edifying, patriotic and topical sorts. However, it was a broiling day. Sun fell ruthlessly on the instruments of the bandsmen. Sargent put his hand on a tuba. 'Feel that,' he said to one of the singers. 'They'll all be out of tune.' And so they were. But exceedingly few in the Wembley populace that day noticed anything wrong. With the sun for spotlight, Sargent was escorted across the green when the time came by two Guards officers with bared swords and took his place on a high rostrum wearing mortar board and doctoral gown over his morning coat.

The day before, Sargent had wondered which of his three doctoral gowns to wear: Oxford, Durham or Liverpool. 'Everything,' ventured Oliver, his valet, 'depends on the weather. The Durham robe of cream silk, black and purple, will look beautiful if it's a fine day. The scarlet Oxford one is better if it's a dull day.' So he took them all, and the Durham won.

Finding a tune and words capable of inspiring

sportsmen from all over the world had been no easy matter. Spyros Samuras had composed a song for the first modern Games, but the music was now considered 'too Greek'. In 1936 Richard Strauss had written an Olympic Hymn but in 1948 he was standing trial in a 'de-Nazification' court in Hamburg, accused of complicity in the Nazi regime. Although Strauss was to be acquitted, a German song was clearly not suitable. The choice made was the English composer Roger Quilter's 1934 choral setting of Rudyard Kipling's 'Non Nobis, Domine' (Not unto us, O Lord). The second verse seemed especially apposite:

> Non nobis domine!
> Not unto us, O Lord!
> And we confess our blame –
> How all too high we hold
> That noise which men call Fame
> That dross which men call Gold.
> For these we undergo
> Our hot and godless days,
> But in our souls we know
> Not unto us the Praise!

As the music died away, Sargent was joined on the rostrum—constructed of scaffolding draped in white sheets—by the Archbishop of York, Dr C.F. Garbitt, who declared, 'No victory in the Games can be gained without the moral qualities of self-control and self-discipline. Honour is due not only to the victors but also the defeated. When the Games are over, those who have taken part in them should return to their homes as torchbearers with the flame of goodwill burning in their hearts, and committed to burn there long after the Olympic flame has been extinguished.' Then the huge choir sang Handel's Hallelujah Chorus. Asked what it was like, conducting a military band, an orchestra and a huge choir in extreme heat, Sir Malcolm replied, 'It was like taking a jellyfish for a walk on an elastic lead.'

After that Wing-Commander Donald Finlay, the captain of the British team, advanced to the rostrum and recited the Olympic oath on behalf of all the teams. The national flags dipped in salute as he held a corner of the Olympic flag and promised to 'take part in these Olympic Games in the true spirit of sportsmanship, for the glory of sport and the honour of our teams.' The chorus then led everyone in the British national anthem after which, one by one, the flag bearers wheeled about on the grass and marched out, followed by their teams. While all eyes were on them, John Mark left through a disguised door behind the podium. It was the last the public heard of him.

Some of the younger spectators did not wait for the athletes to leave but invaded the arena. 'We lads obtained as many autographs as we could on our programmes,' said Malcolm Tappin. 'I managed to get two Americans—Wendall Robbins and Hilary Smart—two Norwegians and a Portuguese. There was no security and no one minded.'

'I suppose, looking back, the opening ceremony wasn't very exciting,' remembered a Londoner called Billy Jones. 'There was little entertainment or stage management, just a lot of people marching around, slightly out of step. But we were all moved in the same way as watching a small

134

child taking its first steps. Britain was taking its first steps after the war. We had made it through.'

Not everyone was so carried away and Bert Bushnell, as usual, spoke his mind:

> They talk about the magnificence of the Olympics. I never saw any, at either Henley or Wembley. With no warning, in the middle of training, we were shuttled off in a bus. We had to stand for hours in the blazing sun in Wembley Stadium. Nobody told us what was going on. We walked round the stadium behind a Boy Scout carrying a flag, sweat pouring off us, standing in the sunshine in our ghastly blazers for three hours. It was dreadful, absolutely dreadful, a complete dereliction of duty to the athletes. You're all lined up and then this bloke with a flaming torch suddenly runs in, and lights the Calor gas. They didn't mind spending money on that, but they didn't give us athletes anything.

For most people, the day was one of pure joy and a cause for celebration. The Czechoslovakian runner Emil Zátopek later wrote:

> I so wanted to see the opening ceremony at Wembley. But because the 10,000 metres was coming up the very next day, our team leader told me that I was not to tire myself out in the hot sun. But I could not miss this great human celebration. So I crept carefully to the back of our delegation, trying to hide myself behind some of the biggest men as we lined up outside. It was only later, in the stadium itself,

that our leader saw me and began to complain about lack of discipline. 'Emil,' he was calling, 'what are you doing here?' But by then the ceremony was beginning, and I whispered back to him, 'The King George is looking at us. How can I go off now?'

For me, it was a liberation of spirit to be there in London. After all those dark days of the war, the bombing, the killing and the starvation, the revival of the Olympics was as if the sun had come out. Suddenly there were no more frontiers, no more barriers. Just the people meeting together. It was wonderfully warm to feel. Men and women who had lost five years of life were back again and there were all the young ones too.

Twenty-five miles away near Stoke Mandeville in Buckinghamshire, something else extraordinary was happening. Ludwig Guttmann, a German-born neurologist, had founded the National Spinal Injuries Centre at Stoke Mandeville Hospital in 1944. He believed that for people with disabilities sport not only helped build physical strength, but also self-respect. On 29 July, the day the Olympics opened in Wembley, the first Stoke Mandeville Games for former servicemen and women with spinal cord injuries took place in the hospital grounds. They competed in archery and wheelchair races and so began what was to become the Paralympic Games.

That evening, and for the next seventeen days, the Olympic flame shone brightly over Wembley Stadium. It was powered by newly invented butane gas cylinders, and constructed with a pilot light, so

136

that at nightfall, when the stadium was empty, the flame could be turned off and fuel saved. This gave rise to a rumour that the gas supply had failed, and a newspaper headline 'The Night The Flame Went Out'.

9

THE FIRST DAY OF COMPETITION

On Friday 30 July, the temperature was even higher than on the previous day and excitement was tangible as crowds poured out of the railway stations and down Olympic Way. Public transport to Wembley was good: there were ten bus services, two mainline stations and Wembley Park on the Metropolitan Underground line, where a new subway, pedestrian bridge and six platforms had been built. For the next two weeks it would be the busiest station in the world. Sir Arthur Elvin noted: 'The Olympic crowd have been very good and easy to handle compared to Speedway, Cup Final and Rugby League crowds.' Larger car parks were prepared, and in central London the first one-way streets were introduced to ease congestion.

The local children were out in force, including Malcolm Tappin:

It was easy to talk to participants waiting around outside. The Egyptians were good value. They signed our books and did little sketches of Pyramids and a gymnast drew some parallel bars—something to show my mates. But the Bermudan runner Hazard Dill got so tired of autograph hunters that he wrote his name in chalk on the pavement and declared 'There it is, now you all have it.' It was a once in a lifetime experience. On the first day I sauntered past the stadium and was asked by some Canadians where their entrance was. As I was very familiar with the place I took them to it. They had a spare ticket and asked me to go in with them. It was the heats for the hurdles, and there were long delays.

It turned out that white lanes had been marked on the cinder track but not the position of the hurdles. And nobody had noticed until the race was due to start.

Commentating on athletic events was shared between the BBC's premier sports commentators Rex Alston, Max Robertson and Harold Abrahams. Alston wrote in 1951:

Harold is a walking encyclopaedia, but Max and I found we had to get to know hundreds of foreign athletes. Our commentary position was some distance from the track, with the result that the runners looked astonishingly alike. Quick recognition was essential, so we spent long hours at Uxbridge camp. We found the coloured men especially difficult to distinguish. I confess that after two or three days my mind was still a jumble of new names and faces, but the wearing of numbers on the vest was a big help. Abrahams not only described the relative positions of the runners, but with his battery of stop-watches he could record lap times for the whole race. His knowledge of tactics enabled him to make critical comment during the race, which a less knowledgeable man would have had to work out afterwards.

The BBC planned to transmit the first heat of the 400 metre hurdles on the radio. Alston remembered:

Abrahams started with preliminary information and talked with great knowledge about individuals. I saw with dismay that the hurdles were being slowly placed in position as officials measured the correct distances between them. Abrahams continued gallantly to talk about past Olympic Games and some future events. No announcement was forthcoming about the start, so there was nothing for it but to return listeners to the studio. What an anti-climax! Intricate arrangements for broadcasting later events were thrown into chaos, and we had difficulty in pacifying foreign broadcasters, some of whom suspected us of sabotage!

William D. Clark of the *Observer* reckoned there was plenty to entertain, even without the races:

For the incurably frivolous there is an infinity of unintended attractions. The participants who before their races seem afflicted with St Vitus's dance and bounce aimlessly up and down, or else lie on their backs and furiously pedal inverted and invisible bicycles; the men's chorus of timekeepers all identically dressed and standing on the rungs of a ladder like Jacob's angels; and the Jury of Appeal, stern and aloof on their white platform all dressed in Mephistophelean scarlet.

The Boy Scouts were kept busy. 'The perk for standing for so long in the sun on the opening day was that we were allowed to sit in the competitors' stands,' said John Glenister. 'We ran around buying them cups of tea. There was a fair amount of that on the first day, when things weren't quite organised.'

Among the waiting hurdlers was Ng Liang Chiang, a clerk at the Singapore Harbour Board, representing China. The eldest of twelve in a poor Teochew family, he had promised his dying mother to bring glory to his family. When he arrived off the boat in London, he was in great pain from an infected tooth but an RAF doctor had advised against an extraction and given him an injection of anaesthetic instead. Now he paced nervously with the others.

Eventually the race got underway. 'The men seemed scarcely to leave the ground,' said Rex Alston. 'So quickly did the front leg go up and the rear leg snap down after it, as though the hurdle didn't exist and they were merely taking an extra big stride.' Apart from 1928, when Lord Burghley had won gold, the Americans had made the 400 metre hurdle their event and Roy Cochran duly did so again. Ng Liang Chiang came in fourth in his heat and was eliminated. His hopes dashed, he returned to Singapore and hung up his spikes.

The first medal ceremony was held later that day. De Coubertin had been determined that the

Olympics should not exaggerate nationalism and the daily presentation of medals featured flags and anthems but no speeches. The committee faced a problem in that many national anthems had changed in the post-war settlement. Yugoslavia had a new one; Italy was planning a change but had not yet made it; and Romania's new anthem had no score available. The recording company EMI had been asked to produce short gramophone records of all fifty-nine anthems but complained there wasn't enough time. The committee had then allocated £150 to prepare musical scores and engaged military brass bands for each of the venues.

The production of the Olympic medals was also the responsibility of the committee. They had to be at least 60mm in diameter and 3mm thick. The gold and silver medals were made of 92.5 per cent silver, with six grams of gilding applied to create the gold one. For the reverse side, the London organisers chose to use Giuseppe Cassioli's 1928 design of a Grecian chariot representing 'Victory for eternity and universality'. The other side was created by Mr Parker, chief designer at the Royal Mint, and featured Big Ben with the words 'XIV Olympiad, London 1948' and the Olympic rings. The medals were presented in boxes, with no ribbons. For the first time, Olympic diplomas were also awarded to the six highest placed competitors in each event.

The first event to be awarded with medals was the women's discus, a new female competition, the discus and shot having been added to the javelin, which had first featured in 1932. Micheline Ostermeyer from France had thrown a discus for the first time only a few weeks earlier. Tall, slim and twenty-eight, she was the great niece of Victor Hugo. Her father was an outstanding rider and her mother a renowned piano teacher. Brought up in Tunisia, she had come second in the shot put in the European athletics championships in 1946 and in the same year won the Premier Prix as a concert pianist at the Paris Conservatoire. A French writer compared her throwing of the discus to her playing of the piano works of Scriabin. 'Sport taught me to relax,' she said. 'And the piano gave me strong biceps. The sense of rhythm which I gained from music definitely helped the flowing technique of jumping and throwing.' Donning dark glasses against the glare, she now threw the discus over forty-one metres, a distance which in the confines of the stadium scared several of the officials. They also showed surprise when, on hearing she had won the gold, she kissed the medal winners Edera Cordiale Gentile from Italy and Jacqueline Mazéas from France. They beat eighteen other women, the last three places going to Miss Pong Sik Pak of Korea and Miss Birtwhistle and Miss Whyte of Great Britain. Ostermeyer later added gold in the shot put to her tally, after which she gave a Beethoven concert in the women's housing centre. Horacio Estel, a journalist from Argentina, admired her for demonstrating 'the unexpected potential of the female athlete's ability'. Her gold medals were stolen while she was still in London but the committee quickly replaced them to avoid adverse publicity.

The terrible heat on that Friday caused many of the athletes competing in the high jump to collapse, and orderlies of the Royal Army Medical

Corps came to the rescue. In the event of a bad fall, Wembley General Hospital was on stand-by with X-ray equipment. A professional masseur was also on hand, and to offset his fee of £15, athletes were charged four shillings per hour. Boots the chemist provided medical supplies for the Games, and at their all-night branch in Piccadilly interpreters were available, as was a small stock of penicillin.

The British high jump hopefuls were Alan Paterson, a nineteen-year-old Glaswegian in the Royal Army Pay Corps, whose policeman father had coached him to a British record in 1947, and the Nigerian Prince Adeghoyega Solaranmi Adedoyin, a medical student at Queen's University, Belfast, who used the very latest 'straddle-style'. Adedoyin was an all-rounder, who excelled at the hop-step-and-jump and was also good over hurdles.

Lloyd Oscar Valberg, the sole entry from Singapore, who had had to raise his flag alone, was entered in the high jump. His story illustrates the amateur nature of the Games. In 1947, when the Singapore Olympic and Sports Council had been established, Valberg had seen some athletes practising and asked if he could join in. In a crude execution of the 'Western Roll' he threw himself diagonally over a bar set well above his head and went on to win the Malay Peninsular championship. A few weeks later, he bought some peanuts wrapped in a newspaper which contained a photo of an athlete jumping using an 'Eastern Cut-Off'. Valberg tried this, throwing himself backwards over the bar, and beat further records. He arrived in London still without a single lesson

143

in high jumping and, after receiving instruction from the Singhalese coach, he competed in the AAA championships at White City. A few days before the Olympics, he fell from a bus and injured his left leg. He nevertheless qualified for the finals and finished equal fourteenth out of twenty-six. Alan Paterson also qualified and came seventh; Adedoyin came twelfth and the gold winner was John Winter, an Australian bank clerk.

The 10,000 metres also took place on that Friday afternoon. Despite a 6 p.m. start, conditions were still very hot and the runners loosened up by trotting up and down the cool dark tunnel beneath the stadium. Lord Burghley mingled with them, cracking jokes about subjects as far removed from athletics as possible. His colleague Sir Arthur Porritt had tried to analyse exactly what it was that made an Olympic athlete:

> Olympians offer considerable variety in physique and personality, but their main common quality is their steely control over mind and body, allowing maximum effort at the critical moment, and an unflagging spirit that will produce just that extra little bit beyond the maximum when the big occasion demands it. Olympic champions are superb athletes, they are the geniuses of their profession and as such they offer much to admire, but little on which to base a concept of the average athlete.

One of the runners, Stan Cox, had been an international athlete before the war, and was keen to continue. He remembered:

It wasn't easy to prepare yourself for top-class athletics, what with food rationing. Having served seven years in the RAF, I was in an ordinary job, earning a low wage and married with two children. I was allowed extra milk rations which caused a headline in the local paper: 'The milkman is leaving an extra pint at Stan Cox's'. In 1948 I became British six-mile champion and was selected for the Olympics, but we all had normal jobs from Monday to Saturday mornings, so fitting in our training was not easy. When it came to the Games themselves, I took the Friday off as a holiday and went back to work on the Monday.

Harold Nelson, representing New Zealand, had carried the flag the previous afternoon:

We had been out in the scorching heat for the Opening and there was no water provided. All that night and the following day I was thirsty but didn't drink. We had been advised not to drink for the day before a race. A dessert-spoon of honey got rid of all the liquid in the stomach. The need to put liquid back into the body was just not understood. We had tried to get used to the cinder track by training on it, but we found that our legs were tightening up.

The field of thirty-one men set off at a cracking pace, he remembered:

I avoided the early jostling by hanging back. When I moved up to the middle of the field on

145

the 10th lap, I got cramp in the stomach. This got steadily more intense and I had to pull out on the 18th. Everything was a red haze and I collapsed unconscious on the track.

Suffering from dehydration and heat exhaustion, Nelson was stretchered off to a cool dressing room.

Among those he left to continue running was Alain Mimoun-o-Kacha, a French-Algerian. He had been eighteen years old at the outbreak of war and had fought for six years in France, Tunisia and Italy where he nearly lost a leg. Following peace, his local athletics club found him a job as a waiter in the Bois de Boulogne in Paris and he ran for an hour each day, to and from work. 'That's all I did to prepare myself,' he said recently. 'It was archaic. For the ten thousand metres I was a bit of a novice compared to all the top flight. It was my first competition.' In the top flight were Viljo Heino, the world champion from Finland, and his compatriot E. Heinstrom. Finns had dominated long-distance running since the 1920s and Heino and Heinstrom took an early lead, lapping the slowest runners in just over a minute, despite the intense heat.

Among the spectators was Eric Hulse, his wife and their six-year-old son. Hulse had taken a holiday from his veterinary practice in Weybridge. 'One man in a scarlet jersey stood out. We had no idea who he was, his cheeks puffing out like a bagpiper.' Few people had heard of the 26-year-old Czech army officer called Emil Zátopek. At five foot eight inches tall, with a large balding head, he did not look at all like a runner. His skinny body moved in an arrhythmic dance of uncoordinated arms and legs, that somehow produced a long stride. Others too were drawn to his ungainly appearance and the way he seemed incapable of running at all.

'When Zátopek ran, he grimaced,' said Mimoun, 'pumping his arms, with his tongue hanging out. He worked like a woodcutter in the forest. But he didn't cut down trees, he cut down other runners.' His style was deceptive. After one lap he already looked exhausted, his head nodding all over the place. However, both Mimoun and Zátopek proceeded to catch the two Finns, who were leading the field. On the eighth lap Zátopek took the lead and Viljo Heino found he could not last the pace. 'With nine laps to go,' wrote Harold Abrahams, 'and a good race between the Czech and the Finn still on the cards, Heino suddenly stopped running.' In fact, Heino almost collapsed before he withdrew, and he was not alone—seventeen others fell one by one onto the grass beside the track. 'Thereafter,' Abrahams continued, 'the only interest was to watch the incredible, forceful if ungainly running of Zátopek, who proceeded to lap all of his opponents. Everyone was shouting for him.'

Zátopek's approach to pace-setting was quite extraordinary and had never been seen before. He ran fast for 400 metres, then slowed for 100, then surged ahead again. This left the other runners totally confused, for each time he slowed, they thought he was finished, and just as they caught up with him, he would break forward. His method of training was also most unusual. 'Neither wind nor rain could ever halt his training,' wrote one of his

147

admirers, the Czech novelist Frantisek Kozik. 'One day he would run twenty sprints over a stretch of 250 metres, the next day twenty times 400 metres, and every day, the four kilometres between the barracks and the wood, there and back. That meant nine to twelve kilometres daily at full speed.' Zátopek trained not in running shoes, but in army boots, and was reputed on occasion to carry his fiancée, the javelin thrower Dana Ingrová, on his back. 'It is better to train under bad conditions,' he said. 'The difference is then a tremendous relief in a race.'

Kozik described the outcome of these efforts:

Zátopek could produce an almost super-human effort to hold off the threat of others. Years of hard training had established in his wiry frame remarkable powers of recovery. His head lolled back and forth, his tongue stuck out like a dog's, his face contorted as if in agony or having a fit. Yet half way in a race, while his competitors were gasping for breath, Zátopek wanted to hold a conversation. As he sped forward beyond the pack he yelled out 'Achtung!' It was enough to discourage the greatest of giants.

Watching him, Arthur Porritt was deeply impressed, but as a doctor and an athlete himself, he understood Zátopek's style. 'The amazing Czech Zátopek had a rhythm which made a gigantic effort look almost effortless. Stamina, developed by months and years of patient practice into speed, was his essential attribute.'

Over the final 4,000 metres, Zátopek lapped

148

every other runner. Then he entered the last bend. 'Though no one had passed him for some time,' wrote Rex Alston, 'with 300 yards to go, Zátopek produced the most astounding burst of speed. He had been looking fit to drop at every stride as he flogged his tired body along, but appearances were obviously deceptive and he tore down the finishing straight as though his very life depended on it.'

Zátopek knocked nearly twelve seconds off the Olympic record and the crowd went wild. Mimoun came in second and the two men hugged each other in delight. Only fourteen others managed to finish. Abrahams, as sharp as ever, noticed from his commentary position that the judges had been so preoccupied with Zátopek's lapping of other runners that they had failed to give Stan Cox his last lap bell. The poor fellow ran an extra circuit, and although he should have been awarded fifth place, he was placed seventh.

The Olympic motto 'Citius, Altius, Fortius', borrowed by de Coubertin from a college in Paris, is usually translated from the Latin as 'Faster, Higher, Stronger'. But *fortius* can also mean 'braver'. The athletes who took part in the London Olympics soon proved to be both strong and brave. Complaints in the press slowed to a trickle once the Games got under way, and interest among Londoners increased rapidly.

10

TELLING THE WORLD

With competitions to report at last, the world's press got down to work. These were the first Olympic Games in which newspapers, radio, film and television were all involved, and organising them was a major undertaking. The press department had begun work in January 1947 with the difficult task of convincing reporters that London was capable of playing host. 'Those on the sports side of newspapers were encouraged, and those with political opinions, either avoided or completely ignored,' wrote R.F. Church of the Olympic press committee. Once it became clear that the Games would go ahead, newspapers began to run more positive stories about the preparation and over 2,000 foreign journalists attended on 29 July, the largest number ever assembled in one place. 'The most glowing leading articles appeared even from the ranks of the bitterest critics,' reported Church, 'despite the counter-attraction of a disturbed international political situation. More space was given to the Games than to any other single event since the end of the war.' The Foreign Office paid for a party of German sports writers to attend, as part of their 'Re-education of Germany' programme.

The newspaper proprietor Lord Rothermere donated £7,000 to convert Wembley Civic Hall, located halfway between the stadium and the pool, into a press centre with a quiet writing room, a canteen, and a bar which had been 'magicked out of a disused laundry'. The committee obtained special permission from the Cabinet to extend the alcohol licence there to 11.30 p.m. on the grounds that 'Normal closure at 10 p.m. would be irksome for foreign correspondents and likely to give an impression of petty and unreasonable restrictions, and a bad effect on our campaign to attract foreign tourists.'

The Organising Committee took considerable trouble identifying suitable hotels and boarding houses for the visiting journalists, who continued to turn up without warning until the last day of the Games. The Central Meteorological Office at Dunstable provided daily weather forecasts and journalists were also given stamps to save them queuing at the post office. At the end of each day, results were typed into a stencil and 2,500 copies duplicated and distributed to the press by Boy Scouts. Despite all this, complaints were received that there was no special press badge, nor free transport around London. Though for anyone wanting to cool down, the 'Oganic' [sic] water-ferry plied between Putney and Tower Bridge on the Thames.

The student volunteer James Pilditch had been moved from the housing centre at Uxbridge to the press office:

There was the press officer, his secretary, five telephones which never stopped ringing, one typewriter, and me. Journalists came from all over to write about their own athletes. They thought I would know where to find them but I hadn't a clue. The man from *The Times* handed

151

me his card and wondered politely if he 'might just have a word with so and so . . .' The chap from the *Daily Mirror* hustled in and said, 'What's the story? If you don't tell me I'll guess.' We never saw the man from *Paris Match*. He shinned over a wall and went into the French team's dormitory without asking. Just round the time that Herb McKenley, a Jamaican who had broken some hurdling record or other went missing, the press officer disappeared for three days, leaving me in charge. Nobody had seen McKenley but all the press in the world wanted to know where he was. How should I know? All day I picked up one phone after the other and said, 'He's not here,' and slammed it down again. McKenley arrived just in time for his race. The rumour was that he'd spent a few days in New York with his girlfriend.

Team managers were suspicious of the press, viewing them more as dangerous gossip-mongers than allies. They had little understanding of how a good story could be used to raise a national profile. 'We were barred from any contact with the Press,' said Maurice Crow. 'It was the same when we arrived back in New Zealand. Officials informed us that if we spoke to the papers, we would never represent our country again.'

Harry Clarke, a sixteen-year-old Wembley schoolboy, got a job as a messenger for the Great Northern Telegraph Company of Denmark. He had to stand next to a Danish reporter and take his cablegrams to an office below:

For this meagre operation, we saw the whole of the Olympic Games and received seven shillings and sixpence per day. One day the French operator stepped up to me and said 'Parlez vous français?', to which I replied in stumbling school French. His machine had broken and he asked what he should do. There followed a great palaver, out of which I eventually managed to tell him he must go to a GPO mechanic, and I stumbled off, sweat pouring down my face from that verbal barrage. Every time the operator saw me after that he would grin broadly and shake me heartily by the hand.

The General Post Office installed a complete telephone exchange at Wembley. It was called 'Corinthian' and was manned by military personnel. In addition, ten telephone operators moved about in the arena, fitted with breastplate transmitters, double headgear receivers and special waterproof plugs.

There was always a queue for the four phones allocated to accredited journalists for international calls, which had to be booked on the previous day. Three-minute calls ranged from six shillings to Paris, one guinea to Moscow, and £3 15s to South America. The public were also well catered for with fifty-seven extra 'press button A' telephones, made in the GPO's Wembley factory. A local call cost four pence, so attendants stood around with supplies of pennies.

A pile of forms was to be found in the Press Bar, the first stage in sending a telegram. After composing his message, the journalist placed the form in a tin canister and dropped it from the window down a length of vertical gutter pipe. A team of Boy Scouts with bicycles waited underneath. When they heard the clang of the canister, one boy caught it, extracted the telegram and pedalled away to the teleprinter, leaving the can to be pulled back up the pipe on a string.

Eileen Mitchell operated one of the eight teleprinter machines for Cable & Wireless Ltd, which sent out results and communicated between the housing centres, the press office and the arenas:

Teleprinting involved typing on an electric keyboard from hard copy. This went by landline from Wembley to Electra House on Victoria embankment, and thence by Morse code to the various countries. We received the messages in whatever language the reporter spoke, but we were all touch-typists so it was no problem. Thankfully, there were no Japanese. I was part of a team of six operators set up in the betting office at Wembley. It was a bit hot. My husband-to-be spoke fluent Portuguese so he was there as an interpreter for the Brazilians. The press were allocated very good seats in the stadium, and as most of them only attended when one of their athletes was performing, we were allowed to use them. So, work permitting, we saw a lot of the Games. I felt quite proud of my home town for putting on a good show so soon after the war.

The magazine *World Sports* had sponsored eighteen spectators from overseas, each of whom had won a local newspaper competition. The French winner was Mlle Huguette Lienard, an eighteen-year-old schoolgirl from France and the daughter of a French air force officer. When told the good news, her mother said, 'My poor dear, it is wonderful but how can you accept? You have no clothes good enough.' The newspaper *France-Soir* stepped in and took Huguette on a shopping spree in Paris. Other winners included Mr Odd-John Holen, a student from Norway, Mrs Karl-Erik Strangler, a post office clerk from Stockholm, and Mrs Jale Gunay from Turkey. They stayed at the Cumberland Hotel at Marble Arch, visited Parliament and took tea with the Lord Mayor of London.

The photographic rights for the Games were sold by the committee to the Olympic Photo Association, a body set up for the occasion composed of the leading picture agencies. They in turn employed forty photographers to cover all the venues. At Wembley Stadium, only eight photographers, wearing numbered arm brassards, were permitted into the arena at any one time. They had to stay in clearly marked positions and move as little as possible. A fleet of motorcyclists were on call to collect exposed photographic plates and despatch them to Fleet Street. In return for exclusive copyright, the Association had to make their photos available for sale to all newspapers, and prints had to be on sale to the public as soon as they were published. They were displayed in the Palace of Engineering next to Wembley Stadium, and public interest was enormous: foreign tourists alone bought over five thousand.

Picture Post devoted a whole issue to the Games.

Its photos ranged from the pageantry in the stadium on the opening day to children standing on soapboxes in order to watch. The *Kingsbury and Kenton News* printed its picture of the opening ceremony sideways, but people in Manchester got to know little of the Games because the printers of all their five daily newspapers were on strike for a rise in their £8 weekly wage.

Many spectators wrote home about what they had seen, and others were keen to collect the special issue of postage stamps. The General Post Office could deliver 23 million letters a day, but even they were somewhat overwhelmed on the opening Thursday when 66,000 letters were posted from Wembley alone. They had set up a temporary post office at the stadium and produced a special issue with values of 2½d, 3d, 6d, and 1/-. The King was responsible for choosing all British stamp designs and the committee worried that he might pick a picture of a cricket match. He chose some dull abstract designs featuring himself and the Olympic rings, and one featuring winged Victory, designed by children's book illustrator Edmund Dulac. It was only the eighth time that commemorative stamps of any kind had been issued since postage was introduced in 1840.

Stamp collector George Stitt-Dibden remembered:

The GPO didn't have a clue. It was bedlam at the Wembley Arena post office. From the moment the doors opened on the stroke of 9 a.m. until they shut at 10 p.m., everyone wanted to buy the special Olympic issue. In a

156

matter of seconds each counter clerk had a queue in front of him and was busily selling 'one of each' at 1/11½d. The whole office remained a mass of people all day long. After the customers had bought their stamps and stuck them on cards and envelopes, the clerks were besieged again by people asking for their post to be specially franked, and given back to them. When it was explained that there was no hand-stamped commemorative postmark, the poor clerk had to face the wrath of many foreigners.

Not even souvenir envelopes were printed by the post office! They missed a trick there. However, an enterprising stamp dealer from Wembley garnered a beautiful harvest by standing outside the office and selling pictorial covers to disappointed customers as they came out. Customers were even more surprised that they could not have their post cancelled, and then take it away.

Extra post boxes were placed around the stadium, by the Empire Pool, by the kennels, opposite the station and at the entrance to the Royal Tunnel. George Stitt-Dibden remarked:

The GPO rigidly observed the rule that no letter once posted could be taken out of the post but had to be forwarded to the addressee by the proper channels. There could be no relaxation, even for a bona-fide philatelist with an empty envelope. The foreign visitors indignantly pointed out the extra revenue the post office gained from placing all four stamps on one envelope. You only needed one tuppence ha'penny stamp really.

Apparently, in Germany in 1936, they used no less than 193 different special Olympic cancellations. Here in London there was one for ordinary letters, and that was it. The Post Office engineering department had carefully fitted special impression metal dies for the franking, with the rings designed into them. But the new dies cut slots into the stamps and envelopes, thus ruining most of them. On top of that, the ink was not kept well supplied, so in many cases you could hardly see the impressions. At any rate, any surviving, undamaged first day covers are now extremely rare.

The BBC was still the world leader in radio and television, both technically and creatively. A Radio Centre was established in the Palace of Arts at Wembley, with forty recording studios and disc reproduction cubicles, two television suites and a bar. This formed a base for the 200 foreign correspondents and a link to the 100 microphones positioned at the thirty different arenas. There were eleven editing rooms and anyone lingering outside them in the early evening would have got an idea of what it must have been like working at the Tower of Babel. On each day, 400 discs and 100 live broadcasts passed through the Radio Centre. At any one moment an engineer might be handling a broadcast from Henley to Radio Globo in Brazil, while next to him a hockey commentary from the Guinness Sportsground beamed out to India. Transmission had to be done in stages, from one radio station to the next, and each station might require a different language. A broadcast to Czechoslovakia was heralded by the words 'Transmission from London to Prague', which was repeated in English, French, German and Czech until the line was safely established across Europe.

'BBC commentators have for months now been familiarising themselves with the intricacies of the hop, step and jump, or the logarithmic scoring system for the yachting,' reported *London Calling* magazine. 'They have been practising their art either at actual sports meetings or before a film of the 1936 Games.' There were thirty-two commentator's positions in Wembley Stadium; at Bisley a single microphone was all that was needed to report on the shooting; at Torbay, a motor boat was fitted with a transmitter to follow the yacht races. 'Lip ribbon' microphones, held close to the mouth under the nose, were used in open-air locations, without the need for a sound box.

'The broadcasters talked excitedly in many languages or listened intently on headphones as they waited to pick up an opening cue from a studio announcer on the other side of the world,' wrote R.F. Church of the press committee. 'Nearby, spectators never complained, for they recognised the part that radio played in enlarging the Olympic audience from thousands to millions.'

The BBC invited applications from bilingual people interested in sport to act as commentators, and Paul Yogi Mayer was one who auditioned:

The running events had been allocated and all that was left for me was the hammer throw. When the green light came on, I had difficulty

159

with my first sentences, but found that I improved with the distance the throws achieved. However, once the hammer had reached its zenith, I could not talk it down. At the final throw I dried up completely. Standing nearby was the best known athletics reporter of the time, Harold Abrahams, who asked me, 'Why did you not use a flower piece?' 'I never heard of it,' I replied. 'Watch me.' He produced a wooden tray which hung from his neck like a balcony, covered with coloured sheets of papers. 'Didn't you prepare descriptions of the scene, details about the competitors, something about the rule of this not-so-well-known event, a review of the competition at previous Games, the standing of the thrower among other competitors?' Of course I didn't.

The BBC radio operation required hundreds of miles of wiring, thousands of pounds worth of equipment and 350 engineers. One of these was Arthur Price, who was demobbed from the Royal Navy in 1946 and then found work as a recording engineer at Bush House, the headquarters of the BBC European and World Services.

I was seconded to Wembley Radio Centre to record features, talks and commentaries by the accredited correspondents of the participating nations. My experience in the European Service stood me in good stead for dealing with the numerous languages. Each recording studio at Wembley had a portable recording machine installed. They were not wonderful,

160

but adequate for the job. They used 12-inch discs of aluminium coated with fine black cellulose paint into which a polished stylus cut the modulation which produced the sound on reproduction. The surface was quite soft so the quality of recording deteriorated with each playing. The glamorous boys of the recording world were those who travelled with the Outdoor Broadcast. Their equipment was carried in a Humber Super Snipe.

Launched earlier that year, these large, pre-war-style cars had independent front suspension, headlamps in the front wings and a gear stick on the steering column. The BBC fitted twelve with portable recording machines, each of which could make eight different recordings at once.

'Listeners on five continents were able to share in the suspense of each event while it was actually taking place,' wrote R.F. Church. 'They were often actually better off than a spectator for he could only be in one place, whereas the radio listener could visit half a dozen venues in as many minutes and could travel from the Empress Hall to Torbay at the twiddle of a knob.'

With so many events taking place in each arena, difficult decisions had to be taken in using the available staff and equipment, which depended on how many nations wanted to receive the broadcasts, how many languages were spoken in each country, and how popular the sport was. Coverage was for about three hours a day, but neither continuous nor programmed. 'We are prepared to break into afternoon programmes where possible for peak events,' conceded the

Light Programme planners. The Games shared the Home Service with 'Music while you work', 'Children's Hour', and Denier Warren and Ike Hatch in 'The Kentucky Minstrels—a black-faced minstrel show'. On the Light Programme they had to compete with 'Woman's Hour', 'Mrs Dale's Diary', and 'Gert and Daisy's Working Party'. If a dull patch occurred, Fredric Bayco played his theatre organ, or Arthur Albury and his orchestra played 'Music for the housewife'.

Thanks to radio, the Olympics affected people far beyond London. Dick Booth, aged eight, and his eleven-year-old brother John lived in Dover. Dick recalled:

We were gripped by the radio commentaries and immediately planned our own Olympics in the garden. We marked out a track round the perimeter of the lawn. It came to only eighty yards but we agreed this was just sufficient. We ran round it interminably with a series of events to match the main Olympic distances. As a very special treat my father lent us his pocket watch which had a small inner dial showing seconds. Times were carefully recorded. We used a cricket ball for putting the shot and a tent pole for a javelin.

*   *   *

Like Sleeping Beauty, British television restarted in June 1946, opening with the same Mickey Mouse cartoon it had closed with in September 1939. It now had an even smaller budget than before the war. In November 1946 the programme

162

planning committee reported that, 'The proposed television version of *How to Furnish a Flat* has now fallen through owing to unavailability of the furniture.'

There was very little news and no politics. *Television Newsreel* started in early 1948, with a weekly fifteen-minute programme following the pattern established by cinema newsreels, featuring mainly animal stories. The Director-General of the BBC, Sir William Haley, who had worked on newspapers, believed that television was not an appropriate medium for news; Clement Attlee disliked television altogether; and Churchill, now the leader of the Opposition, thought the BBC was full of Communists.

Despite this, television's popularity had been greatly enhanced by the wedding of Princess Elizabeth and Prince Philip in November 1947 and the Olympics proved a marvellous opportunity to demonstrate the new wonders of television.

At the start of 1948, 11 million households had wireless sets, while 45,000 had televisions—a threefold increase from the year before. By July, a further 46,000 sets had been purchased, and the *Evening News* reported from London that: 'The television aerial has become the symbol of social superiority down our street.' There was no hire purchase or credit and the cheapest television set with a 9½-inch black-and-white screen cost £50: two months' wages for an industrial worker, or a month's for a male clerk. Although most television owners lived within fifty miles of London, programmes were sometimes picked up further afield, and Jersey's single viewer reported 'excellent entertainment value'.

Although there had been limited use of closed-circuit television at Berlin in 1936, this was the first true television coverage of the Olympics. Getting the Olympics on the BBC was quite a coup—the BBC had failed to persuade either the Grand National, the Football League, the Theatre Council, the Church Council or even the BBC Symphony Orchestra that their events would benefit from television coverage. All felt either that this medium would denigrate their profession, or that it would take away valuable custom. But Sir Arthur Elvin realised the advantage of television and met with the BBC in December 1945 to state that he was 'anxious to have the BBC televise sport'. The BBC sports commentator Kenneth Wolstenholme recognised that Wembley was not only 'a very special place, the home of thrills and excitement, but also the home of perfect organisation'.

The Olympics were an incentive for the BBC to improve their outside broadcasting cameras. 'Never had television images been so good,' wrote the social historian Asa Briggs. 'The very high lighting levels needed in the studios of Alexandra Palace were no longer necessary for televising, and the pictures of the Games on the screen had a "velvety" quality reminiscent of high-grade photographs. From now on it was possible to take pictures in settings which had hitherto been too "dim" to televise.' However, the camera operators found it hard work. 'There was the strain of continuous focussing,' wrote cameraman Stanley Luke. 'And the psychological strain because the camera viewfinder showed the scene upside down.'

'Two mobile television units, at the Empire Pool

and outside the Stadium, each marshalled three cameras,' wrote Asa Briggs, 'controlled from a radio centre in the Palace of Arts, with producers watching events on monitoring screens and drawing on the stories of a dozen commentators. Seventy hours of television were prepared in fifteen days.' On one single day, 7 hours 35 minutes were broadcast, a record only exceeded during political conventions in the USA.

'To watch the water polo was almost to be splashed with water,' commented the *Observer*. 'The outdoor staff of television have been consistently successful in giving viewers the equivalent of a really good seat.'

In the Empire Pool, competitors were brought before the cameras still panting and dripping. Viewers were also introduced to trainers and personalities visiting the Games. Small interviewing studios were constructed at the main venues, and at the conclusion of each race, a 'chaser' gently jogged the winner's elbow in the hope of persuading him or her to be interviewed immediately by either the British team manager Jack Crump, or one of the BBC's two main broadcasters. Gruff Englishman Richard Dimbleby and Welsh hero Wynford Vaughan-Thomas were the BBC's most distinguished and experienced correspondents, both of whom had reported on major events in the war. Dimbleby had already made 4,000 broadcasts, and the day after television resumed had commented on the Victory Parade through London.

The BBC planned to show only the major events, but the Games turned out to be so popular that most of the other programmes were cancelled and

165

at least five hours a day were broadcast live. Television viewing rooms were set up in all the housing centres for the resting competitors to watch the daily *Olympic Sports-reel.*

*   *   *

Television, for all that it offered in novelty and immediacy, was still the junior partner of cine-film. For several months before the 1948 Games began, the Newsreel Association produced weekly black and white 'picture stories' for cinemas about the Olympic preparations. The producer J. Arthur Rank bought the exclusive film rights for £20,000 and set up the Olympic Film Company. He decided that the film should be the first feature-length documentary shot in colour. It was a huge task, with no possibility of reshooting any scenes. While one unit covered the kindling of the Olympic flame in Greece and followed the torchbearer to the Adriatic, a second unit wrote a shooting script and a third tested cameras at Wembley. Few film crews had any experience of either colour photography or the filming of live sporting events, especially in poor light. There were only three Technicolor cameras available in Britain, and Rank realised that at least twenty would be needed. He discovered that a monochrome camera could be converted to colour with the addition of special film magazines.

Castleton Knight, who had filmed the royal wedding in 1947, was appointed director. Three weeks before the opening ceremony, he asked that gantries for his cameras be constructed on the south roof of Wembley Stadium. Elvin remonstrated that not only would it cost an extra £3,000, but the whole stand would probably collapse. Instead, a trolley supporting a 24ft-high metal tower was constructed, which could be pushed around the centre of the stadium by three men. The only camera they possessed with a zoom lens was hoisted up the side on a pulley. Over one hundred camera stands were also erected around the stadium, each linked by telephone and carefully placed not to obscure the spectators' view. 'The newsfilm men,' wrote William Clark in the *Observer*, 'are wheeled about the field on aluminium platforms under green umbrellas looking like African potentates using a street-lamp cleaners' vehicle as their state carriage.' In order to ensure cameramen were aware of the position of the sun, the filming timetables were printed in Greenwich Mean Time, not British Summer Time.

Elsewhere, derelict air-raid shelters were converted into film-loading rooms by sealing the concrete walls and fitting double-lock doors to keep out the light. These underground shelters provided safe, fireproof storage for the flammable film and valuable cameras. Exposed film was rushed by motorbike to processing laboratories at Harmondsworth and then to cutting rooms at Shepherd's Bush.

To protect Rank's rights, public ticket holders and the press were banned from 'taking cinematograph pictures of any kind'. As an extra safeguard against pirate cameramen, the film crews wore distinctive red berets, white jackets bearing the Olympic badge, brown trousers, white shoes and a special tie. 'This resulted in one of the smartest turn-outs ever worn by a cameraman,'

167

boasted R.F. Church in the official report. Not everyone obeyed the rules, including a spectator from New Zealand who shot a wobbly, silent, coloured 8mm film of the teams marching in; and a member of the Peruvian team who was spotted filming as he marched, turning in his path to get shots of his colleagues behind him.

In addition to directing the feature film, Castleton Knight had to produce enough black and white film for a twice-weekly newsreel which was shown in cinemas all over the world. For the duration of the Games, he lived in a caravan in the stadium car park so that he could spend every available moment either directing the filming, or selecting the best material from the 350,000 feet of exposed film. Editing was done at a rate of 20,000 feet per day. This required such concentration that after each day's work, Knight cured his headaches by watching his bowl of goldfish for fifteen minutes.

The incidental music for the film was based on national anthems and recorded by the Royal Philharmonic Orchestra in Watford Town Hall. The commentary was dubbed in English, French and Spanish. Only two weeks after the closing ceremony the film was finished: it had been edited down to 12,000 feet, or twelve reels. *XIV Olympiad—The Glory of Sport* was shown to the press before its official premiere at the Gaumont Cinema in Haymarket.

It was the first full-length feature film to be finished in so short a time. Ten days later it went on general release across Britain. For many it was the first time they had seen a film in 'glorious Technicolor'. The audience in Merton in south west London were surprised to see someone they knew up on the screen. George Mills, a schoolboy at Rutlish Grammar School, remembered:

Our Maths teacher was Mr 'Harry' Hathway. My friends and I were quite surprised to see 'Harry' sitting on the timekeeper's ladder at the finish of the races. This explained an incident when he had almost fallen over a boy's legs during a lesson. He went ballistic and slippered the boy, who couldn't really help it as he was over six feet tall. 'Harry' then took four large pocket watches from his specially made waistcoat, removed their chamois leather covers and carefully checked them, muttering about how they were worth more than the boy! We had often wondered why he had four waistcoat pockets instead of the more normal two, and now we knew. It was rumoured that he took his stop watches to bed at night, to maintain them at a steady temperature.

The government had hoped that the film would also be good propaganda for Britain's achievements, and a Conservative MP, Sir Thomas Moore, asked, 'Will this film also show the rations received by British competitors, so that that also will be known to the world?'

The first moving film of an Olympic Games had been shot in 1906, though the Greek cameramen had been more interested in the kings and queens of Europe than in the athletes. In 1936, the German film-maker Leni Riefenstahl directed *Olympia*, and spent nearly two years editing it down to a three hour film. *Olympia* is considered a masterpiece of sports documentary, even though few people in Britain ever saw it. It begins with twenty minutes of the Acropolis amid steam, followed by scenes of naked young women waving hoops on a beach. When the athletes finally appear in the Berlin stadium, the trumpets and swooping violins accompany one race after another, punctuated by divers, gymnasts, and naked men beating each other with birch twigs. The only amusing part is when a succession of army officers are thrown off their horses into a deep water jump. Medal ceremony follows medal ceremony, with Americans winning as often as Germans. Spectators include Indians, African-Americans, and Hitler chatting to Count Baillet-Latour, the Belgian President of the IOC. Compared to the sharp monochrome and artistic use of shadows of the German *Olympia*, the British *The Glory of Sport*, the first colour film of any Olympics, is somewhat grainy. The straightforward shots of the principal events make it a homely film about ordinary people which fulfilled the aim 'to create a film which could be enjoyed even by those with no taste for sport'. The *Observer*'s film critic Caroline Alice Lejeune felt that it was a mistake to produce the film so quickly and that they should have taken 'time over it, to select and shoot material from the beginning with an artist's care; to compose each individual picture, to cut and arrange every sequence for dramatic and visual effect' just as Riefenstahl did.

The *Manchester Guardian* film critic was also disappointed and found the 2½-hour film too much like an ordinary newsreel. 'The finish of the marathon is spoiled by use of slow motion,' he wrote. 'E. Gailly, the first man into the stadium, ran his last lap at only four miles an hour anyway: to slow his pace down destroys the drama of his failing effort.' However, he appreciated the emotions of the opening ceremony, the excitement of the races and 'the many beautiful shots of the Henley course, the yachting and the cycling in Windsor Great Park.' Whatever the critics said, the film enabled thousands of people who could never afford to go to London, to enjoy this national celebration.

11

THE 100 METRE DASH

'The 100 metres is considered the gold of the gold,' said Scottish sprinter Alastair McCorquodale. 'It is simply the fastest speed a man can run.' Evoe, in *Punch*, gave it the same top billing: 'Undoubtedly it is the speed which captures most easily the imagination of the ordinary man. He sees himself more often in his dreams pursuing the escaped motorbus, running away from the infuriated bull, or dashing to the post office than setting out on a ten-thousand-metre stroll after a day's work is done.'

On Saturday 31 July, the competitors were gathering inside the stadium for one of the showpieces of the Games. Outside the stadium, excitement was mounting. Word had spread rapidly that the Olympics were worth attending, and many arrived without tickets and had to be turned away. Those spectators who could not afford a hotel slept on camp beds in a marquee for five shillings a night in Northwick Park, two stops up the Metropolitan line from Wembley Park.

One of the most famous Englishmen ever to win this race was Harold Abrahams when he took the gold in Paris in 1924—the 'Chariots of Fire' Games. Understanding the importance of a precise length of stride, during training he would place pieces of paper at regular intervals on the track, and then endeavour to pick them up on his spikes. Before a race started, he would measure the length of his first stride with a piece of string and make a small mark on the track.

Apart from 1924, the race had been dominated by the Americans. At Wembley, the 100 metre 'dash', as it was called, produced sixty-six entrants from thirty-seven nations, which included places as far flung as Cuba, Bermuda, Burma and Iceland. Up to three runners from each country were allowed—a rule which favoured nations that could afford large teams, such as the Americans.

There had been two rounds of twelve heats on Friday 30 July, and now the Saturday spectators could watch the semi-finals in the morning and the final that same afternoon. 'For ten months,' wrote the journalist Denzil Batchelor, 'teams of experts, including dozens of athletes and some six or seven eminent scientists, have been making tests of 120 yards of track until the perfect top surface (the recipe for which remains Top Secret) had been found.'

'The track was built with a margin of error of one inch in 1,000 inches; and the length of 400 metres was accurate to 1/8th inch,' wrote Arthur

Elvin, reminding us that imperial and metric measurements were often used together. Some athletes had brought their own trowels with which to dig a starting hole for their back foot but the tight cinder could not be penetrated and a new innovation, starting blocks, were provided. Though the cinder track had been raked and steam-rollered to a near-perfect smoothness, the athletes knew that if they fell, it would be painful. They also had to guard against each other's spiked shoes, first developed in the late 1890s by a British company, J.W. Foster & Sons, now known as Reebok. By 1948, these shoes had soles thicker than the heels, holding four or five spikes. They were laced almost down to the toe.

Nestor Jacono, Malta's sole representative, had been placed in Friday's first heat.

On the day of the race I felt pretty bad and knowing what heat I was in, made me no happier. As far as I was concerned this was a final, for I had some of the fastest runners in the world, Barney Ewell and Alastair McCorquodale. I had not participated in any major race before. I had that empty feeling inside me and I also felt lonely. A fellow athlete with whom I could talk, to relax the strain, would have been a great help. My name was announced over the loudspeakers and I came out into the vast arena and warmed up. Another announcement and we mustered at the far end of the track. By that time I was so worked up that I did not have a clue about what was happening around me. A few words from the starter and we were under his orders.

Then . . . 'On your marks . . . Set . . . Bang . . .' after that, my mind is blank until I realised . . . the race is over! Although I did not win, I was already feeling better with every minute and I stopped to think what had happened. What were the reasons for my failure? With the help of my manager, Mr Zammit Cutajar and the Canadian trainer Mr Brand Little, we arrived at the conclusion that I had made a bad start as it was difficult to hear the gun because of the loud cheering from the huge crowd. Mine was the first heat and after that, the crowd was asked not to cheer while the athletes were under starter's orders. I was also not used to the long pause between 'Get set' and the gun. I must have relaxed a little, maybe for a split second, with a blank mind, owing to the strain. Despite all this, I feel that the final placings would have been the same, because although a very good start is essential in such a short run, the running of the race and the finish are just as important. So to sum up, I trained hard, I went to the Games, I ran, lost and I came back.

Jacono had come last, in the first heat of the first round of the shortest race, but his inexperience met with sympathy from the radio commentators. For their part, they faced their first serious test: 'How many words, intelligible words, can I get out in ten seconds?' asked Rex Alston. 'I must keep my eye on six runners, and indicate not only their relative positions but also the distance they have run. In world-class running such as this, barely a yard may separate all six. It is a desperate task and I doubt whether it can ever be satisfactorily accomplished.'

By mid-afternoon, the stadium was full and the 83,000 spectators ate their sandwiches under a cloudless sky, enjoying a precious day off and waiting patiently. After picking a lane number from a hat, the six runners from America, Britain and Panama lined up on the track for the final. Each man had already completed two heats the day before, and the semi-final only an hour ago. The shining example of Jesse Owens, who had clocked 10.3 seconds in 1936, was before them, but the standard set in the semi-finals was already high: all the finalists had achieved 10.5 seconds.

In the outside lane was the 25-year-old Harrison 'Bones' Dillard of the United States. Dillard was a surprise entrant. The world record holder in the 110 metre hurdles, he had notched up eighty-two consecutive victories during the past year but then failed to qualify in the Olympic trials. He had decided to try for the 100 metre dash instead and scraped into the team in third place. Dillard, nicknamed 'The Ebony Streak', had been thirteen when Owens returned home from the Berlin Olympics a national hero:

I ran to watch Jesse, then I ran home and said, 'Mama, I want to be like Owens.' A year later Owens himself gave me my first pair of running shoes. Before the final I was quite relaxed and lay on a training table for a little nap. My plan was to get out of my blocks as fast as I could. You want the gun to cause an explosion in your body. I knew I had to be in front to win, as it's no good coming up from behind. I was in the sixth lane up against the

175

stand, so I could see the whole field on my left. They hit the gun perfectly and I led from the start but then I saw two or three jerseys coming up and I started praying and tried not to tighten up and become tense.

Next to Dillard was the 27-year-old Trinidadian Emmanuel Macdonald Bailey, running for Britain, who until the previous year had been hot favourite. Macdonald Bailey had begun winning races at the age of six. His role model was the celebrated sprinter J.R.N. Cumberbatch and in 1939 Bailey had come second to his hero when he ran 100 yards in only 10.1 seconds. That year he came to Britain for the national championships. 'I was really excited about coming to England. I'd read all about Sherlock Holmes and the sports writer F.A.M. Webster of Loughborough.' He returned in 1944 to join the Royal Air Force and through the RAF championships had emerged as Britain's finest sprinter. Then, at the end of the 1947 season, he had pulled a thigh muscle while competing at the White City Stadium. In great pain, he had hopped the last twenty-five metres to win the race and wondered if he would ever walk, let alone run, again. Bailey trained through the pain and in 1948 was selected for the British team. He would have preferred to run for his native country, and many Trinidadians felt that he had betrayed them, but at this point Trinidad had no Olympic committee. 'We were still a Crown Colony,' said Bailey. 'So I could run for Britain. My father said to me "Time is running out. If I were you, I'd go ahead and represent Britain, otherwise you might never have another chance." '

In the end, Trinidad did manage to put a team together and Bailey found himself beating his fellow countryman George Lewis in the second round of heats.

Next to Bailey was the other British hope, Alastair McCorquodale, described by Harold Abrahams as 'a rocketing Martello Tower of a Scots Guards officer', who at twenty-three had not run seriously until the previous year. McCorquodale had gone from Harrow School straight into the Army in 1944, where he had won championships while stationed in Germany. 'He had beaten Macdonald Bailey consistently throughout the summer,' wrote Rex Alston, 'though the latter was potentially the better sprinter.'

'McCorquodale was a strong athlete with a natural talent,' Bailey agreed. 'Though he was more interested in printing than sprinting, and didn't train much.' McCorquodale belonged to the family whose firm printed the Olympic programmes.

After I was selected, they gave me some time off to train, but I didn't do a lot. Harold Abrahams told me, 'Join a club such as the London Athletic and get Guy Butler, an ex Olympic athlete, to train you.' I bought some running shoes and Butler worked out a programme. My wife and I lived near Windsor and I ran around in the dark after work. Butler told me to go and run in a quarter mile race, but it made me sick. I'd never raced that far before and I realised that one or two hundred metres was my thing.

177

'While some allowance should be made for Bailey having had an abscess under his left arm lanced 24 hours before the race,' reported Roy Moor in the *Sunday Chronicle*, 'I consider McCorquodale will continue to have the better of the duel of the Macs, so long as Bailey starts his race with such a psychological disadvantage.'

Prior to the 100 metres, McCorquodale had joined the team at the RAF camp in Uxbridge. 'They did their best there. We were well fed because the Americans shared their food. We got a blazer, a tie and an awful beret. I never wore it.' Like many athletes at the time, he continued to smoke cigarettes.

'Sprinters are born, not made,' said Roger Bannister. 'You can't really train for the sprint. You're either born with the right lungs and long legs or you aren't. McCorquodale was naturally fast, but his style was rather wild with his arms flailing.' Arthur Porritt described him as 'Probably one of the untidiest runners of all time, but he had a lion hearted courage.'

Next in line was Lloyd LaBeach who at twenty-four was the only person representing the Republic of Panama. His parents were among the 40,000 Jamaicans who had moved there to build the great canal. LaBeach had first shown his talent in athletics at school. He later received coaching at the University of California where he became the arch rival of Melvin Patton, who was critical of his habit of rolling at the starting blocks. 'You come up on your set and you start and you stop and you move your body backwards and forwards, so that you've already got your body in motion. That gave

178

you quite an advantage,' he commented later.

One of the world's leading sprinters, the thirty-year-old American Norwood 'Barney' Ewell was next, having returned to the track after service in the US army. Since 1939 he had won over twenty championships and was also an outstanding long jumper. During the Olympic trials, he had equalled the current world 100 metre record of 10.2 seconds.

Finally, on the inside lane was another American, Melvin Patton, or 'Pell Mell', who, at twenty-four, was the favourite, having already run a world record 100 yards in 9.3 seconds. Born in Los Angeles, he had been the first member of his family to attend college. He trained for only half an hour a day. 'The coach works with you on such things as how far forward you lean, where your hands are spread, where the pressure points are on your feet and how high your hips are. He attempts to teach you to react to the firing of a gun. After that it is just a matter of practice. You make sure that you are toeing straight ahead rather than toeing out which could lose you valuable time. I think my toes were pointing out that day.'

Predictions were difficult: it was a very close field. Patton had beaten LaBeach for the world record, but then Ewell had beaten him in the trials. Patton remembered: 'I knew I was in a little bit of trouble to begin with because I was a little down in weight because of the heat and maybe the English cooking. I did not adapt well; there was something that was a little bit of out of sync. I wasn't perky, that's for sure.'

The starter ordered the six men into their starting blocks, a hundred metres to the left of the

Royal Box. He wore a white cap and blazer and thick black spectacles. His pistol, connected by a wire to the timer, was held high in the air for all to hear. There was a false start, after which some in the crowd stood for a better view. The runners crouched on their marks for a second time and got away perfectly, running flat out. The commentator Max Robertson admitted that he was as nervous as the sprinters. 'I couldn't afford to stutter, because if I did, I'd lost three seconds and then I was out of the whole race. So I had to be absolutely on the ball.' The spectators were now all on their feet. Jim Parry, an insurance clerk from Lancaster, had decided to take his summer holiday in Northampton and drive to Wembley every day. He had paid 7s 6d for a good seat. 'Everyone was very good and kept quiet until the gun went off. Then they went mad and the noise was enormous.'

'And they're off,' cried Max Robertson. 'And Dillard is on the outside. It's Dillard, LaBeach and Ewell, I wouldn't like to separate them.' The crowd roared as Dillard, travelling at over 20mph, went in front almost at once. 'The muscular action of the sprinter is not wholly on a par with that of the bird nor even of the jet-propelled aeroplane,' commented Evoe in *Punch*. Barney Ewell came from behind at the finish and thought he had broken the tape first. He danced around the track, embracing his colleagues.

'As we approached the tape I went into my lean and tried to reach for it,' said Dillard. 'I threw my chest out and felt that tape strike me. Cotton yarn goes a couple of feet before it pops. From the corner of my eye I saw something. Barney Ewell my room mate was being very ebullient—he

180

thought he'd won. He jumped up and down to celebrate. Lloyd LaBeach said, "No man, you didn't win, Bones won." '

Sixteen-year-old Maurice Graham, who had travelled down from Yorkshire to watch the race, remembered: 'I was sitting opposite the finish. But on the other side of the stadium, a football pitch width away. Next to me was a very pleasant Dutch guy, a little older than me. We were both amazed at the celebrations of Barney Ewell. I turned to my Dutch friend and said "Why is he doing that? He hasn't won." I think the tape had broken on his chest although Harrison Dillard had crossed the line first.' It had been a tremendous finish, with only about a metre separating all six men. Who had actually won, or come second, or third, was not yet clear and new technology was called upon to make the decision.

The 'Photo Chart Camera' had first been demonstrated in July 1939 at the same stadium during a greyhound race, and had come into official use there in the autumn of 1945. Now was the first time it had been applied to athletics. The 'photo-finish' was operated by the inventors, the Race Finishing Recording Company, who charged £480 for their services. The camera was installed sixty feet above the track to one side of the finishing line. On the opposite side was a vertical revolving drum which was painted with the word WEMBLEY, the date and the event number, and synchronised to the camera speed. This ensured that every print showed the lettering and guaranteed identification of the photo against the particular event. Photographic prints of the finish of any race could be produced within ninety

181

seconds of the tape being broken, and officials at the finishing post were then telephoned with the result. LaBeach was right: Dillard had finished a few centimetres ahead of Ewell, with a time of 10.3 seconds, the equal of Jesse Owens.

'Finally the announcement came in reverse order,' said Dillard. 'When they said Ewell, I knew I'd won it.' Considering that he had only just managed to get into the US team, Dillard's achievement was all the more remarkable. Ewell took the news with good grace. At the age of thirty, he was pleased to have won a silver medal. 'Barney should have won,' said Mel Patton. 'But he looked over at me to see if he had beaten me. Maybe, had he not done that, he might not have thrown up his hands prior to getting to the tape. Harrison sneaked in on the inside of him to win that race.'

A photo-finish was also required to establish third and fourth place. Lloyd LaBeach had just pipped McCorquodale to a bronze. 'Alistair was the fastest white man in the world that year,' said his proud wife Rosemary. 'We were desperate for British medals,' remembered Malcolm Tappin, then a schoolboy. 'I was mortified when our great black hope Macdonald Bailey did not win.'

'People are always surprised,' Bailey recalled, 'when they ask me what my greatest achievement has been and I say, "Coming sixth in the 1948 Olympics!"'

Although he came in fifth place, it was the handsome white American Mel Patton and not the black victor Harrison Dillard who featured on the front cover of *Life* magazine two days later.

There were no competitions on 1 August because it was a Sunday. The observance of a day of rest had been a contentious issue at previous Olympics. The US athlete Alvin Craenzlein returned from Paris in 1900 with four medals and was publicly denounced in Philadelphia for having broken the Sabbath. In 1924 Eric Liddell refused to run on a Sunday and forfeited his entry in both the 100 metres and the relay. This time, the London committee had headed off these problems by removing Sunday from their schedule. Competitors were expected to go to church, where on that day, Dr Fisher, the Archbishop of Canterbury, in his sermon recommended that using donors for the artificial insemination of humans should be made a criminal offence.

Nobody, however, seemed to pay much attention to the needs of the 228 Muslim competitors from Turkey, Iraq, Iran, Egypt and Pakistan, who were given no concessions for the fast during Ramadan, which ended on Saturday 7 August. The weightlifters and boxers were fortunate in that their events fell after Eid, but not so the Pakistani hockey players or the Turkish wrestlers, all of whom had to compete while fasting.

The rain fell so heavily early on the morning of Monday 2 August that the driver of a taxi skidded and collided with a milk van in Olympic Way. Mr B. Ricardo of Mill Hill suffered minor injuries and was not detained in hospital. After a few glorious days, the weather had turned nasty across the country—during heavy rain, thunder and lightning, 12,000 people attending the Welsh National

183

Eisteddfod had to wait over an hour while rain on the pavilion roof drowned out the children's solo songs; the crowd entertained themselves by singing hymns. Disappointed holidaymakers trekked home from the coasts as heavy rain put an end to their sunbathing. At Staines, 2,000 vehicles an hour were heading along the Great West Road. Just south of Wembley, the previous days' heat had caused an aqueduct carrying the Grand Union Canal over the North Circular Road to crack. Water cascaded over the edge, creating a deep flood on the road below. The Olympic traffic was diverted via Ealing.

The spectators at Wembley crouched beneath folded newspapers or crowded into the radio commentators' covered positions. 'As if by magic,' wrote H.J. Oaten in the *Evening News*, 'the stadium cleared of all those who had no particular job to do and officials scurried away to return equipped in thick oilskins, lent by the Navy. Umbrellas went up all over the stadium but quite a number had been caught without any protection at all, particularly girls in summer dresses. I saw a single mackintosh shared between six people.' The film crews standing in their steel-lined pits around the edge of the track found themselves up to their knees in water.

'If the shortest of races presents a certain difficulty to the poetic imagination how much harder it is to convey adequately the idea of the longer and more complicated events,' wrote Evoe in *Punch*.

The point about the 800 metres is that there is a good chance of seeing Great Britain win this

184

race. We have won it more often than any other event in the athletics section, which is not perhaps saying very much, and we have won it as often as all other countries put together, which is saying quite a lot. This year there is a certain John Parlett who should be closely observed. A month or so ago he won a half-mile against such formidable gentlemen as Messrs Wint of Jamaica and Harris of New Zealand, and did it in a time which has only twice been beaten in this country. *Punch* readers will not need to be reminded that I am referring to Sydney Wooderson's world record made in 1938.

New Zealanders had high expectations too. 'I sat on the track-side with some of our boys for Doug Harris's 800 metre race,' said Ngaire Lane. 'Doug was our big hope for a gold medal as he was first in the world ratings.' As a child, Harris had suffered a badly shattered arm and a piece of bone had been taken from his leg and grafted into it. Now a tall and powerful athlete aged nineteen, he was studying at Loughborough Sports College. In the build-up to the Games, he had been quietly confident, though he had not run on a cinder track before. During Friday's preliminary heats, he was halfway through the first lap and running comfortably towards the back of the field, when, with no warning, the man immediately in front of him changed his stride. To avoid a collision, Harris side-stepped into the path of a Danish runner called Christiansen, who caught him with his shoe so that three spikes went into the back of Harris's heel. Thus entangled, Harris lifted Christiansen clear off the ground, and the Dane fell sideways and broke his leg. Harris continued to run, unaware of the damage done both to Christiansen and himself. He finished second and qualified for the semi-finals the following day. However, the spikes had damaged his Achilles tendon and he required an injection of painkiller from Arthur Porritt before he could make the start.

'In the semi-final,' wrote the New Zealand captain, Harold Nelson, 'Doug Harris had picked Arthur Wint as his most dangerous opponent and ran his race with that in mind.' Harris was running easily in third position, with 200 metres to go when he moved into an attacking position. Suddenly he stumbled in pain and collapsed on the track: his tendon had torn and he was stretchered out of Wembley in agony. Porritt, himself a New Zealander, took personal care of him at St Mary's Hospital in Paddington. 'Doug was operated on today,' Nelson wrote in his diary. 'The opening in the leg was twelve inches long, extending from the heel up to the middle of the calf. He goes into tears over the whole business. It is a pity because he has no other interest in life but athletics and now he is lost.'

Two days later, the 800 metres final got under way, watched by Christiansen wrapped in a tarpaulin against the rain and propped up on his stretcher. The nine runners, three from the USA, two from France and one apiece from Denmark, Great Britain, Jamaica and Sweden, bunched tightly at the start, which was close to a bend. Robert Chef d'Hôtel of France started in the lead. The British contestant John Parlett had peaked too soon and was feeling, if anything, too relaxed:

'I ran quite well in my heat and then faster in the semi-final, but by the final I had done enough. I was so familiar with being in London that I did not feel sufficiently worked up to get the adrenalin going.' At the halfway bell there was a scramble for position and a 23-year-old US Air Force Sergeant called Mal Whitfield went into the lead.

'Whitfield,' wrote Abrahams, 'running with beautiful ease, was never seriously challenged, and won in a time which beat the Olympic record. Wint of Jamaica ran a restrained and well-judged race and came in three metres behind.' Britain's hopes were unfulfilled again when Parlett came last. 'Having run a dismal final,' he said sadly, 'I did not regard the Olympics as an enjoyable occasion.'

Spectator Maurice Graham recounted:

Afterwards, I got on the tube at Wembley Park to go to the Central YMCA where I was staying. On got Mal Whitfield in his tracksuit, carrying his bag which presumably contained his gold medal. We all recognised him but were too shy to speak. At the next stop, which was Neasden, an elderly lady got on and sat next to him. She looked him up and down and said, 'Oh, you are an athlete, aren't you?'

Mal very politely replied, 'Yes ma'am.' Others in the carriage who were listening, smiled and nudged each other.

'Are you competing in the Olympic Games?' asked the lady.

'Yes ma'am, I am,' said Mal.

'What is your event?' asked the lady.

'Eight hundred metres ma'am,' said Mal.

'How very interesting,' said the lady and got

off at Willesden Green.

*   *   *

When the pole vault final began at 2.30 p.m. it was raining heavily. The floodlighting had been removed from the stadium track and all the events had to take place during daylight, so the programme could not be suspended and the competitors just had to brave it. No one expected records to be broken that day.

America had won every Olympic pole vault since 1896 but their champion, Cornelius Warmerdam, had been banned from the Games after he was paid as a coach. Britain's entry was Richard Webster from Bedford. Born in 1914, he was the son of Captain F.A.M. Webster, the author of *Great Moments in Athletics*, published the previous year, and the founder of athletics coaching at Loughborough College. During the First World War, Captain Webster had been invalided out of the Army and had come under the guidance of the charismatic coach Sam Mussabini who also trained Harold Abrahams. 'What Sam didn't know about getting athletes fit wasn't worth knowing,' Webster wrote. 'I learnt from him the wisdom of working up slowly and the utter folly of doing anything that might cause one to produce a peak performance too soon.'

Webster had passed on his skills to his children. Richard and his two sisters, Peggy and Joan, made themselves a gym in their garden. One summer his father went to Scandinavia and brought back a child-sized bamboo vaulting pole. 'We always played at athletics,' Richard remembered. 'I

188

started pole vaulting at six. You have to have strong arms. We had a rope in a tree to hang from. This American chap I knew had his staircase replaced with a rope to strengthen his arms. You had to learn to jump and vault at a low height so that you could practise landing. We fell on to sand which was very hard.' In 1937 he joined the 2nd Searchlight Regiment and after the war he remained in the Army and took up athletics again. 'I hadn't touched the pole since 1939. Once I was firmly accepted for the Olympics I got an extra ration card and the local butcher gave us all extra meat. The Army didn't provide any extra food.'

Webster's wife, Beryl, came to watch. 'We could hardly see the pole vault, it was so far away in the corner.' The vaulters took turns to run along the sodden track, carrying bamboo poles borrowed from the Army Physical Training Corps. They had to ignore the roars of the crowd watching the track events. Their clothes were soaking wet and heavy, and their hands slipped down the poles as they leapt. They landed on a solid pile of wet sand and wood shavings. 'There was a worry that the bamboo poles would crack just as I was at the top,' Webster said. 'By then I was thirty-four years old, and I didn't come anywhere near.' He was among seven vaulters who were not placed. Guinn Smith of the USA won gold, despite having an injured knee. He was the last man to win an Olympic medal using a bamboo pole.

*   *   *

The last big event on the Monday was the final of the 5,000 metres. In his heat at the weekend,

Harold Nelson had been determined to make up for his poor performance in Friday's 10,000 metres but the timetabling of the races so close together told against him. 'Over the first lap and a half, I led and the pace was slow. Then a Dane shot past me, led for a lap and collapsed on the track. When the pressure was on, I felt curiously listless and finished sixth, which was not good enough to qualify for the final.'

By late afternoon the rain had saturated the track and there was standing water as the twelve runners lined up soon after five o'clock. They included Gaston Reiff from Belgium, Alain Mimoun-o-Kacha, and the 'Human Locomotive' Emil Zátopek, who had won the 10,000 metres three days before. 'There was much speculation as to whether Zátopek would win the 5,000 metres too, the double having been accomplished only once before in 1912,' wrote Abrahams. The 5,000 metre heats had been held on Saturday. 'The most astonishing thing about the heats had been the totally unnecessary duel between Zátopek and Ahlden of Sweden. Though they were well over 100 metres ahead on the last lap and qualifying with ease, they elected to stage a spirited battle, much to the delight of the crowd. They raced on as if their lives depended on the issue.' Ahlden had won on that occasion but the struggle may have had a greater affect on Zátopek two days later. 'By the half-distance,' Abraham continued, 'the contest was between Zátopek, Gaston Reiff, Willem Slijkhuis from the Netherlands and Ahlden. With four laps to go, Reiff broke away from the others, and at the bell was twenty yards ahead of the Dutchman, with Zátopek another thirty yards away.'

'Reiff put on a spurt which took him yards ahead of his two rivals and he looked an easy winner,' wrote Bill Nankeville. 'Then, the incredible Zátopek pulled out all the stops. He had already made himself a favourite with the crowd, and as he demolished the gap between himself and Reiff, they yelled their heads off.' As Zátopek moved into top gear, the crowd, sensing that something extraordinary was happening, picked up the chant of his Czech supporters, 'Zá-to-Pek! Zá-to-Pek!' The whole stadium was with him as he went down the straight, his back drenched in mud, every step apparently the biggest effort of his life, his tongue hanging out and huge head rolling. Many thought he was about to have a heart attack, running his third long race in three days.

'Zá-to-Pek! ZÁ-TO-PEK! *ZÁ-TO-PEK!*' the chanting rose to a crescendo. 'Throwing all caution aside,' wrote Rex Alston, 'with arms flailing, body swaying, he tore after the other two and quickly passed Slijkhuis. The roar of cheers from the crowd was almost deafening. Stride by stride he brought Reiff back to him.'

'The crowd rose to their feet and gave him even more energy,' continued Abrahams. 'He made an extraordinary 200 metre sprint at the end to catch up and with every stride he gained on Reiff. His last lap must have been achieved in about sixty seconds: it was phenomenal running. With less than ten yards to go, Reiff suddenly sensed the danger from the shouting of the crowd and won by a couple of strides.' Zátopek literally hurled himself across the finishing line but he had lost by just 0.2 of a second. Slijkhuis came in nine seconds later.

Derek Wood was a seventeen-year-old spectator from Barnet. 'I saw the greatest and most exciting race that Emil Zátopek failed to win.' Zátopek later said that he had felt overwhelmed by his 10,000 metre victory, that he thought the 'double' was impossible and, with two laps to go, he had felt content to come third. Then he suddenly decided to go after Slijkuis, and once he had caught him, his strength revived and he set off to beat Reiff.

Of course, to the British public I was not a name until after my 10,000 metre victory. Then, perhaps they took me to their heart a little more when I ran that incredibly stupid tactical 5,000 metres race against Reiff, getting left behind so far. It was all so silly. Suddenly I was saying here is the last lap and maybe I can win. I tried and I came so close to Reiff at the finish and the crowd at London cheered for me, but when I got back to Czechoslovakia they asked, 'How could you be so stupid?'

12

THE GENTLER SEX

Women have always had to fight hard to compete in athletics. Their first appearance at the Olympic Games was in 1900 in the croquet programme. In 1904 at St Louis, women were given their own archery events, which by 1908 drew thirty-six entries. The British winner that year was Sybil

'Queenie' Newall, who was fifty-three and is still the oldest woman ever to win Olympic gold. The runner-up was Charlotte Dod, an exceptional athlete who had won the Wimbledon tennis singles on five occasions, the British Ladies golf crown, had represented England at hockey, and also excelled at skating and tobogganing. Three female swimming and diving events were introduced in 1912 and five kinds of athletic events in 1928. One was the 100 metre dash, at which three Canadian finalists horrified the predominantly male audience by hugging and kissing each other. That same year women raced over 800 metres but unfortunately some collapsed at the end, leading doctors to claim that women would suffer early senility if they undertook such 'feats of endurance'. Despite the fact that men often collapse after races, the IOC president, Count Baillet-Latour, wanted to revert to an all-male Games. The IOC as a whole were a little more generous and concluded that 200 metres was far enough to test women's delicate bodies.

In 1943, even when women were fully employed in the war effort, employers were advised to 'Give every girl an adequate number of rest periods during the day. You have to make some allowances for feminine psychology. A girl has more confidence and is more efficient if she can keep her hair tidied, apply fresh lipstick and wash her hands several times a day.' The 1944 Education Act, which established free secondary education for all, still expected girls to ignore sport and cultivate the feminine graces. Many schools for girls rejected athletics because of the perceived danger of displacing internal organs.

Even in 1948, of the 4,000 athletes competing in London, only 385 were women. They were permitted to compete in only nine athletics events, which included long jump and shot putting. They were still considered unfit to swim further than 400 metres, and though the British woman Violet Piercy had run the marathon in 1926 at Chiswick in 3 hours 40 minutes, the IOC still considered that women were not strong enough to run long distances. The equestrian, shooting and rowing events were among those that women were still barred from. In gymnastics, they could only compete as teams, not in individual events. In the sailing events, the Royal Yacht Association was only informed by the IOC in May 1948 that women were banned. Even the most stalwart Royal Navy types were amazed by 'this unexpected bombshell', for women had competed in earlier Games: Frances Clytie Rivett-Carnac had crewed for her husband in 1908, winning gold; and the 38-year-old Virginie Heriot had won gold with her French crew in 1928. The RYA protested but to no avail. Sigfrid Edström arrived at the opening ceremony in Torquay with the welcome news that women would be admitted in future, but the decision came too late for Mrs Winifred Pritchard who was forced to withdraw after winning all four races in the British trials.

At the European Championships in 1946, two of the fastest women athletes had afterwards been discovered to be men, so in 1948 sex testing was introduced. Much to everyone's embarrassment, this involved a doctor looking into the underpants of female competitors to check for 'sexual abnormalities' such as an overlarge clitoris.

194

In 1939, the British high jumper Dorothy Odam (later Tyler) had broken the world record, only to be informed that the German athlete Dora Ratjen had already jumped higher. She was enraged about this because she had watched Ratjen closely at the Berlin Games in 1936: the German had a deep voice and always bathed on her own, and Dorothy was convinced she was really a man. Pressed, the German authorities conducted an examination and admitted that Ratjen was a hermaphrodite who would be withdrawn from competition. It was not until 1957 that Herr Hermann Ratjen told his story: he had been forced by the Hitler Youth to compete as a woman.

It was in this atmosphere of distrust that a woman became the undoubted star of the London Olympics, and one of the most famous of all twentieth century athletes. Fanny Blankers-Koen was born in the Netherlands in 1918 and made her Olympic debut as a high jumper in 1936. When she was a child, her father, who was a farmer, insisted that she drank whale-liver oil every day. At home she never bothered to open the garden gate, but vaulted or even hurdled it. As a sixteen-year-old she set a Dutch 800 metres record and at twenty gained her first world record in the 100 metres dash. By then she was being coached by Jan Blankers, the Olympic triple jumper, and in 1940 they married. In 1943, two years after the birth of her first child, she broke world records in the 100 metres, high jump and long jump. After the birth of her daughter five years later, she took her children with her when training, feeding the baby in the changing-room while her son played in the sand pit of the long jump. Tall, sharp-featured and

195

flaxen haired, she was now a world record holder in six events and nick-named 'the Flying Housewife'.

One person who wanted to watch all the women's events was fifteen-year-old Phoebe Tyson from Hampshire:

My father, a doctor, was given tickets for the Olympics. He could only manage to go on one day so my brother and I went to Wembley each day by ourselves on the milk train. I was a schoolgirl in a cotton frock, white ankle socks and brown sandals, and my school navy gabardine mackintosh. The train was always packed, so we aimed for the guard's van, where one could perch on a hamper. We didn't have to worry about how to get to Wembley as everyone was going the same way. As we came out of the station we joined the great crowd walking down the middle of the road towards those two majestic towers. Our seats were right on the front row, beside the competitors' entrance. There was a tremendous camaraderie in the crowd: everyone was so glad to be there, proud of the effort that Britain had put into staging the Games, and excited to see competitors from other countries. Even on the days when it poured with rain, and most of the spectators and all the competitors got soaked, I never heard a word of complaint from anyone. Many of the athletes smiled and spoke to us. My proudest moment came when Fanny Blankers-Koen gave me her cardigan to hold whilst she ran.

Douglas Burns, a former navigator in the RAF, was another who came under her spell. 'One day we were on the underground train from Piccadilly and standing next to me, hanging on a strap, was Fanny Blankers-Koen. She told me she had entered four events and although she would definitely run the 100 metres, it would depend on how the others were programmed for the rest.'

The heats for the women's 100 metre dash had been run on Saturday, and on Monday 2 August the semi-final was scheduled for 3.30 p.m. with the final an hour later. It was raining. Dorothy Manley, aged twenty-one, was the favourite among three British runners. 'My preparation was very low key. I had a full-time job as a typist in the City for the Suez Canal Company, so I could only train after work for a couple of hours, four evenings a week. I always thought my ability to run was a God-given talent, and nothing to do with me. People say that you cannot hear the crowd cheering, but I was aware of them and many were cheering for me, including my parents and my fiancé.' For the first time, women were permitted to wear sleeveless vests and shorts. It was Manley's first international event and she had only switched from the high jump to sprinting a few months earlier. She had sailed through her semi-final and joined Blankers-Koen in the final:

Fanny was a marvellous athlete. I'd never met her or even heard of her before. I was expecting to win, but everyone else was expecting her to. The whole atmosphere was quite awe-inspiring. I was so petrified before the race that if I could have run away I would

197

have done. The gun went and I got a good start, but I thought it had been a flyer and that we would be recalled. That did for me. I would never have beaten Fanny, but I think I could have got closer to her. She was completely focused, whereas I was probably thinking about other things.

Julian Potter was seventeen when he and his brother Andrew went to Wembley. 'London was a dreary place and it was a rather grey, wet day. But we cheered up when we saw Fanny Blankers-Koen running. She had very long legs and long paces.' With a high knee-lift and head held back, wearing baggy home-made orange cotton shorts, Blankers-Koen won the gold and Manley took silver. Manley stood on the podium with tears in her eyes. 'Some newspapers wrote that I was crying because I hadn't won,' she remembered. 'It was absolute nonsense. I was just choked with delight. I lost by a few feet. Even so, I had a great sense of achievement. My father reminded me not to let it go to my head. Afterwards I ate some nice toad-in-the-hole.'

The bronze went to 23-year-old Shirley Strickland from Australia, who grew up running barefoot around her father's farm and took up competitive sport while studying nuclear physics at university.

On the following morning, Tuesday 3 August, Blankers-Koen returned to the warming-up track behind Wembley Stadium to prepare herself for the hurdling event. The weather was now even worse. 'Nobody could ever have been so nervous before a race. I wasn't even in the mood to sign my autograph for all those enthusiastic boys and girls clamouring for it.' She went through her usual warming-up routine but her mind was not on it. 'All the time I was waiting for a glimpse of my rival Maureen Gardner, whom I had never seen before. I had read about her and though I had set the world record earlier that year, I knew only too well how many factors can upset form in sprinting races.'

Maureen Gardner, pretty with dimples and curly hair, was a nineteen-year-old English ballet teacher who had met her coach Geoff Dyson whilst jogging to recover from a dance injury. 'I saw that Maureen had brought her own hurdles,' Blankers-Koen continued. 'She must really be in the top class, I thought. There were no other hurdles available and I summoned up my courage and asked if I could use hers. We shook hands and I noticed immediately that I was not the only one who was nervous. Both of us were on tenterhooks because all the sports writers of my country had marked me down as favourite, and all the British experts had tipped Maureen for the gold medal.'

Ian Adams and his brother Bob were Glaswegians who had just got out of the Army. They and twenty friends went down to London by train and stayed for a week in a small hotel near Wembley. He remembered:

Only the keenest people went in the mornings when there were the heats. We went back to the hotel for lunch and then came back to the stadium in the afternoon. In the evening we would go out on the town. One day we were on a packed train to Wembley from central

London and Maureen Gardner and Geoff Dyson, her coach, came in. Everybody stood up so that she could lie down on the long seats for a rest. Maureen Gardner was the pin-up girl of modern athletics. We all talked about her.

The women's hurdle track was 80 metres long and the ten hurdles were 30 centimetres lower than the men's. Both Gardner and Blankers-Koen won their heats and were in separate semi-finals that same afternoon. In her semi-final, Gardner had scraped a hurdle and lost her balance, but still came third to gain a place in the final. Jan Blankers, still coaching his wife, warned Fanny that she had to concentrate on the hurdles. 'This English girl knows her business,' he said. 'An athlete who can recover as Maureen did is obviously a very dangerous rival.' That night Blankers-Koen slept badly because in her mind she was running hundreds of 80-metre hurdles races. 'What does it matter if you lose?' she asked herself. 'After all, you have already won the 100 metres title. Be satisfied.' Another part of her answered, 'Why be content? Why should you lose? Maureen Gardner is no better than you are. Go out and win. Of course you can do it.'

The next morning, after she had been warming up for the final, Blankers said to his wife, 'You are too old, Fanny.' He was quoting Jack Crump, the British team manager who had announced publicly that she was far too old for the Olympics. 'It was just the thing to rouse me,' she remembered, 'to make me go out there and prove to them that, even if I was thirty years old and the mother of two children, I could still be a champion. Too old, was I? I would show them.' But her self-confidence was shattered when she got off to a late start:

The rest of the field were a yard ahead of me. What is a yard? What is a fraction of a second? Not much, you may say, but in a race over 80 metres it can mean the difference between defeat and victory.

I raced after Maureen, sprinting as I had never sprinted before. Nobody could have felt less like a champion, and my knees trembled. How glad I was that we had trained to meet such a crisis; to keep a cool head. By the time we reached the fifth hurdle I was level with Maureen, but I was going so fast that I went too close to the hurdle, hit it and lost my balance. After that is just a blurred memory. It was a grim struggle, in which my hurdling style went to pieces. I staggered like a drunkard.

She leant so far forward at the end, that the tape cut her neck, leaving blood on her vest. 'It was quite a jolt for me to hear the British national anthem being played. Had Maureen, then, won after all? No—the band were saluting the Royal Family, who had just arrived at the stadium.' The suspense was not over: it was a photo-finish. When the result came up, Blankers-Koen jumped for joy. 'I was proud to have beaten such a brilliant athlete.'

'Well done, Fanny,' said her husband. 'You aren't too old, after all.' Geoff Dyson gave Maureen a long kiss. A spectator noted, 'That's the difference between an engaged couple and a staid old married pair.' Gardner and Blankers-Koen shared the same time, 11.2 seconds, which was a new world and Olympic record.

By the end of Wednesday 4 August, Fanny Blankers-Koen had been competing for six days and the strain of her success was getting to her. 'I was missing my children and while the heats were okay because I was with the other Dutch girls, now I was very lonely. I was crying and I just wanted to go home and see my children. I had had enough of it.' Jo Pfann, the Dutch women's team manager, could not persuade her to compete in the 200 metre dash which had heats and semi-finals the next day. Jan Blankers told his wife, 'If you don't want to run, it doesn't matter. Just go out there and try to make the final, that will be enough. You will be sorry afterwards if you don't at least try.' 'He was right,' Fanny wrote later. 'So I had a good cry and felt much better.'

Sylvia Cheeseman was a nineteen-year-old reporter with the *Evening Star* when she was selected to run in the 200 metres. Years afterwards, she remembered:

As a child I was aware that I was a fast runner because no one had ever beaten me. I joined an athletics club when I was sixteen because it was the cheapest club to belong to and I ran my first few races in a pair of Woolworth's plimsolls. We trained three times a week after work in Richmond Park, surrounded by people walking their dogs. Athletics was regarded as a strange thing for a girl to do. People thought you had to be ugly and musclebound with piano stool legs, so I tried to show that women

202

athletes could be feminine. I always made an effort to dress properly and wear make-up. When I was selected for the British team I was terribly proud. I felt very nervous, but if you are not nervous, then you will not run well. The crowd was supportive and excited.

Cheeseman was beaten in the semi-finals by fellow Briton Audrey Williamson who made it to the finals, on the Friday. Blankers-Koen's mood improved as soon as she too had qualified.

Williamson was twenty-one, a strongly built servicewoman in the Royal Army Corps and an army champion. She had a bustling running action which gave no sign of undue strain. 'It was desperate weather that day. We arrived at the start very chilled. I was in the fourth lane, Fanny was on the inside.' The track was inundated with puddles and the lines marking the lanes had almost disappeared. Also running in the final was Mickey Patterson, who had almost missed out on the US trials when she had burnt her leg with an iron. As if this wasn't enough, minutes before the start she got locked inside the dressing room and had to sprint to the line. It was all worth it though, because she came third and became the first ever African-American woman to win an Olympic medal. The *Times* correspondent was once again impressed. 'Miss Williamson, running with the utmost determination, forged a little ahead of the others, passed Miss Strickland, but still had to contend with the long stride of Miss Patterson. Miss Williamson did well to gain the second place in such a gruelling race—a shade too gruelling for women as many thought.' Blankers-Koen and

Williamson were in a photo-finish from which Blankers-Koen emerged with her third gold, and Williamson took silver, half a second behind. Mr and Mrs Blankers-Koen celebrated with supper at a Lyons Corner House in the West End. Eighteen years later the photo-finish was re-examined by a sports enthusiast who noticed that the Australian Shirley Strickland had actually been centimetres ahead of Patterson and should have received bronze.

'How strange that I had made so many people happy,' wrote Blankers-Koen. 'It made me proud to know I had been able to bring joy into people's lives. My winning those medals was good propaganda for all women.' Almost single-handedly she transformed women's athletics from a sideshow into a central feature of future Olympics. The British athletes Dorothy Manley, Audrey Williamson and Maureen Gardner are probably better known for having come second to Blankers-Koen than they would have been had they won.

13

THE EMPIRE POOL

'The empire pool is a pretty sight,' reported the *Manchester Guardian*. 'Flags of competing nations hang from the great roof span, and intrusive sparrows twitter daylong. While below, men and women from the US, all of them sensationally photogenic, practise the butterfly breaststroke in turquoise water or dive from intimidating heights.'

The swimming heats got underway in the Empire Pool close to the Stadium on the day following the Opening Ceremony. The pool's architect was Owen Williams, and in 1934 it was considered a feat of modern engineering with its cantilevered concrete arms which removed the necessity for interior pillars. There was seating for eight thousand spectators, who enjoyed a light and airy space enclosed by large amounts of glass. 'The Empire Pool surprised me,' Sir Arthur Elvin told the *News of the World*:

No one has seen this magnificent swimming pool since the day war was declared and the bathers were turned out of the water. Over the top had been constructed an ice rink and now the ice has been thawed out and the false floor removed. It meant shifting ten miles of tubular scaffolding, three and a half miles of brine piping, seventy tons of sand and a double deck wooden floor. The pool now revealed is magnificent with its gleaming new paint and 700,000 gallons of specially sterilised and filtered water.

The hand rails were removed 'to prevent contaminating the water with rust'. The temperature of the pool was 73 degrees Fahrenheit (23 Centigrade), which the Americans, whose trials had coincided with a heatwave in Detroit, found 'uncomfortably cold'. Spectators were charged one shilling to watch the training sessions, and all the race days were sold out well in advance. Notices reminded the public, 'If possible, smoking

205

is prohibited.'

With so many photogenic swimmers on display, Castleton Knight was keen to film the event. Filming in colour had not been carried out in a pool in Britain before and there were fears that artificial lighting might distract the swimmers and divers or even create a risk of electrocution. Wartime black-out paint still covered the huge glass roof and a gang of men had to spend ten days scraping it off in order to increase the natural light. The pool was very long—sixty-six metres—and to create the Olympic length a racing bridge was constructed exactly fifty metres from the deep end. The pool's retaining walls were above ground, with portholes inserted along the side which allowed Knight to film underwater. 'The ends of the pool were flat and high with no rail to grab and therefore a spin turn was a must, using both hands,' said Don Bland, a swimmer from Northumberland.

'The Empire Pool was very cold, everyone suffered,' said Peter Elliot, a young British diver from London. 'You dived, ran into a hot pool and waited for the next dive which might be an hour. I wore all my clothes and a tracksuit on top of that and a scarf. The one free thing we got was plenty of hot Bovril.'

Competitive swimming had become more sophisticated since the first Olympics in 1896, when the 100 metre freestyle was held in a sea bay near Piraeus, watched by 20,000 people from the shore. Only two swimmers made it through the choppy and unseasonably cold water, following a course marked by hollowed-out pumpkins bobbing on the surface. At the 1900 Olympics in Paris there was an *underwater* race and an obstacle course in the River Seine.

The number of entrants in 1948 set an Olympic record, with nearly 500 swimmers and divers, 111 of them women, from 37 countries. The pool could accommodate eight lanes but, even so, the events took eight days and went on until ten o'clock at night.

Harry Walker, the headmaster of the Pitmarston Road Primary School in Birmingham, was a judge with the Amateur Swimming Association and was employed by the BBC as their swimming correspondent. 'It was during the holidays and I had to be at the Empire Pool from 8 a.m. until 11 p.m. every day to watch every heat and dive. You could hear the roar of the stadium in the distance. Radio was nearly all live, and every spare moment I was interviewing or getting background material.' Announcements were made in French and English and there were three interpreters who could speak ten languages between them. The starter was provided with three pistols and a red hat, and swimmers were given two towels each at the poolside. Despite these efforts, the Empire Pool proved a daunting experience for many competitors.

'I had never swum in front of such huge numbers of spectators,' said the New Zealander Ngaire Lane. 'It was totally unnerving. Before our event we were all marched out and were lined up and introduced by name and country. Our boys were all there to watch. Suddenly they jumped up and did the *haka*, the Maori war dance. It is done to spur the team on but it nearly was my undoing. It was very emotional and must have been somewhat

207

amazing to all the people in the grandstand!'

The pool itself was a shock for the US diver Vicki Draves. 'I had no idea it would be an indoor pool. I had never dived off platforms indoors. It was all such a different feeling, with a roof above you. Also, the competition was held over a period of five days. It was difficult to keep this edge up. I was very nervous and I had all this time between dives to watch all the other competition.'

Philip Hipkin of Wembley County School was a messenger at the pool. 'One evening we collected all the cartridge cases from the blanks fired by the starter. The topic next day was not who had seen the epic 400 metres, but who had got the cartridge case that started it.'

The Organising Committee had decided that medal ceremonies should take place 'in the heat of the victory' rather than waiting to the end of each day. When Sigfrid Edström arrived at the Empire Pool to present the first of them, Viscount Portal of the Organising Committee was dismayed to find that there were 'Neither flags, nor medals, nor *even* a band.' He quickly found some medals and flags, and hired a band for £30.

*   *   *

As soon as she had arrived in London, Ngaire Lane had been anxious to begin preparing properly:

Our manager only saw me for training once. I could have been sightseeing and he would never have known. My training consisted of about half the distance anyone else was doing,

208

with little sprinting practice. The basic breast-stroke had changed quite a lot and I had never seen the 'new' tumble turn. I eventually found the Vauxhall Pool opposite the Houses of Parliament but I had to swim lengths while everyone else was jumping in and bobbing about just everywhere. Eventually the British trainer took me into his squad and helped me. I learned the new turn and also increased my distance training. It was simply wonderful to have the comradeship of the British girls to train alongside.

Ngaire came seventh in the semi-final, a disappointment for her, since she had swum faster before.

The approach of Britain's coach Harry Koskie of Newcastle was clear from the manner in which he wrote to those selected:

NOTHING should be allowed to interfere with the OBJECTIVE. I will set such a pace that it will require all the guts that you possess. There is no other way to the top. The time has come for the kid gloves to come off, so here are my suggestions to prepare the BODY and the MIND. TRAINING RULES: remember that REGULAR HABITS are the basis for physical well-being. Go to bed at 10 p.m., arise at a regular time, take your meals at specified times. REGULARITY, REGULARITY, REGULARITY. NO smoking. NO alcohol. Eight miles walking during the weekend. Keep away from water on the seventh day so that your MIND, the controller and dictator is rested. Excessive and continuous swimming dulls the driving force of enthusiasm. You want to maintain the URGE to get into the water and swim and swim.

Koskie later reported, 'The result of common sense, as opposed to slogging, was apparent.' He was also grateful for 'Sun-ray and Infra-red equipment lent by the Hanovia Company of Slough, of which regular doses were given to the swimmers. The psychological effect of all this attention was obvious.' However, he did not have matters all his own way. On arrival in London, he was furious to discover that his swimmers would have to train in Uxbridge Municipal Pool. 'Owing to the hot weather the pool was swamped with bathers. On one occasion we trekked half-way across London only to find that a practice water polo match was being played, so we could only use the shallow end. There is no doubt that the edge was taken off the whole team.'

Don Bland was the son of the Durham five-mile swimming champion. He was working in the engineering workshop of a coal mine when Harry Koskie came to visit:

He was very disappointed to see the poor quality of my swimming, and thought he'd wasted his weekend. It was considered unfair to train too hard. When I bought a set of chest expanders, my dad tried to persuade me not to use them. I would not give up my pleasure for sport. I gave up beer but not my cigarettes. The swimming world said I would soon be burnt out due to swimming two races over two weeks. Koskie's training exercises included,

'Hop on one leg. Shake the arms and fingers. Hug the knees,' and he introduced the kicking board. Mine was very heavy, made at the local colliery from a plank.

Bland trained in the Dawdon Colliery Pool, watched by his Scottie dog:

There were no poolside clocks to test our timing. In addition, huge amounts of chlorine were used. We had no goggles and our eyes were always sore. Warming up in the pool was never considered. Once, before a gala at Gateshead, a Swedish team dived into the pool. The pool manager was furious because they had disturbed his beautiful blue flat water before the spectators arrived!
   Early in 1948, as an Olympic potential, my father wrote to the National Coal Board asking permission for me to start work at 8, instead of 7 a.m., and to have some leave for the Olympics. We were informed that I would lose pay as 'absent' and lose my bonus which was the equivalent to 50 days' pay. The letter concluded that it was necessary to point out 'The effect this would have on the absentee figures of the coal field.' There were 100,000 men in the Durham mines and I was sixteen!

Nothing daunted, Bland joined other swimmers at a training camp in Loughborough:

They said, we'll go a steady thousand yards and I said 'Blow that' and did my usual 440 yards. Little did I know that in three weeks' time I

211

would race the 1,500 metre heat, semi final and final in successive days. I swam so slowly that day that the team manager wanted me to go home.

The Olympics was my very first international and in the heat I raced the winner all the way to be second. I found I had improved, probably because I had not been working in the coal field from 7 a.m. each day. I came fourth in the semi to qualify for the final and was left on my own that evening to prepare. Supper in the camp cafeteria consisted of a ham salad and two free bottles of Pepsi. The final was tough although I was first into the water.

Bland came seventh.

Ray Legg was brought up in Bristol, the son of a factory worker, and at thirteen was national junior champion at the 100 yards freestyle. 'During the war the roof of our pool got holed by incendiary bombs, but we carried on swimming the next day.' He was sixteen and still at school when he was picked as a reserve for Britain.

We were issued with Olympic swimming trunks and a bar of soap each. You had to wear 'slips' underneath because swimming trunks often fell off. They peered in your trunks to check before you raced. The local council gave me twenty minutes water time to practise on my own but I really had to train with the general public. There were no lanes and this made me very unpopular. A Canadian swimming club adopted me and once a month a parcel of strange tins of oranges and peaches came. We didn't know what to do with them.

Legg left school and joined Bristol Tramways as a junior clerk. 'They let me off for the Olympics and even paid me. My parents couldn't afford to come to London and watch. The Empire Pool felt enormous and it was quite cold even though it was August. As a reserve I didn't actually take part, but it didn't matter. I wore the blazer quite a lot after the Olympics because it was the tidiest thing I owned and we got a pair of new fangled Y-front pants.'

*   *   *

The tensions that had festered since the Irish team arrived now came to a head in the swimming events. While Bland, Legg and others were busy training, the Irish were once again embroiled in a row over eligibility. Both Ernest McCartney and William Fitzell Jones had been refused permission to swim for Ireland, because they had been born in the North. They felt this to be grossly unfair because the Irish Olympic Council had not objected to the eight men born in the South who were competing for Britain. Under Irish law, McCartney had become a citizen of the Irish Free State in 1922, and Jones had acquired an Irish passport under the Irish Nationality and Citizenship Act of 1935.

The two sides convened a meeting at the Empire Pool and both then claimed that the other had not turned up. The Irish manager, Chisholm, who was said to be a quiet man, grew enraged once again. Letters flew between the antagonists and the reason for disallowing the Irish swimmers changed from their place of birth to their voting eligibility. Chisholm pointed out that this was an entirely new rule which, if applied, would bar everyone under twenty-one years old from taking part in the Olympics, or else render eligible all sorts of people previously ineligible because of their place of birth. What is clear from the dozens of letters exchanged is that neither the Irish nor the British were prepared to give way. The IOC stepped in to resolve the matter, finding in favour of the British and breaking their own rule in the process. The Irish Olympic Council was still feeling aggrieved in its report six months later: 'We have very little reason to thank the British Organising Committee. The Irish Olympic officials went out of their way to establish friendly relations and even travelled to London for this purpose. We listened to pretty speeches about Olympic ideals but behind the scenes the old political game was played for all its worth.'

*   *   *

The swimming competition brought with it an unexpected and important stylistic innovation. Many contestants in the breaststroke class were found to be using a new, faster and more powerful technique which was dubbed the 'butterfly-dolphin'. Roy Romaine, who made it to the semi-finals of the 200 metres breaststroke, was one of the first British swimmers to use it. The new style broke none of the rules governing breaststroke but those who adopted it clearly gained a considerable advantage. 'The butterfly variation swept orthodox breaststroke from the field,' wrote the British swimming coach Carl Wootton in *John Bull* magazine. There were fears that unless the rules were changed, breaststroke would only be used by women and would cease to be swum by men in competitions.

The youngest of the British swimmers was Helen Gordon, a fifteen-year-old secretary from Hamilton in Scotland, whose father coached her in the local 25-yard pool. 'Most sessions were for men only, and this did reduce the time when I could train.' She nevertheless became Scottish junior breaststroke champion at only thirteen. 'Luckily my boss was understanding about me being away for the Olympics. We set off by train from Scotland with our ration books, towels, soap and some eggs. It was the day before the opening ceremony, so there wasn't any time to practise. I'd never seen a 50 metre pool before and just looking at it made the hair on my arms prickle.' She swam the 200 metre breaststroke. 'I would have won if everyone else had used orthodox breaststroke like me. But some used the new butterfly and I was knocked out in the first heat, a wee disappointed little girl.' From 1947 on, Gordon won the senior breaststroke championship for eleven years running—the only Scottish swimmer ever to win on so many occasions.

National swimming associations got together after 1948 and agreed that 'butterfly breaststroke' and 'orthodox breaststroke' should be considered as separate classes, representing two distinct styles of swimming. Henceforth they were not swum in the same competition.

Swimmers were always on the lookout for ways

of improving speed. The American Walter Ris was coached in the 100 metres freestyle by James 'Doc' Counsilman from Alabama, using radical techniques. Analysing film shot underwater, Counsilman realised that the pull in front-crawl should be made with a bent arm rather than the traditional straight one. His training was severe— he posted the words 'Hurt', 'Pain' and 'Agony' around the pool, though he also made the sessions fun with the aid of music and jelly beans. It worked, for the strains of the US national anthem became almost as familiar during the competition as the announcement 'New Olympic record': the USA won twelve events, Denmark two and Holland and Italy one each.

*   *   *

As Castleton Knight had foreseen, the women's swimming events provided a wonderful opportunity to show photographs of beautiful, scantily clad young women, that were nonetheless all in good taste. This did not prevent one reader from writing to *Picture Post* to complain that their photos were 'deeply un-Christian'.

The eleven young women in the British team were sturdily built and used to training outdoors in cold water. The bikini had first appeared in 1947 but it was certainly not permitted for competitive swimming. Instead they were given tight-fitting silk costumes manufactured by Jannsen knitting mills and North's Rubber Company donated rubber swimming hats.

'Crack! Splash!' wrote W.J. Howcroft in *Illustrated* magazine:

216

As Margaret Wellington dives, the two sounds appear to be simultaneous. Her mental responses to the starting signal are so quick and her flight through the air so direct that she has an unfair advantage over rivals. This auburn haired, slim Sydenham girl, aged twenty-one, flashed from the obscurity of suburban club circles to national repute within a few brief months. Starting at seven, Miss Wellington swam in the London Schools Championships and now works in a suburban bank. Taking all sorts of risks, Miss Wellington kept training where ever she could, despite blitzed baths and blackout. She is mentally alert and her turning is electrically slick with a fast, very fast, push off.

Despite this accolade Wellington was eliminated in the first heat of both the 100 and 400 metres freestyle.

'Cathy Gibson's figure is not the usual one associated with champion women swimmers,' reported *John Bull* magazine. 'Though her shoulders are broad, she is slim and small. The danger to her present excellent form is if she burns herself out before the Olympics. Cathy works in an office all day and swimming four or even five hours after this is, she admits, a bit of a strain.' Cathy Gibson was from Scotland, a dark-haired, blue-eyed seventeen-year-old with lots of determination. 'I was born in Motherwell in a family of five, where my father was the assistant bath master who taught me to swim as soon as I could walk. My mother fed me up on home-made soup.' In 1947 she had beaten the French champion Monique Berlioux in the 100 metre backstroke. 'As soon as I was selected for the Olympics I was given time off for training. They even paid my wages. The atmosphere at Wembley was out of this world. It was absolutely amazing, wonderful. The Empire Pool looked very long; the water was tepid which was good. I had to do three heats. I won them all and if my father had been allowed on the poolside, I might have won a gold medal but no coaches were allowed near the pool.' David Morgan was present as a schoolboy messenger. 'I saw our own Cathy Gibson in the television room. She seemed very excited as she had just won her race and was still very much out of breath.' She won bronze medal for the 400 metre freestyle and was surprised to be celebrated beyond the pool. 'I wore the uniform blazer and beret a lot afterwards,' she said. 'They were my smartest clothes. I was taken to Madame Tussaud's wax works to see myself, and it looked just like me. Amazing!'

Helen Gordon was not the youngest swimmer in 1948. 'I didn't feel especially young at fifteen—dozens of the other girls were still teenagers.' Margaret McQuane of Victoria was thirteen, the youngest Australian ever to be nominated for the Games. She came sixth in the semi-final of the 100 metre freestyle, which was won by Greta Andersen of Denmark with tremendous strength and dash. When Andersen entered the first round of the 400 metres freestyle, however, she passed out in the deep end and was rescued by the Hungarian swimmer Elemer Szathmary and carried off on a stretcher. It had been her fifth race in as many days, but even so she helped the Danish relay team to win a silver medal on the following day. A year later, she swam the English Channel, and in 1964, at the age of thirty-six, she swam it for a sixth time in 13 hours and 14 minutes.

*   *   *

If the swimmers were a feast for the eyes, the men and women who specialised in diving were deemed to be positively glamorous, especially the Americans. 'The world was longing to know what real American girls looked like—they had only ever seen film stars,' said Sammy Lee, a diver from Los Angeles. 'They were not disappointed. Our girls were beautiful with good figures.'

'The girls wore clinging black costumes,' remembered the young British diver Peter Elliot. 'I fell in love with a French diver called Maddie Moreau; she was so beautiful. However, we didn't think much about all these half-naked lovely women because diving took so much concentration. Mind you, Vicki Draves was beautiful even with a hat on.'

'It was like Hollywood had arrived,' remembered the French contestant Nicola Pellisard. 'The place was full of swimming stars. The Americans had figure-hugging shiny costumes made of silk, with latex caps. They were infinitely more glamorous than us. Everything was very elegant. I was in love with the whole male diving team.'

The USA had dominated Olympic diving since it was introduced in 1904, and had won all the gold medals since 1920. Plain high diving was discontinued after 1924 and the names of the dives were changed. A jack-knife became a swan dive, a half-gainer was now a reverse dive, and a cut-away jack-knife—the inward dive pike. 'We had scheduled workouts every day,' remembered Vicki Draves. 'Sometimes I would practise early in the morning and sometimes early evening. There was just one pool for everyone and diving practice was dangerous because of the swimmers underneath. Some people wanted to swim widths so as to practise their turn-rounds, and others swam lengths. It was mayhem.' Most of the US divers had never competed indoors and they found it difficult contending with the noise made by spectators and the glare of the film crew's lights.

In 1944 Vicki had met the diving coach Lyle Draves. He had learned to swim in rivers, and taught himself new dives by observing contestants on cinema newsreels. He had qualified for the 1932 Games but could not afford the train fare to Los Angeles. 'I was absolutely amazed because he had a reason for doing everything,' said Vicki. 'Before, my diving had relied on my talent more than technique. I had to learn how to walk on the board first. He taught me as if I had never dived before. It was like buying a new hat. I went home with stars in my eyes, thinking about how I was really going to learn how to dive.' The two grew fond of each other and when Vicki was yet again refused entry to a competition on account of her mixed race, Draves too quit in protest at the racism. In 1946 they married. Lyle knew he had ruined his chances of selection in 1948 when he accepted a coaching job and some film work, but he coached Vicki every morning before work. She remembered:

I was doing pretty well in the first four dives off the springboard. But I was having a lot of problems with my last dive. I prayed a lot that night. 'Please, God, help me with my back one and a half.' I was so nervous that I would shake between each dive. I said to Sammy Lee, 'I can't do this Sammy. I am not going to make it.' He said, 'You came all this distance and you are going to give up? Get up there and do what you are supposed to do.' I got up there, and I tell you it was like somebody else did that dive for me. I sort of sailed through it, and I knew I hit it when I was underwater and I thought, 'Oh boy. Thank you, God.' It was just a beautiful feeling.

There was only half a point between Vicki Draves and Zoe Ann Olsen, another protégée of Lyle Draves, and Vicki won the gold. The victory ceremony was held as soon as the event was finished. 'It is overwhelming when you hear your national anthem, especially with three Americans on the podium and you see the Stars and Stripes go up.'

Three days later she competed in the highboard diving:

Platform diving scared me to death. The first time I tried to dive off the lower platform, which is five metres high, I stood up there for about a half an hour before I got off. In platform diving, you really have the feeling of going through the air, like you're flying. You set your dive and you're out there for what

221

seems like a long time. It's scary, and you hit the water with a great deal of force.

Up at the top platform, I had the standing swan dive and the running swan dive, and I was not pleased with my performance. For my running half gainer, I was so nervous that I forgot about stepping on it. I was hop, skipping and jumping up there, and I thought, 'I'm going to miss this dive.' Somehow or other I hit.

Vicki entered the water perfectly, with hardly a ripple. Even before her head emerged, the 8,000 spectators were applauding. 'I couldn't believe I had won again. It was just the most thrilling thing in all the world.' Her success made a perfect story for the cinema newsreels, especially the shots taken through the poolside port-holes as she entered the water. Vicki Draves was the first woman to win gold medals in both springboard and highboard diving. For the newspapers in America it was front-page news: 'Women's diving: USA, USA, USA.'

The first to dive in the men's competition was the Bermudan Francis Gosling, nicknamed 'Goose'. The pool was eerily silent as he prepared to leap up from the springboard three metres above the smooth water. He hit the board perfectly, spinning into his first somersault and was almost ready to straighten himself out from his second somersault when a camera shutter whirred. The sound threw him off balance and he lost ten points on the dive. Gosling didn't protest but the next diver, Capilla Perez from Mexico, refused to compete until all the cameras had been silenced.

The judges eventually agreed and cleared the photographers from the gallery and poolside. When Gosling finished in tenth place, the *Gazette* called him 'A good sport. He even obtained the autograph on his pith helmet from the guilty cameraman.' Perez didn't win a medal in springboard, but he did win bronze in platform diving.

Britain's best diver was the eighteen-year-old Peter Elliot, the son of a circus owner and a Spanish Gypsy clairvoyant. During the war his father had run a pub called the Noah's Ark in Blackfriars, the scene of dramatic happenings. 'I was blown up three times in the blitz,' Elliot said. 'As my sister was being born, the roof of the pub was blown off. Nobody was hurt. One day I was sent across the road to get change and as I opened the side door of the pub opposite, the door flew backwards about twenty feet. I landed underneath the door but the pub was blown up by a V2 rocket. All my father saw was a big hole and assumed I was in it.'

Elliot's father taught him to trampoline, and the flying trapeze, which made him a courageous diver:

When I was about thirteen, a friend took me to the Marshall Street pool, near Oxford Street. I dived off the five-metre board and a man asked me if I'd like to learn to dive properly. This Sid Dalton came to the pub to see my father that night. He said, 'Your son has great legs and good feet, he could make a great diver. I will coach him for the national championships and then for the Olympics.' My father wanted to know how much money I would make. Of course, there was no money, it was for the glory of our country. I said, 'Please Dad, let me.' He said, 'OK, you can do it for a year.' I left school at fifteen, and Sid my coach asked me to work in his antiques restoration shop as a tea boy. It was across the road from Marshall Street baths. So every lunchtime I was coached in diving. Then we used to go to a café in Carnaby Street called Oscars with all the Palladium Theatre stars such as Max Bygraves. I won the Middlesex county championships and then all the county championships.

Divers are quite different from swimmers. We do our own thing in the air. It is more like trapeze work. You have to be very acrobatic. The only thing we need the water for is landing in. We were in trouble when it came to competing though, because Britain had no up-to-date diving equipment. We had to get it from America. I had never used an aluminium board before and I fell in the first time because I wasn't used to the spring. Divers require considerable courage, much more than in any other job. You could break your ribs or dislocate your knees.

On one occasion during training, Elliot was diving from a ten-metre board when he hit the water flat after a three-and-a-half somersault. 'I almost split my stomach open.'

At the Olympics, Elliot and the other divers performed five compulsory and five dives of their own choice. 'The thing about diving is there are no class barriers. All that matters is if you can do it. But even so, I tried to improve my cockney accent for the officials.' Elliot came twenty-third out of twenty-five.

As in other sports, the diving competition had its war heroes. Miller Anderson was twenty years old when he won the US diving championship in 1942. He then joined the US air force as a fighter pilot and flew 112 missions before being forced to parachute from his aircraft over Italy, when his leg was almost torn off by the tail-plane. He spent a month in a German hospital before it was captured by Allied troops. An American surgeon inserted a silver plate in his thigh and, once recovered, Anderson set himself to relearn diving from scratch. He went on to become the first to perform a forward one-and-a-half somersault with two twists, and a backward one-and-a-half with one twist, and at the London Games he won the silver medal on the springboard. Anderson died from a heart attack at the age of forty-two.

Sammy Lee was a stocky, 28-year-old Korean-American doctor who worked at the Port Surgeon's office in Los Angeles. He chose a forward three-and-a-half somersault as his last dive from the highboard, ten metres above the water. On a previous occasion he had performed a similar dive and mistaken the sky for the water and pulled out too soon. Now, with no sky visible in the Empire Pool, he was afraid something else would go wrong. 'I dove, hit the water, felt numb and tingling and decided I did a belly flop.' When he popped up to the surface he discovered that, far from belly flopping, his dive had been rated almost perfect. 'I just walked on water out of that pool,' he recalled. Lee was the first Asian-American to win an Olympic gold.

Although the Americans were winning more medals, the British team were not downhearted—they were winning in other ways. 'As the week progressed,' wrote Carl Wootton, 'it appeared that London had achieved a success far surpassing anything at Berlin. For, in place of glamour and brilliant showmanship, we had substituted the spirit of *camaraderie* and good sportsmanship. The whole meeting was characterised by an intimate informality and friendliness. Naturally one heard some criticisms. Some of the visiting swimmers complained, quite mildly, of the arrangements to practise in the pool. But all the same, they all joined good naturedly in the general scramble. Those midday periods in the pool with everyone "mucking in" together was one of the happiest features of the week. One day, breaking all rules, I put one of my own young swimmers in the water to swim with the USA stars. The chief USA trainer broke off from coaching one of his world record breakers to put my young boy through his paces, and to give him advice and encouragement. Could such a thing have happened anywhere else?'

14

WINNERS AND LOSERS

So far, the British had not shone in the Track and Field events, but hopes were high that a local hero might be found in the 110 metre hurdles. 'Hurdling is a peculiar combination of gymnastics and athletics,' wrote the *Observer*, 'requiring self-control of nerves and accurate judgement, and more brains, patience and courage than any other sport.' Two of the British competitors had awakened the public's interest: one a veteran, the other a youngster. The world record holder was Harrison Dillard but since he had been eliminated in the US trials, the favourite was Wing Commander Donald Finlay, seven times international hurdles champion and winner of Olympic medals in 1932 and 1936. Finlay had fought in Burma during the war, and now aged thirty-nine and grey-haired, he was captain of the British team and had taken the Olympic oath on behalf of all the competitors.

The other great British hope was an eighteen-year-old called Joe Birrell who was at Barrow-in-Furness Grammar School. Six foot three inches tall, Birrell was the son of a submarine engine fitter at Barrow shipyard. Despite making his own hurdles and having no trainer, he had won schools championships, the North Counties Open and the Nationals. The *Barrow Mail* described him as 'tall and dark, with the quiet manner we like to associate with young sportsmen'. It continued: 'The day after he won his Northern AAA senior title at Billingham-on-Tees, he was busy taking his Sunday school class as usual.'

On 2 July, just two days after he had sat his School Certificate, Birrell had taken part in the Olympic trials at the White City. 'With his examination papers stuffed in his pocket, Joe Birrell hurtled out of school to catch a train to London—and to athletic fame,' wrote the *Sunday Dispatch*. His school had persuaded the Joint Matriculation Board to move the final School Certificate exam forward by an hour, thus giving him ten minutes to catch the last train from Barrow to London. Although 45,000 spectators paid to attend these trials, the rules of amateurism meant that the maximum prize allowed to competitors was seven guineas or a dinner at the Dorchester Hotel. 'When he came up against all the "crack" athletes Birrell was completely cool and undisturbed and acted like a champion from the start,' said the *Barrow Mail*. 'This Lancashire lad yesterday streaked past two Australian hurdlers to beat the field.' His parents had to wait at home for a reporter to telephone a neighbour, who came down the street to tell them the good news: their son had won the AAA hurdle championship and was now in the Olympic Team. The spectators at White City rose to Birrell as he received the trophy from Lord Burghley, who himself had won it three times in the pre-war years. Asked how he would like to celebrate, Birrell suggested a half-day holiday for his school. The *Kenya Weekly News* reported: 'We had been looking for a hurdler to follow in the footsteps of

Don Finlay, and here he unexpectedly fell into our laps like a bolt from the blue. Birrell's style and speed were beautifully blended.' India's *The Statesman* also reported, 'An unknown 18-year-old Lancashire schoolboy stole the limelight in the Amateur Athletics Association Championships at the White City here today in which Australian Olympic athletes won five titles.'

The day after Birrell's triumph in the trials, his parents were visited by Mr Price, Joe's headmaster. 'They learnt how Joe left his running kit at his hotel and ran the first heat in borrowed gear with his shorts pinned up,' said the *Barrow Mail*. 'And still he was first. Mr Price dashed back to the hotel by taxi to retrieve the forgotten kit for the final. "Part of his success is his own hard work, but also his Sunday school has given him grand help in forming his ideals," said Mr Price.'

Harold Abrahams wrote in the *Sunday Graphic*: 'Joseph Birrell certainly was a surprise. When I saw his entry I wondered if it had slipped in by mistake. But there was no mistake about the performance of this 18-year-old. My only concern will be that this young man will realise what a long way he still has to go.'

The Mayor of Barrow, Mrs E. Smythe, was at the station to congratulate Birrell on his return, but his mother Mary was not going to let her son's success go to his head or spoil her family. 'Joe's sister, six-year-old June, and his two brothers Bobby who is ten and Jack who is fifteen, have all won prizes for running too,' she said as she sewed the Union Jack badge on to his running vest. With only three weeks to prepare for the Games, it was too late to receive food parcels, but a daily steak arrived from an anonymous donor. Years later the Birrells learned it had been from the local butcher; but they never discovered who had sent bananas—an exceptionally rare treat.

Following his success in the trials, Birrell's training continued to be minimal. His coach was Mr Delamere, his physics teacher, who played rugby but had never actually hurdled. 'We concentrated on my hurdling style,' remembered Birrell. 'But there was no strength training. You just ran and if you were any good, you won.' Once again, he set off for London accompanied by Mr Price and Mr Delamere. The Barrow stationmaster had decked out the railway station with bunting, and a banner reading 'GOOD LUCK JOE' was strung above the platform. The train compartment too had been decorated for his journey south. Birrell's parents again stayed at home with the younger children: 'There was no television that far North, but they listened on the wireless.'

The Olympics was only the fourth time I had ever hurdled at 3 foot 6 inches and the first time I had run on cinders. We had only two days to practise. We'd never seen starting blocks either. The school bought me a new pair of spike shoes and I ran in the shorts that my mother had made me. They were far too long and tended to sweep the top of the hurdle.

We weren't allowed on the actual track at Wembley until the day of our event and then I found the track was so good that I went too fast. My stride pattern between each hurdle was different and I missed the hurdle—my

230

leading foot was too far ahead and I kept knocking them over. I was about to start my heat when they announced the results of the wrestling which had taken place at the Empress Hall in Earl's Court. Then the Guards Band played the Turkish national anthem no less than six times. It was rather distracting. However I did have one advantage. Coming from up North I was used to running in bad weather.

To the great disappointment of the British crowd, Birrell came fourth in his heat and was eliminated. He had done no worse than the third British hurdler, Ray Barkway, whom nobody had paid attention to because he was twenty-five years old.

Finlay ran in the fifth heat. John Macadam of the *Daily Express* wrote:

The crowds rose to the veteran as he took hurdle after hurdle with the polished ease they expected of him. As he came to the last hurdle, they prepared to shout him home the clear winner, when the cheering died in their throats. Finlay hit the last hurdle, toppled it, and himself crashed to the track and rolled over and over to finish up on the greensward at the feet of the judges. This was the end of the great Olympian. He picked himself up, waved to somebody and then trotted quietly off the field into the athletes' quarters, while the crowd still called his name.

The final of the 110 metre hurdles occurred two

days later, on Wednesday 4 August. Taking part was Craig Dixon, a youngster from Los Angeles. Despite reaching the finals, he reckoned the biggest mistake he had made in his whole career was attending the Olympic Opening Ceremony. 'There was a big sign down at the end of Wembley Stadium which read, "The important thing in life is competing not conquering." Well, I wish I had never seen it, because that made a big impression on me. I thought, "That's right, just being here and competing is the important thing." I had made it and I believed I did not have to worry about concentrating. It was a bad influence because I took that message literally.' The message, although often attributed to Baron de Coubertin, had actually been based on a sermon given by the Bishop of Central Pennsylvania, Ethelbert Talbot, in St Paul's Cathedral in 1908.

As the starter called 'On your mark. Get set,' an American woman in the crowd had shouted out 'Come on, Bill!' which distracted Dixon's team mate William Porter, in the adjoining lane, so that he made a false start. Had he done this a second time he would have been disqualified, so he took extra care. 'I think Porter was over the first hurdle before me,' said Dixon. 'I was first over the second and in the middle of the race I was leading. I was feeling good and thought I had the race won. That was my big mistake. At the last hurdle I was a little high and I just wasn't driving to the tape and Porter passed me. I should have won but I had been taken in by that quotation, and I lost my concentration.' Porter hit three hurdles, but his perfect rhythm helped him to set a new Olympic record. The USA won gold, silver and bronze.

British Olympic hopefuls train at Butlins Holiday Camp,
Clacton-on-Sea. *(Getty Images)*

The Olympic transport fleet, mainly Women's Voluntary
Service drivers. *(Getty Images)*

Preparing signs at Richmond Park Olympic Camp. *(Getty Images)*

The telephone room in the Press Club at the Civic Hall, Wembley.

Members of the
Argentinean and
Austrian teams
inspecting their
lunch boxes
before setting off
for their
competitions.
Each received a
cheese sandwich,
an apple and
an egg.
(Getty Images)

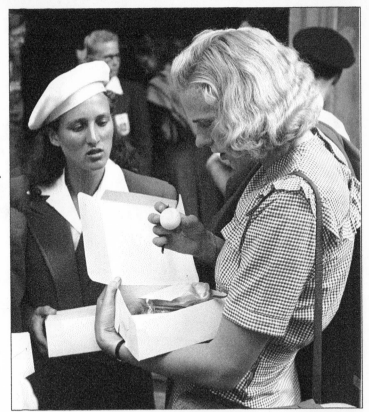

Some of the women competitors who stayed in Southlands
College in Wimbledon going by bus to Wembley. *(Getty Images)*

The Olympic torch is carried through Bari by an Italian captain, en route from Olympia to Wembley. *(Getty Images)*

Spectators surging up Olympic Way towards the Empire Stadium, Wembley for the Opening Ceremony on 31 July 1948. *(Getty Images)*

Inside the stadium, the Guards Band marches past Boy Scouts waiting with crates of pigeons. *(Getty Images)*

Waiting to march in: British fencers on the left chat to American competitors under a tree outside the stadium. The temperature was 93ºF, the hottest day for nearly fifty years. *(Getty Images)*

The final of the 100-metre dash, the first time that photo-finish was used in the Olympics to determine the winner. *(Getty Images)*

Film cameras in position for the first race, the 400 metres hurdles. The portable camera trolley and static stands are in the arena

Left to right: Emil Zátopek of Czechoslovakia, Erik Ahlden of Sweden, Gaston Reiff of Belgium and Willem Slijkhuis of Holland during the 5,000 metres on Monday 2 August, after the weather had turned to torrential rain. *(Getty Images)*

The women's 80 metre hurdles, with Fanny Blankers-Koen of Holland on the right and Maureen Gardner of Britain beside her, on Wednesday 4 August. *(Getty Images)*

Olympic judges prepare for a race on the first, sweltering day.
(Getty Images)

Competitors in the decathlon wait their turn in the rain, wearing oilskins lent by the Admiralty.
(Getty Images)

Concert pianist Micheline Ostermeyer of France throwing the discus. *(Getty Images)*

British high-jumper Dorothy Tyler training in her London back garden by leaping over her babies' nappies. *(Getty Images)*

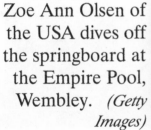

Zoe Ann Olsen of the USA dives off the springboard at the Empire Pool, Wembley. *(Getty Images)*

Glamorous divers from the USA in training at Epsom Baths, Surrey. Left to right: Vicki Draves, Juno Stover, Zoe Ann Olsen and Patricia Elsener. *(Getty Images)*

The boxing ring erected on the 'bridge' over the Empire Pool.

Bantamweight Joe De Pietro of USA lifts 112kg in the two-hand jerk at the Empress Hall, Earl's Court. *(Getty Images)*

Rowing at Henley-on-Thames: Ran Laurie and Jack Wilson of Britain just ahead of Felice Fanetti and Bruno Boniat of Italy, in the Pairs without Cox race. *(Getty Images)*

Giovanni Rossi of Switzerland changing his tyre during the cycle road race at Windsor Great Park. *(Getty Images)*

Alec Wales of Britain on the rings, watched by the British
gymnastic team at the Empress Hall, Earl's Court. Helmut
Bantz is among them in his Olympic blazer and tie.

Paul Elvstrøm of Denmark, aged twenty, preparing to race round Torbay.
(Getty Images)

Firefly dinghies gathered in Torquay harbour.

Yugoslavians in dark shirts and British footballers in white in the semi-final at the Empire Stadium, Wembley. Bob Hardisty has just headed the ball while Harry McIlvenny (9) and Denis Kelleher (10) look on. *(Getty Images)*

In the modern pentathlon, Charles Palant of France tackles a jump at Tweseldown Racecourse on a British army horse.

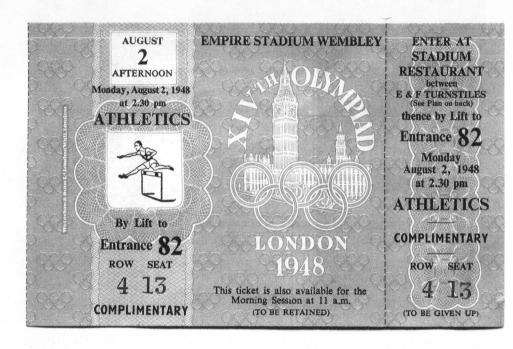

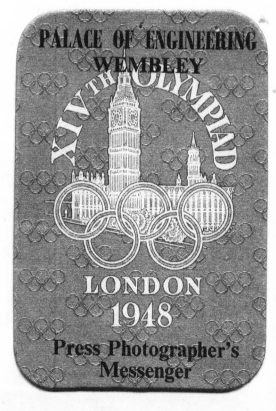

Olympic stamps chosen by King George VI, a press pass for
fencing and a ticket for athletics.

*   *   *

Now a spectator, Joe Birrell settled down to enjoy the first round of the 3,000 metre steeplechase. 'There was a special competitors' enclosure near the finishing line, but no refreshments were available for us, not even a free cup of tea. I had no money for treats like lemonade.'

The 3,000 metre steeplechase was seven and a half laps round Wembley Stadium, with twenty-eight solid hurdles, which could be stepped on, and a water jump—a hedge followed by two feet of water—constructed in front of the competitors' tunnel. The first such standardised Olympic steeplechase had been won in 1920 by Percy Hodge of Britain, who could jump a hurdle while carrying a tray with a bottle and filled glasses. 'The first British man over the jump fell into the water,' Birrell remembered. 'The others all just ran straight over him. Every time he got his head up out of the water, somebody else leapt onto him and carried on, until the poor fellow was almost drowned.' British hurdler Geoffrey Tudor remembered:

We had no indoor training facilities, so were badly unprepared. All our training was done over standard light hurdles which we would occasionally clip and topple. It was only when we got to the Olympic trials that we discovered we had to clear the solid, heavy steeplechase hurdles. It was not a good idea to bash into those, so we had to plan our approach more carefully. On the way to the trials, I was caught

233

in a Tube hold-up for nearly an hour. I had to run all the way to the White City as my warm up, change quickly and go straight onto the track.

The three Britons, Thomas Curry, Tudor and Rene Howell, all failed to complete the first round.

The final was held on Thursday 5 August, at 4.15 p.m., by which time it was raining again. The track was heavy and punished those who didn't measure out their energy carefully. Erik Elmsäter of Sweden set a pace calculated to knock his opponents out of the race, one by one. The 1946 European Champion, Pujazon of France, was probably his greatest threat but with two laps to go, Pujazon dropped out. At the final hurdle, Tore Sjöstrand, another Swede, put on a spurt. 'Elmsäter always used to beat me,' Sjöstrand said, 'but I decided that at the Olympics I would beat him.' Elmsäter was unable to match Sjöstrand, who took the gold. A third Swede, Göte Hagström, was in fifth place with one lap to go when the Finn Siltaloppi fell head first into the water jump. This gave Hagström the encouragement to overtake the Frenchman Cuyodo and add the bronze as well for Sweden. 'Winning the steeplechase was just like life,' said Sjöstrand. 'You run around in circles slogging your guts out and then suddenly you come up against a bunch of obstacles.'

Sjöstrand was another who later had problems with the IOC's strict amateur policy. In November 1948 he was accused of competing as a professional after accepting a prize of 100 kronor (about £7) for a race in southern Sweden. 'As a photographer it is difficult to make ends meet. I have never competed for money but sometimes for the cost of transport,' he told *Se* magazine. 'I am a sportsman because of the friendship it gives. Being a sportsman takes a great deal of time. During the Olympics I ran about five hours per day. I have nothing to hide. Once I had achieved the gold, I stopped all serious training and only took part in minor events.' Eventually the case was dropped.

*   *   *

The same day as the 110 metre hurdles final, the Wembley crowd was watching the javelin contest. Sitting among the spectators that Wednesday was the man who would probably have won gold for that event. Janice Stendzeniek was widely recognised as the world's best, but in 1944 his homeland of Latvia had been absorbed into the Soviet Union. Now a stateless refugee, he worked in a factory in Lincoln.

Javelin throwing had been introduced to the Olympics at the London Games of 1908. Finland had held the Olympic record since 1932. In 1948 the two British competitors were Morville Chote from Luton and Malcolm Dalrymple who lived in Bedford. Both had been trained by Malcolm's father Jock, who had competed in Paris in 1924. Jock Dalrymple had been gassed during the First World War and invalided out of the Army. 'He was determined to rebuild his strength,' remembered Malcolm:

Employed as a railway-carriage cleaner in Bedford, he trained before work, during his lunch break and in the evenings, throwing both the javelin and the hammer in the station yard. When it came to my turn, my father really put me through the mill. Every morning there was a pair of dumb-bells waiting for me before I went to school, and I threw my first javelin at twelve years old. My father also organised a Health and Strength Club in the evenings under the railway arches. We would run six miles, and in the winter we played football. He wielded the whip all right!

At sixteen, Malcolm Dalrymple had been county junior champion at the shot, hammer and javelin, and in 1947 he had set a new British record. After leaving school he had become a pattern-maker at W.H. Allen's, a marine engineering company:

Every evening my father and I threw javelins by the railway sidings. One day, during the freezing winter of 1947, the managing director called me over. 'I understand you're throwing javelins after dark at night.' 'Yes,' I said. 'Not any more, you aren't,' he said. 'You and your father will each have an extra hour at lunch to train at the sports ground. But you'll make the extra time up at night.'

The javelins were eight feet long and cost a lot—the bamboo or birch had to be imported. Luckily my dad had saved enough wood to last the war. Very few people had ever seen javelin throwing in those days. When we went to the park to train in the summer, the cricketers would stop to watch what we were up to.

There was no rule about the distance of the run-up to the throw, but spinning round before a throw was illegal, because it could confuse onlookers as to which direction the javelin might fly. Even so, accidents did happen. At an international meeting in Antwerp, Dalrymple's javelin hit a runner as he unexpectedly came round the outside of the track. Fortunately, although embedded in his head, it had not penetrated the skull and was easily pulled out.

Jock and I were the only father and son to have both taken part in the Olympic javelin. Though I could throw a javelin 215 feet, the actual Games were a disappointment. You were allowed three throws and my first was a good one, one of the best I had ever done. But the judge said it was a 'no throw' and disqualified it. I argued the matter but he was a teacher in Bedford and I knew him, which made it worse. He said my foot had crossed the line. I must have been discouraged by this as my other two throws were not as good.

Neither Dalrymple nor Chote made it into the finals. When Dalrymple returned home to Bedford, the chairman of W.H. Allen's called him in. 'He was delighted that I had represented Britain in the Olympics, but I got no paid time off for it.' Dalrymple later joined the police and his three sons kept up the family tradition. The eldest threw javelin for the RAF, the second represented Bedfordshire schools, and the third trained in Finland for the 1980 Olympics but injured his shoulder.

Kari Tapio Rautavaara from Finland won the

gold. Two years later he became world champion in archery and went on to have a successful career as a folk singer and filmstar. One day in 1979, while posing for photographs, he tripped and cracked his head fatally on the floor.

Among the participants in the women's javelin that same day was Emil Zátopek's fiancée, Dana Ingrová, who finished seventh. The two British women came last. The gold medal was won by Hermine Bauma, the 33-year-old daughter of a tram worker in Vienna, who had come fourth in the Berlin Olympics. 'I was only really aware of winning gold when I returned to the girls' hostel in London,' she said. 'My friends congratulated me with little presents: sweets, biscuits, sandwiches, a bunch of wild flowers. They were modest gifts but came from the heart.'

*   *   *

For the first time in the Olympics, in 1948 the 'standing jump' for women was replaced by the 'long jump'—allowing them to sprint prior to take-off. This placed good runners at an advantage. Phyllis Lightbourn from Bermuda was hoping to make up for the disappointment she had suffered in the semi-finals of the women's 200 metres, when, close to winning, she had collapsed just before the tape. Sadly though, her best jump of eighteen feet was disqualified. 'My toe must have been over the take-off board by a hair. They used a magnifying glass to see the nick.'

The British entrant was Lorna Lee-Price, aged just seventeen. Though only five foot three, she was an able sprinter with natural ability. 'The first time I jumped at my school in Wycombe, I cleared the end of the pit, and they had to dig it longer.' In 1947 she had won the All England Schools championship with a jump of over eighteen feet and then had left school to work for the Chrystalate Company in Kent, which made gramophone records.

They were very supportive—they even dug me a special jumping pit in the grounds so that I could practise during the lunch hour. They gave me extra time off to compete, and when I was selected for the Olympics, they gave me an engraved gold watch. It was nice to get food parcels from Canada, though they were mostly chocolate powder. There were eight children in our family and I had to share the tinned peaches with them all, so it didn't do much to build me up! For our kit we were sent ribbons and a small Union Jack to sew onto our vests and shorts. The vests were sleeveless, which was quite daring, with a square neck, but the fabric wasn't stretchy. Our shorts had to be four inches from the ground when you were kneeling and this made jumping quite tricky. You couldn't really stretch your legs properly, so I split the side seams a few inches up, to allow for more movement. When the team manager noticed, she said I was a brazen hussy!

Lee-Price was critical of the confusion around the new run-up rule. 'They said we weren't allowed to mark the start of our run-up, which we needed to do to make sure that we jumped off at the closest point. As a result, not one of us three British girls jumped nearly as far as we had jumped before.' Only eight of the twenty-six participants managed to reach the qualifying length and none of the British women made it into the finals. 'It was terrible. It broke my heart that night, knowing I could have done so much better and hadn't. I had let my father down too. He had paid £10 for a special pair of spiked jumping shoes.' Only two weeks later, Lee-Price jumped well over the qualifying length. Her jumping career ended four years later when she caught tuberculosis and had to have a kidney removed.

The gold medal was won by a Hungarian, Olga Gyarmati, even though her distance was two feet short of the existing world record held by Blankers-Koen. The silver went to Noèmi Simonetto de Portela of Argentina, prompting admiration from the journalist Horacio Estol in the newspaper *Maribel*:

The women from across the globe who took part in the Olympics stole the show. Despite only nine events for women, they were the sensation of this sporting competition. Noèmi Simonetto de Portela proved her exceptional ability, smiling as though the responsibility was too much and she would like to shrug it off. Her modesty does not mean she is not worthy, just as being an athlete does not mean she is not feminine. 'I only did what anyone would have done', she simply stated. 'We would all like to win. After all, I am only an Olympic silver medallist by nine centimetres.'

*   *   *

On the morning of 5 August, thirty-five male competitors prepared themselves at Wembley for the decathlon. According to Olympic rules, the ten events have to be completed within two days, irrespective of the weather, and the rain continued to pour that Thursday. The men were first required to sprint 100 metres, then contest the long jump, and then the 16lb shot put. At four o'clock that afternoon they began the high jump and at 5.30 p.m. they raced 400 metres. The best high jumpers were hampered by the added weight of their wet clothes and only managed to reach their own heights. Friday's rain was even worse. They began the day with the 110 metre hurdles, then took turns throwing the discus. After lunch they pole-vaulted and after tea threw the javelin. Finally, from 6.30 p.m. onwards, they each ran a timed 1,500 metres.

There were entries from twenty-three countries, but none from Britain. Two of the competitors in this gruelling contest were from the tiny European state of Liechtenstein. 'Naturally we tried to offer our best possible team,' wrote their manager, Xavier Frick. 'This meant our two decathletes, Gebhard Buchel who was several times champion in our country, and Josef Seger, who was spending time in London on a language course.' Buchel had to give up after the 100 metre dash because of a knee injury, and despite Seger's sparkling performance in the 400 metres, he tripped and fell while hurdling and had to drop out prior to the pole vault.

After the five events of the first day, the

241

Argentinean Enrique Kistenmacher was in first place, the Frenchman Ignace Heinrich second and Bob Mathias from the USA third. Mathias, aged seventeen and a half, was the youngest of the decathletes, having graduated from high school in California just two months earlier. He was an all-round athlete who had taken up the decathlon four months before the Games and had only competed twice before. The sprinter Clifford Bourland had taken him under his wing.

I was a little older. I became friendly with Bob aboard ship, and when we arrived I decided to watch out for him. No matter what Bob did, he did well. For example, he hadn't played table tennis before, but pretty soon he beat everyone, including guys who had been playing for years. The little town of Uxbridge was beautiful, with bowling on the green. Bob, Mel Patton and I went over there and were invited to play. Bob beat everyone. He just had natural ability, and he was a nice kid.

The competitors spent most of the second day huddled under wet blankets, with no food to sustain them except what was in the cardboard lunch boxes they had brought from their housing centres. The rain slowed everything down, making it unlikely that the events would all be completed within the time limit. Mathias was in one of the last hurdles heats which began at 10.30 a.m. but he could hardly have supposed that he would still be running nearly twelve hours later. His day began to go wrong during the discus competition, when an official tried to dodge one and accidentally

242

knocked over the marker indicating Mathias's best distance. Mathias, clad in his wet vest, spent half an hour with two raincoated officials and two other US competitors, hunting on their hands and knees for the tiny hole left by the small flag. It was finally discovered at forty-four metres, almost three metres beyond everyone else.

With three events to go, Mathias was now in the lead. It was not until 9.15 p.m., however, his sodden shorts sticking to his tired legs and his vest drenched, that he arrived at the pole vault. Others were back in the changing rooms, having completed all ten events, and it was growing dark. With the stadium's floodlights all removed, the only light now came from the flickering Olympic torch high up on its stand. A colleague helped out by pointing an electric torch at the bar and Mathias took careful aim with his pole, leapt forward and swung up into the gloom, clearing 3.5 metres. Once again, he had beaten the field.

Though the take-off mark for the javelin was also obscured by darkness, Mathias hurled it fifty metres. This left the tenth and final event, the timed 1,500 metre run, in which Mathias had to beat 5 minutes 49 seconds. It was now 10.30 p.m. and the stadium was deserted. He sloshed around the track, through ever-deepening puddles, in just over five minutes. It was the third slowest time, but his overall score of 7,139 gave him victory by 165 points. He had overcome inexperience, foul weather, obstacles, darkness, hunger and exhaustion to become the youngest athlete in Olympic history to win a gold medal for a men's athletics event.

'Bob Mathias was younger than me by three

weeks and I could hardly believe that someone our age could shine as he did,' said Maurice Graham. 'He was the first of the teenage superheroes.'

Asked what he would do to celebrate, Mathias replied, 'I'll start shaving, I guess.'

* * *

On the same day as Mathias's triumph came the final of the Olympics equivalent of the mile. 'On August 6th we must be back here again for the final of the 1500 metres,' wrote Evoe in *Punch*. 'We shall hardly hope to see a British or even an Empire win in this event, but of all the races it is the most exciting; and there will almost certainly be the spectacle of a Swede beating Lovelock's 1936 record by several seconds. Since about 1942 one Swede after another has been whittling the time down. The reason for this outbreak by the Swedes is obscure. Perhaps neutrality made them restless.'

Doug Wilson, aged twenty-eight, was the British mile champion in 1946. During the war he had been in the London Rescue Service and he now worked for the Institute of British Launderers. 'I had run against Bannister and beaten him a couple of times,' he remembered. 'Then in early 1948 I pulled a muscle and thought I wouldn't be picked.' Wilson went to Butlins holiday camp to train, where he met Olympians from other sports for the first time. 'My employers were quite enthusiastic so long as it didn't affect them. I had to take my annual holiday during the Olympics. At Uxbridge we did more training, and I did well in the trial against Nankeville.'

Bill Nankeville was eighteen years old when he joined the Army in 1944 and was sent to Germany. After the war ended, he was coached by German Olympic athletes, and became British mile champion in early 1948. After that, the only way he could afford to train for the Olympics was to stay in the Army: they posted him back home to England as a PT instructor and later gave him a month's leave. 'We trained for around ninety minutes, six days a week with long slow jogs of six miles under the eagle eye of the legendary coach Bill Thomas.' Two weeks before the Olympics, Nankeville ran in Ireland:

On the way back to Liverpool from Dublin there was a storm, and I was very ill. I was so ill that I couldn't stand up. The *Daily Mirror* columnist Arnold Milne helped me home but I had lost a whole stone in weight. However, Bill Thomas was no believer in throwing in the sponge and he told me to run slowly, lap after lap, twenty-five laps of a quarter of a mile on the grass to build up my strength. He gave me sherry and egg twice a day, mixed with sugar. It worked well and I was soon running a quarter of a mile fast, and three quarters slowly.

After one hard afternoon's training at Uxbridge, Bill Thomas had told Nankeville to run a trial against Doug Wilson. Nankeville felt he had done enough for that day and was appalled. 'Little did I realise that Bill Thomas wanted to prove, both to himself and to me, that I was fully recovered, that I was fit enough both in mind and body to be in for the race of my life.' Both ran very fast, finishing within less than a second of each other.

Nankeville was in the first of four heats, two days before the final. 'I was fortunate because mine was leisurely compared with the other heats. Eriksson of Sweden set a hot pace, but nobody tried to stop him and I ran in second.' Wilson was not so lucky. 'I got so cold that I didn't even qualify,' he said. 'I felt very miserable. It should have been the highlight of my athletic career. I was very deflated and I slumped in the bath.'

The final took place late on the Friday afternoon when it was raining hard. Rain poured off the policemen's helmets and onto their capes. Some spectators wore folded newspaper hats with headlines such as 'Stalin to talk about Berlin' and 'Tito rounds up secrets'. The athletes huddled under mackintoshes on the muddy grass in the middle of the stadium.

'Unfortunately,' recalled Nankeville, 'the weather decided to treat us to a cloudburst just before the start, so we had to line up on a track soft and sluggish and pitted with pools of water.' Workmen had spent the afternoon piercing the track with garden forks to encourage it to drain, but to little effect. 'Despite this, the atmosphere was electric, and I felt a dryness in my throat as I limbered up before the vast crowd. People had been talking of a new Olympic record, but the rain had washed that possibility away. With the exception of the vociferous Swedes, who kept up their chant of "Hiya! Hiya! Hiya!", the crowd was on my side but this couldn't stop those butterflies fluttering about in my stomach.' There were twelve finalists. Hansenne of France set the early pace but faded at halfway. 'The three Swedes were all

246

potential candidates for the gold medal. Sweden would have been in a state of national mourning if none had managed to win the race.' After one kilometre the Swedes picked up speed and swept past the rest of the field. Nankeville ran on at his own steady pace. 'I was hoping to surprise everyone with a finishing burst. I felt confident I could pull out some speed despite the sodden track. Some 300 metres from home I made my effort. I was well back but as I speeded up I set the crowd a-roaring and before I knew it, I was in fourth place.' Sadly, everyone else speeded up too. 'I couldn't hold on. The Swedes really burned up the track on the finishing straight, with Eriksson taking the lead most definitely. I was bursting my lungs to make some impression but it was no use, and I had to be satisfied with sixth place.' As predicted, both the gold and the silver medals went to Sweden and Slijkhuis of Holland won bronze. 'Sure I was disappointed,' said Nankeville. 'But I felt no sense of shame or of disgrace when I walked off the track and into the dressing room for a much-needed bath.'

15

TIME OFF FOR FUN

Although the competitors were expected to train hard all day and go to bed early, for those near London plenty of entertainment was available once they had competed. In the West End, *Revudeville*, the naked cabaret at the Windmill

Theatre, was going strong in its seventeenth year. The Andrews Sisters—Patty, Maxine and Laverne—were making their successful debut at the London Palladium. On general release was Powell and Pressburger's *The Red Shoes* starring Moira Shearer, along with Korda's *Anna Karenina* starring Vivien Leigh, and Alicia Markova and Anton Dolin were dancing at Covent Garden. Those who preferred to go early to bed could read Agatha Christie's latest Hercule Poirot murder mystery, *Taken at the Flood*, or Graham Greene's *Heart of the Matter*, or cheer themselves up with Monica Dickens' new novel *Joy and Josephine,* described by John Betjeman in the *Daily Herald* as 'a rich and humorous description of street life in the Portobello Road'.

For the Olympic officials, unrestricted by the constraints of training, grander entertainments were laid on. In the days before the Opening Ceremony, they had embarked on a marathon of gourmandising. On Monday 26 July, the IOC gave a dinner for 300 people at the Dorchester Hotel. On Tuesday the 27th, Viscount Portal hosted a dinner at Claridge's for the IOC and 250 foreign and British VIPs, while their wives were taken by bus to the Odeon Cinema in Leicester Square where Mrs J. Arthur Rank entertained them with a screening of the new *Hamlet* starring Laurence Olivier. On Wednesday the 28th, the British Organising Committee gave another dinner at the Dorchester presided over by Lord Burghley. On Thursday the 29th, the Lord Mayor of London invited Olympic VIPs to dine at the Mansion House. Cocktail parties were also held at the Savoy Hotel, the Lyceum, and the Grocer's Hall hosted by the Masters of the twelve Great Livery Companies. On Sunday 1 August, Sir Eugen and Lady Effie Millington-Drake gave a luncheon garden party, followed by a special service at St Paul's Cathedral, and another at Westminster Cathedral for Roman Catholics. The Hungarian Olympic Committee gave a dinner at Hendon Technical College and the Danish Olympic Team gave a party in the Paramount Dance Hall with 'Bombe Danoise' for dessert, followed by dancing.

Xavier Frick was one visitor who took advantage of all the invitations going:

As the team manager I had to look after the Liechtenstein press. A famous English newspaper put on a reception in the Dorchester Hotel. Why shouldn't I go along? The porter saw the coat of arms on my blazer and said in Swiss German, 'Liechtenstein: ha, I was at school in Wallastadt. Welcome.' The guest of honour was the British Minister of Health. After dinner there was a cabaret programme in which I saw for the first time in my life a tummy speaker [ventriloquist]! That was something quite new for me and I suspected a trick.

The evening held yet more surprises for Frick:

As I struggled towards the exit I saw what was clearly curfew and the bobbies were all there ready to clear the venue. Then I faced my next problem. It was Sunday and the Underground stopped very early. My friend the porter advised me to leg it quickly to the nearest

Underground station but by that time, the entrance was closed. Instead there were just some helpful ladies hanging around on the street. I walked round several blocks. I asked a policeman how I might get to Uxbridge, 20 miles away. He struck a deal with a taxi driver who asked for three pounds. Even at black market rates that was 30 francs!

Determined not to be outdone, the worshipful Mayor of Wembley, Councillor H.S. Sirkett, JP, felt that 'This historic occasion should be marked in some special way, and the Borough Council has accordingly prepared a splendid programme of entertainment. We hope to prove to the world that our borough can provide a variety of first class entertainments in one of the finest Assembly Halls in London, an international centre of enjoyment and good fellowship.' The planned attractions included a Punch & Judy show in King Edward VII park, a display of health exercises by the Women's League of Health and Beauty, the Wembley finals of the London children's talent competition at 2d a seat, and dancing in Wembley Town Hall with a competition between Slough and Wembley Old Time dancing clubs. The Bathing Beauty Queen of Wembley would be chosen by Alderman Marshall and Councillor Ormsby-Taylor, and presented with a prize by 'A Famous Film Star (whose name will be announced)'.

The Mayor of Hammersmith, Alderman Reginald J. Buckingham, JP, invited all competitors to a reception on Saturday 7 August, with dancing to the orchestra of Geoffrey Swift. 'Our town hall is one of the newest and best equipped in London. I am sure you will find a visit most interesting and I hope entertaining,' he said. Also present would be the Chairman of the Metropolitan Water Board, and mayors of seventeen London boroughs from Battersea to Woolwich. Floral decorations were provided by the Borough Engineers Department.

Not all the entertainments were appreciated. The *Wembley News* reported:

> The 'small audience' bogey again haunted Wembley Philharmonic Society when they presented 'England' on Sunday afternoon. Playing to a half empty hall the orchestra and choir presented an interesting, if rather long, tribute of 43 items in prose, poetry and music. George Eskdale's trumpet voluntary was one of the high spots. The orchestra was not at its best. Even conductor Harry L. Willis seemed a little off his usual excellent form. The Borough Engineer is still endeavouring to divine means of excluding draughts from the town hall.

The royal family played their part in making visitors welcome. Queen Elizabeth celebrated her forty-eighth birthday on 4 August with a lunch for the International Olympic Committee at Buckingham Palace, and afterwards she and the King were joined by other members of their family at a party given at Buckingham Palace for three hundred Olympic competitors.

'In a most democratic manner their Majesties conversed amicably with each guest,' reported the *News of the World*. The footballer Chia Boon Leong from Singapore had been chosen to represent the Chinese team. 'We all lined up and I shook hands with the King and Queen. The old Queen Mother was there too. We had been told before not to take photos or ask for autographs. Then we went into another room with lots of tea and cakes. Prince Philip was very charming, and I took the opportunity of talking to Princess Margaret. She was very pretty and full of smiles.'

Once again, Xavier Frick was in the thick of it, this time accompanied by his team of two decathletes. 'This was great social event for us,' Frick reported. 'To be invited to a do with the Royal Family. In the entrance hall, I was informed that our Prince, Franz-Josef II, had been to visit the King and Queen. After we were greeted by the royal couple we were ordered to go before Queen Mary and she was particularly impressed by our Olympic uniforms. That was a big compliment to our tailor.'

As the national representatives were being lined up by Mr Holt, the Director of Organisation in the Ante-Chamber, once again the vexed question of whether Chisholm was managing a team from Eire or Ireland arose. This time, his spirited determination paid off. His team found itself as usual behind Egypt but as they approached the Throne Room, the King's equerry asked how they would like to be announced. 'Ireland,' said Chisholm firmly. The King did not seem to mind.

The British team was the last to be presented. 'Old Queen Mary, the Queen Mother, was standing by the door with her tasselled umbrella,' said Mary Glen Haig. 'As I walked past in my Bourne and Hollingsworth dress and blazer embellished with the Union Jack she said, "And

252

which country do you represent, dear?" The whole length of a long room was laid out as a buffet.'

The New Zealand team were delighted with the occasion. 'To us it was one of the most unforgettable moments of our lives,' Harold Nelson confided to his diary. 'Dr Porritt, surgeon to the Royal household, has done the most to make our stay in London as pleasant as possible. He is well liked, capable and respected. We were all personally introduced by him to the King, Queen and Princess Margaret. They are looking forward to their visit to New Zealand. The King appears older looking than the photos would have you believe. It is evident that the strain of work is taking its toll. The Queen, always charming, appears to dominate the family. She has no affectation, and showed an interest that appears to be personal for the few minutes that she had with us.'

Princess Elizabeth, married the year before, was now five months pregnant with the future heir to the throne. Nelson wrote:

We were surprised to see Princess Elizabeth present in view of the Happy Event. She had given a statement that she would not be attending any more functions till after the birth. She is very like her mother both in her looks and her mannerisms. She said she would not have missed the party for the world, & said she hoped it would be a boy. Turning to Dutch she said 'And what do you do Mr Holland?' Dutch replied in a high-pitched squeaky voice 'I'm a Hurdler, Princess.' We all had to laugh. Princess Margaret is obviously very different to the rest. Very petite, quite pretty, she is perhaps the rebel of the family. The Duchess of Kent I caught alone in a corner. She is an acknowledged Leader of Fashion in London.

The British gymnast George Wheedon was less impressed by the royal tea party. 'It was nothing special really. We shook hands with some royalty. There was some tea and a few buns, but no champagne.'

16

MEDALS FOR ARTISTS

'The original aim of the Greek Olympics was the improvement of the whole man,' wrote Roger Bannister in 1955. 'For a long time specialisation was discouraged and athletes competed within a stone's throw of the auditorium where dramatic performances took place. Alcibiades was a fine example of an athlete who was also a writer and thinker and it was for the victors at the Olympic Games that Pindar wrote many of his odes.'

Baron de Coubertin had hoped that his revival of the Games would help to create a complete man, developed in both mind and body through art and sport, though it was not until Stockholm in 1912 that the Arts appeared as an official competition. Only thirty-five people submitted their work that year, but gold medals were awarded in five categories: architecture, painting, sculpture, literature and music. At Amsterdam in 1928 over

1,100 works were exhibited and the British artist William Nicholson, famous for his illustrated alphabet, won the lithograph class. All the exhibits were later sold, a strange decision given the IOC's policy on amateurism.

Prior to 1948, the IOC had discussed abandoning the arts event but the idea was rejected. Colonel Evan Hunter wrote: 'To suggest the exclusion of Art would be regarded by the most cultured and influential people in the international Olympic spheres as a retrograde step. There would be more resistance for the removal of Art than for many of the non-universal activities.' All the countries competing in London were invited to submit original works inspired by sport. Painters in the USA had shown little interest in 1936, so the US Olympic Committee did not even bother to ask for entries. But the committees in Czechoslovakia and Italy were enthusiastic and Ireland sent a great many entries, valued at £1,387. Liechtenstein and New Zealand were unable to participate because of the high cost of freight and insurance. The British had trouble recruiting entries because potential competitors who had already established their reputations preferred to judge, rather than be judged. 'British exponents of Sport in Art are somewhat few and far between,' reported the Olympic Fine Art Committee. 'A certain war-weariness, together with a serious shortage of canvas and brushes, is undoubtedly affecting the entries. The rule that all work must have been carried out since January 1944 is also a misfortune, since most of our younger artists have been engaged upon a different kind of work since then.' Sir Alfred Munnings, the President of the Royal

Academy and a leading painter of horses, submitted twenty-four paintings, none of which was eligible because he had painted them some years before. They included *Their Majesties' Return from Ascot*, showing the King and Queen in a horse-drawn carriage, hardly a sport, painted in 1925.

'Nothing appropriate has been produced either,' the committee added, 'in the architectural world in this period.' Given the pressing need for basic housing, it was hardly surprising that sports arenas had been a low priority for most British architects. The Architectural Association ran a qualifying competition but the only entry was for a sailing club designed by P.B. Horsbrugh, which nevertheless received an Honourable Mention when submitted for the Olympic competition. Switzerland and Finland entered models of sports centres while Italy and Yugoslavia had hopefully submitted plans of their own Olympic stadiums, and Canada plumped for a golf club. The gold medal for architecture was won by the Austrian architect Adolf Hoch, for his model of a ski jump. Despite the amateur rule, many of the contributors were working architects.

The judges felt that the standard was often too low to merit medals, and in six of the fourteen classes only Honourable Mentions were awarded. The best exhibits were displayed in seven galleries at the Victoria and Albert museum, where the floors were repolished, the walls painted 'a warm grey', and trees in tubs were procured for the sculpture gallery. 'To assemble close on four hundred works of art from twenty-five countries, and to arrange and light them so as to provide a semblance of some international Exposition, is no mean undertaking and a round of praise is due to Major Longden, the Olympic Director of Art,' wrote the art critic Neville Wallis in *Punch*.

Painting was the most popular class, although several of the pictures depicted activities not featured in the Olympics, such as fishing, children playing, rugby football and even buck hunting. The *Romany Belles* featured in Dame Laura Knight's painting were at least standing beside a racecourse. The Chinese artist Tsong-Wei Sung contributed a watercolour of *Tibetan Dancing*. Miss Letitia Hamilton of Ireland won a bronze medal for her oil painting *Meath Hunt Point-to-Point Race* and Walter Battiss of South Africa achieved an Honourable Mention for *The Quagga Race*. The quagga is an extinct form of zebra.

Critics seemed undecided as to whether they were more concerned with sport or with art. 'Cricket is represented only by William Fisher's *Village Cricket* which has to compete with the sweep and sparkle of Charles Cundall's *Henley Regatta*,' wrote Neville Wallis. The gold medal for oil painting was won by a Royal Academician and former boxer, A.R. Thomson, for his impressionistic depiction of the *London Amateur Boxing Championships in the Albert Hall*.

The commercial artist Alex Walter Diggelmann of Switzerland had won a gold medal for his sports poster in 1936, and in 1948 he won both silver and bronze for two more, depicting cycling and ice hockey, and an Honourable Mention for his *Swiss Roller-skating Championship Medal*. The gold medal for etching was won by a French artist, Albert Decaris, for his homoerotic etching of men at a swimming pool. 'It was remarkably composed and executed,' wrote the critic Pierre Jeannerat, 'suggesting all the delights of water frolics.'

Sculpture was sub-divided into statues, reliefs and medals. This gave artists the opportunity to submit nudes, some moving and some still. 'In the sculpture section I would single out a powerful granite *Head of a Boxer* by a Dane, Knud Nellemose,' wrote Neville Wallis. 'A bronze statuette *Wrestler Relaxing* by the Italian Emilio Greco and two other sensitive bronzes by his compatriot Filippo Sgarlata of boar hunting.' The silver medal went to sculptor Chintamoni Kar from India, who had studied in Paris and was a member of the Royal Society of British Sculptors. His *Skating the Stag* in stone was inspired by a photograph of Barbara Ann Scott from Canada performing one of the leaps that in January had won her the gold medal at St Moritz for figure skating. The gold medal was awarded to Gustaf Nordahl of Sweden for his full-size nude couple *Homage to Ling*. Pehr Ling had developed Swedish gymnastics, as a means to create beauty of bearing and movement. A demonstration of Ling Swedish gymnastics was given in the Wembley Stadium by 400 Swedish men and women just before the football final. Pierre Jeannerat felt that, 'However capable as a specimen of straightforward modelling, *Homage to Ling* lacked real sporting interest. A boy and a girl stand motionless—and sport, surely, is motion.'

In the Medals class, the judges were so dissatisfied with the standard that they only awarded one medal. Edwin Grienauer, an enthusiastic sportsman from Vienna, had dreamed as a young man of winning Olympic gold for his rowing. Now fifty-seven years old, his bronze medal was awarded for a plaque of naked rowers. Rosamund Fletcher of Britain also won a bronze for the only entry in Relief Sculpture, a stone carving of two pheasants called *The End of a Covert*.

*   *   *

Chair of the Literature Committee was Sir Alan Herbert, who wrote brilliant libretti for comic operas, witty verses for *Punch* and, as an Independent member of parliament, had helped to improve the English divorce laws. 'Dramatic and epic works of Literature' could be submitted in any language and were sent to the BBC for translation. The first Olympic gold medal for Literature had been awarded in 1912 to Georg Hohrod and Martin Eschbach for their *Ode to Sport*, an exuberant piece in German which began, 'O sport, delight of the gods, distillation of life', continued 'O sport, you are beauty! O sport, you are daring! O sport, you are honour!', and ended 'O sport, you are peace!' De Coubertin had later admitted he had written it himself in an attempt to encourage others. Avery Brundage had entered literary works of his own at the 1932 and 1936 Olympics but they had won no prizes.

At the London Games, there was a conspicuous absence of any well known British writers, many of whom saw sport as uncreative. Stanislaus Lynch of Ireland was awarded a diploma in the Epic Works class for *Echoes of the Hunting Horn*. The Danish writer Josef Petersen, aged sixty-seven, who had won silver for *Euryale* in 1924 and *The Argonauts* in 1932, added a third Epic with *The Olympic Champion*. Petersen was well-known for his many historical novels, and his grandfather, Johan Sebastian Welhaven, had fought in the last known duel in Denmark in 1913.

In the Lyrics class, Aale Tynni of Finland won gold for her poem 'Laurel of Hellas'. Tynni had been publishing poems since 1938 and after 1945 her poetry reflected the contrast between the destruction of war and the life force of motherhood. She was married to a history professor and was a distinguished translator into Finnish of Shakespeare, Ibsen and Wordsworth. The South African Ernst van Heerden won silver for his *Ses gedigte*—six poems in Afrikaans including 'Vliegenier' (Pilot), 'Die Boogskuuter' (The Sniper) and 'Die Gewigopteller' (The Weightlifter).

Die Gewigopteller

Die taai klou van die grond
vermenigvuldig elke pond
die ruie vlegsel van die spier
is—triomfantelik!—'n dier
wat met een kap blitssnel
die swaartepunt verstel

The weightlifter

The sticky grip of the ground
multiplies every pound
the rough braid of the muscle
is—triumphantly!—a brute animal
which with one lightning quick snatch
260

Van Heerden was both an amateur weightlifter and a university professor of creative writing. At a time when it risked prosecution under South African law, he lived openly as a homosexual. In 1952 he captained the South African weightlifting team at the Helsinki Olympics. He published fifteen volumes of poetry, received four honorary doctorates and died in 1997.

Gilbert Prouteau was another for whom sport and art came together satisfactorily. Prouteau was a 21-year-old jumper from France who had recently been injured while training. 'I tore my quadriceps landing after a triple jump on to hard ground. I cried because it was the end of my career as an athlete.' Deeply disappointed that he could no longer compete, he travelled to London as a journalist. 'At Wembley I visited some of my friends in the dressing room and breathed in that characteristic smell of sweat you find in there. It was the nearest I was going to get to taking part in the Olympics. In the afternoon I watched the events with some regret. For me it was both absolutely wonderful and totally horrible because I wasn't in it. It would have been a second heartbreak to watch the triple jump.' This turned out to be more true than he realised, as France failed to qualify for the finals.

Prouteau recently recalled:

I was back in the dressing room, writing my report when I heard my name called out. I thought it was a poor joke so I didn't move. Then they kept on calling it so I went and they told me they were giving out medals for Art. I had won a bronze medal for poetry! My publisher had sent in my book of poems which I had forgotten I had even written. It was a kind of justice because what I didn't win with my legs, I won with my hands. It was Fate laughing for me. I had dreamt so much about winning a medal, and then I won for literature!

Prouteau's poem, first published in 1942, was called 'Rythme du Stade'. He went on to write thirty-seven books and film scripts, including *God Chose Paris* and *Le Dernier matin d'Arthur Rimbaud*.

*   *   *

Music was also included in the arts, but attracting a high standard of songs, instrumental compositions and orchestral works 'relating to the Olympic idea in the broadest sense' had always proved to be a challenge. At the 1924 Games in Paris, Igor Stravinsky was a judge and he awarded no medals at all; nor were any prizes awarded in 1928, and only a silver was granted in 1932. In 1948 the BBC offered to judge the music entries and to broadcast the winning composition to its country of origin. Honourable Mentions went to the Irish composer Gerard Victory for his song 'True Greatness', and to Miss Ina Boyle, also of Ireland, for her arrangement for tenor and strings of 'Lament for Bion (from the Greek)'. Zbigniew Turski of Poland won the gold medal for his *Olympic Symphony*. But the BBC judged the general standard to be so lamentable that none of the compositions were performed in London, let alone broadcast.

On the last afternoon of the Games, athletes and artists attended a concert given in the Royal Albert Hall by the Olympic Symphony Orchestra. Mercifully, the hall had cooled down since Miss Eileen Joyce had played Tchaikovsky's First Piano Concerto at the Proms the previous Thursday. It had been so hot on that evening that she had passed out on the keyboard as she played the last notes. After the concert, the competitors wandered down Exhibition Road to the Victoria and Albert Museum, where Lord Burghley presented the medals for the arts, and everyone agreed that they had done a splendid job.

After the London Games, the IOC decided that in future Art at the Olympics would be exhibited without the awarding of medals. Although the Games have continued to inspire writers, artists and film makers, 1948 was the last year in which these competitions were held. Thus ended Pierre de Coubertin's original concept of the Whole Man.

17

THE END OF THE FIRST WEEK

The end of the first week arrived on Saturday 7 August, and *The Times* was in a mood to celebrate: 'The Stadium at Wembley and its most popular neighbour the Empire Pool represent only a fraction of an enterprise deserving that overworked epithet "Colossal". One man could not see all, or nearly all of it, but on his various excursions he could gain some impression of its greatness and complexity.' Halfway through the Games some of the most exciting events were programmed for that day, including the 4 x 100 and 4 x 400 metre relay finals, for both men and women, the women's high jump, and the marathon.

The men's 4 x 100 metre relay final featured the world's fastest runners. The British team was for once truly representative, as it contained an Irishman, a Welshman, an Englishman and a Scotsman, Alastair McCorquodale. 'We had never run as a relay team before,' McCorquodale remembered. 'We didn't even know who would be in it until the night before the heat. But at least the relays were at the end of the athletics, so we had a week to practise, though we didn't practise much. I ran the first leg, so I only had to hand the baton to Mr Gregory.'

Jack Gregory, born in Northern Ireland, was a surprise inclusion in the British team because the Irish had hoped he would run for them, given that he had lived in the South since the age of two and was the all-Ireland 100 yards champion in 1947. He was a brilliant rugby player who had been suspended by the Rugby Union for allegedly playing for Huddersfield Rugby League club while stationed near the town as a soldier. This ruling did not affect his status as an amateur athlete. The Englishman was John Archer, European sprinting champion, and the Welshman Ken Jones, who taught at Newport High School and wrote on Welsh rugby for the *Sunday Express*. Jones had won the 100 yard dash in the All-India Games in

1945 and played rugby for Wales, gaining forty-four caps between 1947 and 1957; he became a leading sports journalist.

The US team included Mel Patton, Harrison Dillard and Barney Ewell, together with Lorenzo Wright. Patton remembered:

The weather had cooled down and I had a lot more energy and vim and vigour and vitality. It was a very slow track and wet and cold, so we decided there was no way we could break the Olympic record. The only thing to do was run for a gold. Our biggest competition was the Brits but we could outrun each one of them individually, man for man. We cut back our mark which meant that the person coming in would overrun and make sure we did not disqualify on the baton pass.

Patton was right to be wary of overrunning, since take-over judges were posted at each stage of the course to check that batons were passed within the twenty-metre passing zone. Ewell was already in the lead when he passed the baton to Wright, who shot ahead and handed it to Dillard. The teams from Italy, Hungary and Canada were not in with a chance of catching them but the British hung on and came second by eight metres.

'Well, it is the thrill of a lifetime,' Patton said. 'If it doesn't bring tears to your eyes, you are not a human being.' However, to everyone's amazement, the US team was disqualified for overrunning at the first change. The judge declared that Ewell had handed the baton to Wright outside the passing zone. When it was announced that the US victory had been ruled out and the gold now belonged to Great Britain, the news was received by the crowd almost in silence, even though this was Britain's first gold of the Games. Young Maurice Graham was among the spectators:

The crowd had become great supporters of Barney Ewell after he failed to win the 100 metre dash. We all thought it was grossly unfair when the USA was disqualified. Barney came over and examined the change-over spot for some time. I had a small box Brownie camera and I called out to Barney to face us and 'Give us a smile'. He treated us with the contempt we deserved but no expletives came from his mouth. I had to be content with a photo of a distraught Barney's back view as he walked sadly away.

McCorquodale, too, was unable to enjoy his moment of triumph. 'The four of us stood on the podium, and they played *God Save the King*. But we knew we had been beaten. It was a hollow victory.'

Patton said: 'We stood there with our hands in our pockets watching what was going on. I had such a low feeling, a sinking feeling. We were doggone better than the Brits and we knew doggone well that we had beat them. We were able to sit down and analyse it in a calm and more or less realistic mode. We came to the conclusion that we were legal. The coach was a bit reluctant to complain but we convinced him to make an official protest.' The Jury of Appeal examined the film of the race and three days later they announced that

266

the decision had been reversed and the USA had won after all. 'It all worked out, we ended up with the medals and the records were corrected,' said Patton.

'I was not surprised that one of the take-over judges had made a mistake,' wrote Rex Alston. 'How any of them ever succeeded in keeping their eyes on their particular two was a miracle, when twelve sprinters were flashing past them, seemingly all together.'

So the Americans added a ninth to their tally of gold medals, leaving Britain once more with none. The American newspapers paid warm tribute to Britain's show of good feeling and their sprinters particularly appreciated the way Ken Jones made the journey back from Wales to return his gold medal. The Italians exchanged their silver medals for bronze, which the Hungarians had to hand theirs back. It took nearly a month to put the correct medals in the post.

'As soon as it was all over, I went home by train and worked on the harvest into the night,' said McCorquodale. The following Monday he returned to work at his family's printing firm near London Bridge, turning out the Olympic programmes. 'Afterwards I ran for the British Empire in a relay with two Australians. We beat the Americans and then I never ran again.' He returned to his real love, cricket, and played for Middlesex. Ten years later, he gave up smoking.

* * *

The first women's Olympic high jump took place in 1928, when the Canadian pianist Ethel

Catherwood entranced everybody with her beauty and her ability to leap over five feet in the air. Now, on 7 August, it was the last of the women's athletic events. There were no qualifying heats but with nineteen entrants it took all afternoon to find a winner.

'I don't know why they always hold the women's high jump on the last day,' commented Dorothy Tyler, one of the British competitors. 'It makes it very difficult to enjoy the rest of the athletics.' Tyler was Britain's best hope for the high jump, despite being twenty-eight and a mother of two. At only sixteen, as Dorothy Odam, she had jumped for Britain at the 1936 Olympics, beating the eighteen-year-old Fanny Blankers-Koen. 'Berlin was awe-inspiring,' she remembered. 'We were greeted at the station by brass bands and Hitler Youth. You couldn't help being impressed by the Teutonic efficiency. The shop assistants greeted us with a Nazi salute and "Guten Morgen. Heil Hitler." So I did a Girl Guide salute and said, "Heil King George".' Dorothy and her team mates had joined Hitler and crowned heads of Europe at a party thrown by the Goebbels family on Schwanenwerder Island near Berlin. Watched by the Nazi leaders, the women's high jump competition that year had lasted three hours. Fanny Blankers-Koen had finished sixth, well beaten by Dorothy who, though she cleared the same height as the Hungarian, Ibolya Csak, had to be content with second place in the jump-off. Under modern rules she would have won gold.

During the war, Dorothy had been a PT instructor and a driver for the Dambuster Squadron of the RAF before she met and married

Dick Tyler. After the birth of her second son in 1947 she was determined to compete again in the Olympics. 'When Barry was two months old, I started training for real.' She took the baby in his pram to the local club.

> I had very little time to train, no coach and no help from anyone as I wasn't a probable or even a possible. I just ran from anywhere, at any angle, at the bar, did a scissor jump over and then landed on grass cuttings and sand. It was way above my own height, but somehow I managed not to injure myself. Once I jumped so high that I didn't tell anyone in case it was a mistake and I couldn't do it again. The bar was much lighter in those days; if your shorts touched it, it fell off. I had once seen a man do a high jump with the Western Roll but I didn't know how to do it.

The local papers made much of her training methods. 'Housework keeps her fit,' claimed the *Sunday Graphic*. 'She crawls under the tables to polish the legs.'

'Actually I never did any housework,' she said. 'And not much training either. I did get an extra ration card and tinned fruit from Canada. I always sent my husband to the butcher because they gave more meat to male customers.' The women had to make their own sports kits, on to which they sewed red, white and blue ribbons. Instead of tracksuits, most British athletes wore casual trousers and jumpers in between their races. Dorothy Tyler wore the tracksuit she had kept since the 1936 Olympics.

No other British woman had beaten her 1939 record, so despite her age Dorothy was selected for the London Olympics.

At last I had the chance to jump in front of my friends and compatriots, with the undoubted advantage of their vocal support. The easy-going atmosphere of the London Games was very different from the formalities of Berlin. It came as a great relief after the war and provided a true sign that it was all over. In spite of the austerity, everything was well organised. Sport took on a new glow, it was like the sun finally coming out.

Dick Tyler left the boys with their granny to be in the crowd that Saturday afternoon. 'It was easy to get to Wembley,' he said. 'There was very little traffic and lots of trains and buses. Dorothy wasn't given any free tickets: I had to buy my own but the facilities were excellent. No complaints there.'

There was stiff competition for Tyler from within the British team. Mrs Bertha Crowther was a PT teacher at Wembley County School and a pentathlon champion as well as a high jumper. 'Bertha Crowther told everyone that she would beat me,' said Tyler. 'That got me going—I was even more determined to win then. I had no idea who I would be jumping against as there was no list of competitors. I was hoping to jump against Fanny Blankers-Koen, who had broken my world record during the war, but she had already won three individual gold medals and she wasn't competing.'

As the afternoon wore on, Dorothy's adversary

Bertha Crowther dropped out in sixth place. Micheline Ostermeyer of France won the bronze, her third medal. Tyler and the African-American Alice Coachman then became engaged in a protracted fight for the gold medal. 'The women's high jump was one of the most thrilling duels imaginable,' wrote Harold Abrahams in the official report. Coachman cleared the bar at 1.68 metres at her first attempt. Tyler failed this the first time, but cleared it on her second jump. The bar was put up to 1.7 metres and Coachman failed on all three attempts. Tyler jumped last. 'On the third attempt,' she said, 'I was running towards the jump when my bra strap broke and I lost my concentration. If it wasn't for that bra, I might have won the gold. As it was, I was again placed second, after jumping the same height as Alice Coachman. But there was some consolation in having my name bracketed with hers as the new record-holder.' Coachman was the first African-American woman to win gold and her countrymen didn't quite know what to do with her. On her return to Georgia, a motorcade travelled the 175 miles to Albany to honour her. But when they arrived at the Municipal Auditorium, officials there informed her that owing to racial segregation laws, she would not be permitted to speak.

*   *   *

While trying to concentrate on their jumping, the women had to cope with the distraction of the 4 x 400 metre men's relay final. The favourites were the Jamaican team, who had three very tall

271

sprinters and one short one. Herbert McKenley, who was to run last, and Arthur Wint, running third, had been at school together in Kingston. At six foot five, Wint had dominated the British running scene since 1946, when he had arrived to join the RAF as a bomber pilot. 'Arthur Wint was a great fellow as well as being a great athlete,' said Bill Nankeville. 'We first met in the officers' mess in Dusseldorf at one o'clock in the morning. We were sitting yarning and drinking beer, and I soon realised why the Jamaican had become one of the most popular athletes in the world.' By 1948, Wint had resigned his commission to study medicine at St Bartholomew's Hospital, London. His untroubled, leisurely, devouring stride had already won him a silver medal in the 800 metres. In the 400 metres, he snatched victory in the last few strides from McKenley, who was world record holder, to win Jamaica's first-ever gold medal. Roger Bannister remembered that people had grown a little weary of hearing the US national anthem played at successive victory ceremonies:

The tiny island of Jamaica then tried to win the relay title. We hoped that with a Jamaican victory, we might hear an unofficial calypso from the West Indian spectators, the crowd's sympathies being with the small man against the giant, though this term applied only to the geography. No one in the American team could ever top the two giants, Wint and McKenley.

The Americans had a strong team, one of whom was Clifford Bourland. 'The coach asked me to run both the relays,' said Bourland. 'But I told him that I would be taking someone else's place and that would make us both unpopular, so I chose the 4 x 400 metres.' Bourland was twenty-seven, the child of a German mother and Californian father living in a poor neighbourhood of Los Angeles. 'After school I repaired bicycles for 10 cents an hour, drove a truck, delivered groceries and worked as an usher in the Metro. I basically supported myself from the age of 12 years.' Bourland's athleticism won him a scholarship to college, which paid for tuition but was not as generous as a football scholarship:

I was smart enough to hang around the football players because they got me free meals and books. I raked leaves around the campus for 40 cents an hour and worked as an extra on movies with Gary Cooper and Jennifer Jones. When I graduated I went to midshipman's school. They were going to start landings out in the Pacific Ocean someplace, so they put me in charge of a Landing Craft. A kamikaze pilot ditched his airplane close to where we were and my crew captured him. This guy was very young, wearing a pure white uniform. He had an injured leg and he was scared to death. I had the crew take him over to the hospital ship. It was hit and sank about nine hours later.

Putting these horrors behind him, Bourland began training again after the war and qualified for the Olympics. 'Jamaica was far and above the best relay team,' he said. 'The night before the

273

race we decided that our slowest guy, Glenn Hardin, should go first against their slowest guy, Rhoden. I decided to run against Laing. He was a little, short, stocky guy who was very strong. Roy Cochran was going to run against Herb McKenley and we matched Mal Whitfield with Arthur Wint.'

In the heats, Italy had created a surprise by running the second fastest time, but tragedy struck in the final when they dropped the baton. The spectator Gordon Broughton from Gloucestershire saw the mishap from close at hand. 'Right in front of us an Italian runner dropped his baton. He flung himself on the ground and beat the track with his fists in shame and anger. The other Italian hit him over the head. That was them out of the race.' As expected, battle was joined between the Americans and Jamaicans. 'Our first guy and Jamaica's first guy were neck and neck,' said Bourland. 'On the last leg, Whitfield had an eight- or nine-yard lead and he ran it beautifully. Then Arthur Wint took four or five big strides that just went bang, bang, bang, and all of a sudden Arthur was running as hard as only he can.'

'We all stopped the high jump to watch the relay,' said Dorothy Tyler. 'The Jamaicans were now streaks ahead and Arthur Wint was going all out as he came past us. He appeared to cover the ground without effort. Everybody was shouting him on, when suddenly he fell to the ground with a pulled muscle. He lay there beating the cinders with his baton in despair, as Mal Whitfield sailed past him.'

So once again, the USA had won the gold. France came second, with a time slower than the

Italians had achieved in the heats.

*   *   *

The climax of the Olympic's toughest event was about to take place. As Dorothy and the other women tried to focus once more on the high jump, news came from outside the stadium that the marathon runners were approaching.

'Once again, I completely forgot my own event,' Tyler said. 'We all rushed to the edge of the track to yell the marathon runners on, especially Tom Richards who had been a member of my club.'

The first marathon runner, an Athenian messenger called Pheidippides, was reputed to have dropped dead as he handed over the news of the Greek victory over the Persians in 490 BC; though as Plutarch wrote the story 500 years later it may not be strictly accurate. From 1876, the poet Robert Browning's telling of the story became accepted as a historic legend and the first modern Olympics in 1896 included a race over the twenty-five miles from Marathon to the Greek capital. A Greek shepherd, Spyridon Louis, fasted for a day, prayed for two nights, set off and won. The winner of the 1904 marathon in St Louis only finished the course after receiving shots of strychnine. For the London 1908 Games, the starting line was outside a window of Windsor Castle from which one half of the royal family could watch, and the finish was in front of the royal box in the White City Stadium, where the King and Queen sat. This was 26 miles and 385 yards (42.2 kilometres) and it became the standard length of a marathon.

In 1936 a new marathon record of 2 hours 29

minutes was set by Son Ki-Jung running for Japan. He was not in fact Japanese at all but a Korean whose country had been annexed by Japan in 1910, so that Son Ki-Jung was forced to adopt the Japanese name Kitei Son and represent his conquerors. Japan's defeat in 1945 had led to Korea's occupation by US and Soviet troops pending establishment of an independent government. In August 1948 Kee-chung Sohn led the national team in London, just weeks before the US-backed south and Soviet-backed north of his country were to proclaim two rival republics. The Korean team included no less than three marathon runners.

Plans for the marathon route had begun as early as March 1946, when Lord Burghley informed the Ministry of Transport about improvements needed to the roads around Wembley. The route chosen was one of the most gruelling yet designed. Only the start and finish, involving laps in the stadium, were on the level and the route went steadily uphill through Stanmore, Edgware and Mill Hill and then on through the fields of Radlett as far as Elstree Cross. The runners had climbed over 300 feet before they began their descent via Watling Street. Two policemen on horseback rode ahead to clear the way for the forty-one men from twenty-one nations, followed by more policemen on bicycles. Specially adapted cars carrying cameras filmed the progress of the race from strategic places. Two hundred Boy Scouts stood along the route as distance markers, each of whom had been provided with a boxed lunch. To refresh the runners, eight mobile canteens provided sweetened warm or cold tea, barley water, sugar cubes, lemons and grape sugar. An official waited in each public telephone kiosk along the route and telephoned the runners' positions back to the press office at Wembley.

John Lyne was a seventeen-year-old schoolboy from south east London, who went with his grandfather to watch the race. 'The underground station was packed like sardines. The stadium was full. It was almost impossible to get tickets for that afternoon. The best marathon runner was Jack Holden from Tipton Harriers. He had won numerous events and was the fastest in the world that year. The speaker system announced that at five kilometres he was leading.' Jack Holden, who was forty-one years old, had been a top runner for two decades. He was four times winner of the International Cross Country Championships and three times the national champion. A short, stockily built, rather taciturn man with great confidence in his ability, he had only turned to road running in 1946 and had immediately won the AAA Marathon championship. Up to ten kilometres he was at the front, but then he developed blisters and started to fall behind and at the mid point he retired.

Etienne Gailly was among those who took immediate advantage. At twenty-five he was one of the youngest runners; it was also remarkable that he was there at all. Three years after the Germans occupied his native Belgium, he had made his way through France, hoping to reach Britain via Spain. He was arrested in the Pyrenees, and spent six months in a Spanish gaol before making it to Gibraltar. Arriving in London, he had enlisted in the Belgian Brigade and trained as a parachutist.

277

In his spare time he ran cross-country with the Belgravia Harriers, where he made friends with some of the men against whom he was now competing. After the liberation of Europe, Second-Lieutenant Gailly had been reunited with his family in Belgium. He continued to run and by 1948 was the Belgian marathon champion.

Gailly had planned to run the marathon in exactly 2 hours 30 minutes. He took the lead from Holden and went well ahead but his pace had failed to take into account either the hills or the humidity.

I was convinced the others would soon re-establish contact with me. I was often glancing back, expecting Jack Holden to appear at my side. I considered him to be my most dangerous rival. Then after about 32 kilometres Yun Chil Choi of Korea passed me and I found I could not respond. I asked myself: 'Is he travelling so fast or am I fading?' My strength had left me temporarily. I could only watch how fast Choi was running. I was not unduly alarmed. I had been alone in the lead for 27 kilometres: but I felt nothing more than a normal tiredness which I hoped to overcome soon.

At thirty-three kilometres Choi was leading, with Gailly close behind him. At thirty-six kilometres Choi slowed to a walk, began to limp and then gave up altogether. Coming up behind Gailly now was Delfo Cabrera, a 29-year-old Argentinean fireman with a dapper moustache and large smile, who was running in his first marathon. In the early stages of the race he had been ably assisted by his two compatriots. 'Cabrera's team mate Guinez,' wrote the Argentinean journalist Horacio Estol, 'broke away and set the pace. He made every effort to destroy those that could have prevented Argentina from taking the marathon, and his intuition told him that Cabrera, who was increasing his effort, keeping his cool, and pushing without collapsing, would be the first.'

For a couple of kilometres Gailly flagged, as Cabrera moved nearly a minute ahead. 'Then I suddenly felt my rhythm coming back,' said Gailly. 'I had got my second—or was it my third?—wind. No sooner had I got into the Argentinean's slipstream than I decided to spurt without delay. I passed Cabrera, and having regained the lead, seemed to be travelling well. Certainly I was tired, but I was quite convinced that I would last the distance. It was then that I committed my biggest blunder. I drew away from him too quickly.'

Large crowds lined Olympic Way as the thirty remaining runners neared the stadium. An exhausted Etienne Gailly still led, but two men were doggedly trailing him. John Lyne recalled:

They announced that the leaders were approaching. And into the stadium came Etienne Gailly, staggering all over the place; then Delfo Cabrera and behind him a British runner. The stadium went wild. Everyone shouted 'Come on, Jack, come on, Jack.' They thought it was Holden. But it wasn't. We knew their names but not what the runners looked like. It was Tom Richards, who was relatively unknown. Everyone was shouting. The whole

279

stadium was in uproar.

Tom Richards, stocky and bald at thirty-eight, with a ready smile, was a psychiatric nurse at Tooting Bec Hospital in London, where the athletics team included both staff and patients.

'I cheered my head off for Gailly, the man who, although Belgian, was a club mate of mine,' wrote Bill Nankeville. 'But as he began to run that final lap, so often the undoing of marathon runners, he was running in a clockwise instead of an anti-clockwise direction. Shouts and signals showed him the correct way, but he could only stagger.' Gailly was now so physically drained that he could only totter round the track, looking behind him for his pursuers. Ashen-faced and with eyes bulging, he was in obvious distress and had lost his confident stride. Gailly remembered:

I had no premonition of collapsing. But at the very moment when I stepped on to the track, exhaustion overcame me like a powerful drug. This last lap was hard for me, it was like the progress of a martyr. I was horribly weak, I almost fainted. I was no longer fighting the other runners but an awful engulfing weakness, wanting more than anything to get to that unbelievably distant finishing line. First Cabrera and then Richards passed me, as if behind a veil.

Cabrera found the reserves of energy needed to take the gold and Richards crossed the line sixteen seconds behind him and flopped to the ground.

'Gailly reached the final straight,' wrote Rex

Alston, 'and then hesitated. Some hidden spark of strength remained and he pulled himself together and tottered over the line, half a minute ahead of the next runner. I never want to see a repetition of such a horrid sight.'

Delfo Cabrera meanwhile had been carried off on the shoulders of his fans. Horacio Estol was beside himself:

> Our modest yet indefatigable Delfo Cabrera won the toughest event, and returned a glorious winner. His brilliant success rests entirely on his strength of character— persistent, relentless and vigorous. He had never run more than 10 kilometres, and could not possibly have been a candidate to win an event that demands such extreme exhaustion. His victory is down to legs of steel and a noble heart. Delfo Cabrera's victory belongs also to Guinez and to the humble Sensini, who is strong. Delfo won't let us forget this, since his heart, as well as having plenty of stamina, is a generous and good one, as big as Argentina. His home in Santa Fé is today elated that it has produced a hero. Guinez and Sensini should also return home victorious, since it is not only those that finish first, that win.

Cabrera had won in 2 hours 34 minutes, only five minutes more than the Olympic record.

'The marathon is the saddest and most sublime of all races,' wrote Denzil Batchelor. 'Gailly stumbled from the pinnacle to third place in a single lap of the stadium, running with paper-white face and staggering legs.' He was carried off on a stretcher and although the spectators were thrilled by Richards' medal, the first for a Welsh athlete, it was Gailly's heroic struggle that seized their attention and his name that they chanted. Just three years later a land mine shattered his left foot while he was serving as a volunteer with UN troops in the Korean war.

* * *

The Olympic rules governing the 1948 Games stated that no single person could enter more than four separate events. Given the records she had already broken, Fanny Blankers-Koen could have won gold medals in at least six. Had she competed in the long jump she would almost certainly have won, as the Hungarian winner, Olga Gyarmati, could only come within twenty-two inches of the world record that Blankers-Koen herself had set a few months earlier. Blankers-Koen was also the world record holder in the high jump, but she decided that it would be fairer to make her fourth event the women's 4 x 100 metre relay with three of her friends. It did mean that she would have to run the relay heat half an hour before the 200 metres final on Friday 6 August. Nothing daunted, the Dutch team duly won their heat and were through to the final on the Saturday afternoon. Blankers-Koen very nearly missed the final because she had gone shopping in the West End for a beige raincoat. Arriving late at Wembley, she had no time to warm up and when she took the baton as fourth runner, she was well behind the Australians. 'I thought to myself when I got the baton: "I can never win this, never, never, never."

282

Then with fifty metres to go, I thought, "Maybe I have a chance." I ran faster than I have ever run, getting closer all the time, until a couple of metres from the line, I went into the lead. We thought it was impossible to win but it was so nice to race together with the other girls. It was lovely for them to win medals too.'

'Mrs Blankers-Koen from Holland, with her orange shorts and her fair floating hair, strode home to victory with all the irresistible surge of the great men sprinters, and stealing half their thunder,' reported *The Times*. The Australian team led by Shirley Strickland came second, and Canada third. Great Britain, with Dorothy Manley and Maureen Gardner in the team, came fourth.

Despite the long period away from Olympic competition between 1936 and 1948, over eight days Fanny Blankers-Koen had now competed eleven times in heats and finals and had won every race she entered. John Macadam commented:

When you look back on the 1936 Olympics with their pettiness and jealousies, it is good to think of this big-hearted Dutch Mother—so nicely called the fastest mother in the world, who pounded round the Wembley track to win all her races, and could still get breath after she had done it and shake Maureen Gardner by the hand and tell her she would be the big Olympic noise in 1952. She was the personality of these Games.

Bruce Peppin, a speed skater in the Winter Olympics, was employed as a surveyor near Wembley. 'We were working on Gypsy Corner station and I was on the roof when the procession of competitors' buses went past. It was great to see them from all over the world. Fanny Blankers-Koen was on everyone's lips. It wasn't that we found her attractive—we weren't interested in the looks of athletes in those days, it was their skill that counted.'

Sir Arthur Porritt also had a soft spot for Fanny. 'Apart from her unique physical prowess, she has a quiet, self-contained but essentially friendly temperament which allows her to face up to the big occasion with an apparent cool equanimity. But anyone who has seen her run one hundred percent and then a little more, concentration evident on her face in the last few strides of a race, will know the remarkable intensity of the effort that is being so beautifully produced.'

Blankers-Koen remembered that when she arrived back home in Holland after the Games, the Customs Officer asked if she had anything to declare.

'Any gold, for instance?' he asked with a smile.

'Yes,' she confessed, 'four gold medals.'

'They are only silver-gilt,' said the officer, who fancied himself an expert on the Olympics. 'But they ought to be made of diamonds.'

'Before I went to England,' Fanny wrote, 'I said to my family and my husband that it would be nice to reach the finals. I didn't really expect to win one gold let alone four.' Her remarkable tally was celebrated by the whole of the Netherlands. Thousands of people lined the streets of Amsterdam to watch her pass in a carriage drawn by four grey horses. It wasn't only the Dutch who celebrated her success. Her homely personality, crooked teeth and embarrassed self-deprecation enchanted the British public. Years later a British autograph hunter said to her, 'After being angry with you for depriving us of three gold medals, I decided you really belonged to us.' After that, she said, she felt as much at home in Britain as in Holland.

James Pilditch wrote:

To celebrate Fanny's gold medals, the Dutch students working at Uxbridge held a dance for her and we were all invited. We all wore our best suits but the nearest that the Dutch students could get to this was their pyjama jackets with their collars turned up. It was amazing that Fanny did so well, considering how under-nourished most Europeans still were. They only had a small chance against the well-fed athletes from the United States.

18

THE MUSCLEMEN

'The difference between Greco-Roman wrestling and Cast-as-catch-can, so the Olympic Games Official Souvenir (5 shillings) tells me,' wrote H.F. Ellis in *Punch*, 'is that in the former the legs may not be used for attack or defence. They can, however, be used to stand on, as we shall see when we go to Earl's Court.' The Empress Hall at Earl's Court, like the Empire Pool in Wembley, was a modernistic design of cantilevered reinforced concrete. Before the wrestling could begin on 29 July, an army of builders worked night and day to remove the remains of an ice rink and install a new wooden floor donated by Finland. The 8,000 seats afforded a clear view of the entire arena to every spectator, but only about 300 people turned up to watch the twenty-seven nations compete. Maybe some had gone by mistake to the Olympia Hall across the street. According to the London *Evening News*, there they would have found 'Both quiet and beauty, recaptured in the Olympia Flower Show. All the colours of an artist's palette and the delicate perfumes of nearly a thousand English gardens.'

Each morning for six days, the 220 wrestlers were ready for their weigh-in by 7 a.m. 'Absolutely no allowance over the correct weight is tolerated,' wrote the wrestling coach George Mackenzie. 'It is quite common to see a huge light-heavyweight man weighing about 13 stone 9 pounds remove his wrist watch to enable him to pass the scales. I once saw a man have his hair and nails trimmed to make the proper weight.' After the weigh-in they were allowed a cooked breakfast.

There were fifteen different sets of wrestling medals to be won, ranging from the 'Greco-Roman flyweight' for men weighing up to 52kg, to the 'heavyweight' at over 87kg. Three bouts took place at once in the arena, on canvas mats lent by the Swedes. Wrestlers flew through the air and writhed in a tangle. At times the judge was down on his hands and knees to check on a hold. In a quarter of all the matches, the judges were unable to agree, and some observers felt that the Turkish spectators had an undue influence on their

286

decisions by roaring their feelings.

Seven of the sixteen British wrestlers came from the Ashdoan Athletic Club in Islington, where George Mackenzie was their trainer. He had fought in five earlier Olympics. In June, the Health and Strength League had invited the British wrestling team to attend a week's training at the Sunshine Holiday Camp on Hayling Island on the south coast. The Greco-Roman wrestler Leonard Pidduck, a French-polisher from London, aged twenty-one, entertained the campers by fighting practice bouts with the handsome Johnny Sullivan. The team also agreed to judge the camp's Mr and Miss Sunshine competition, though sadly the sun shone very little that week.

'To be a good wrestler you have to have a thick neck,' said Kenneth Richmond, a British whaleship crewman who came fifth in the light-heavyweight class. He went on to appear in the 1950 film *Night and the City* and was also one of three half-naked men who beat the giant gong at the start of films produced by J. Arthur Rank. Richmond enjoyed a long active life, winning competitions in roller-skating and windsurfing in his sixties. On his death bed in 2006 he revealed that the gong had been made of papier-mâché. 'Hitting a real gong that size would have deafened me,' he said.

One third of the Turkish team were wrestlers and they put up a strong challenge in both Freestyle and Greco-Roman wrestling, winning six gold and four silvers. 'Strong as a Turk is an almost proverbial expression and the Turkish wrestlers proved themselves worthy of the saying,' wrote George Mackenzie. 'Not only were they strong but their technique showed the advantage taken of the skilled instructors during the preceding two or three years. The condition of the men was magnificent.'

Iranians included Abbas Zandi, a 17-year-old schoolboy and the youngest member of the team.

My father was a businessman and my mother a housewife. I grew up in a very sport-liking family and my uncle was a very well-known wrestler. The parliament did not approve a government budget to finance the Olympic delegation, so the Shah of Iran personally paid all our expenses. My coach was Hassan Sadian, aged twenty-three, and he was in the Iranian Olympic wrestling team too. I competed eight times in welterweight freestyle, against four wrestlers.

Zandi beat Estrada Ojeda of Mexico, drew with Jean Leclere of France and was beaten by Yashar Dogu of Turkey, who won the gold medal.

It was my first trip to a foreign country and was wonderful. For one day we stayed with Indians and Pakistanis. On that single day we did not have good food. Then we stayed in a school where the food was good. We attended two receptions, the one hosted by the Iranian Ambassador and another by the Mayor of Acton. It remained my best memory of my life and travels.

On his return home, Zandi was a local hero. 'We were very welcomed by the people and the Mayor of Tehran gave a reception in the City Hall with many officials participating. I became popular and other students paid a lot of attention to me. It had a positive effect on my future life, marriage and job.' In 1954 Zandi was the first Iranian to win the World Wrestling Championship, after which he became a full Colonel and a military judge.

New Zealand had hoped to be represented in wrestling by their national champion Charlie 'Cooga' Adams. But after he was caught riding his cycle on a public footpath and fined five shillings, the New Zealand Olympic Committee decided that this made him a convicted criminal and he was dropped from the team.

Friday 6 August turned out to be the most successful day in Swedish Olympic history. It began with gold and silver medals in the 1,500 metres and then eight Greco-Roman wrestling finals produced five gold and two silver medals. Despite bleeding from a wound on his forehead, Gösta Andersson defeated his Hungarian opponent in the welterweight class, and following the middleweight final, Axel Grönberg was so exhausted—after beating Taifur from Turkey and winning gold—that he had to be carried off on a stretcher.

*   *   *

Weightlifting took over from wrestling in the Empress Hall on Monday 9 August. There were six classes—bantam, feather, light, middle, light-heavy and heavyweight—and it was the most international competition that the sport had yet held. In Britain, weightlifting was a working-class pursuit that attracted very little financial support. The Olympic team included a docker, a miner, a physical training instructor, an engine driver, a bricklayer and a butcher.

Training conditions were very poor for weightlifters. 'There was no money in weightlifting, it didn't even attract gamblers,' remembered David Webster, the Chair of Commonwealth Weightlifting for Scotland:

> Many trained on the communal landings of tenement blocks. It was the only place where there was room in the winter. Cellars were popular too—they were cheap, and they had solid floors but there was no ventilation and they had very low ceilings. Very few people had showers to clean up after, but there was usually a cold tap with a hose attached outside. No one had an easy time. We had to really want to do it because there were no rewards or prestige. Most of us had had tough lives, but wanted to improve them. There was a great camaraderie, with no class pretensions, or colour prejudice.

Ron Eland, a 25-year-old school teacher from South Africa, was based in England and had hoped to represent his home country. However, the new apartheid laws meant that only white South Africans could represent their country. Instead, he won his way through to British selection, a significant victory for black people. A few had paved the way for him. 'When Dick Turpin became the British middleweight boxing champion in March 1948,' noted John Macadam, 'he became the first coloured man to be permitted to fight for a British title. The idea of a colour bar has always been distasteful to most British sportsmen and this decision by the boxing authorities removed at least one blot on the face of British sport.'

'The recent spurt for our athletes of additional food in the training camps has come too late to be of practical value, but it will save us, we hope, from complete ignominy,' reported *Health and Strength*, the journal for weightlifters, wrestlers and bodybuilders. 'Informed critics declare in moments of optimism that we may even take a gold medal or two.'

Bob Woolger, a retired weightlifter, ran the Sunshine Holiday Camp on Hayling Island and had been promised work as an announcer at the Olympic weightlifting contest. The weightlifting team followed the wrestlers for a week's training there. They were a great draw for the other holidaymakers, all of whom that week were also bodybuilders and members of the Health and Strength League.

'Every workout was carried out with a snap and a sparkle that was a pleasure to see,' wrote Oscar State, secretary of the British Weightlifters Association, in *Health and Strength*:

There arose the team spirit that I was so anxious to create; moreover it came spontaneously without any urging. All the boys were backing one another the whole time, coaching and criticising in a grand, all-out effort to improve the standards of the whole team. Every one of them returned to London refreshed and invigorated and feeling they had a good solid foundation on which to continue. The special demonstration by Jim Halliday was rapturously received by the scores of weightlifting fans who attended the camp. Jim snatched 250½ pounds for a new quadruple British record at middleweight, another step nearer the world record. Special shows were reduced to a minimum which gave the men and their families time to enjoy something of a holiday. Maung Chaw Yin, Burma's lightweight lifter, and three other Indian weightlifters were also at the camp.

Most of the British weightlifters were trained by Bill 'Dad' Pullum. As a child he had suffered from tuberculosis of the bones and lungs and at seventeen he had decided to overcome his feeble state with disciplined exercise. He was so successful that a year later he was employed by the Slade brothers, three strongmen in a music hall act. He went on to become 'The Wizard of Weightlifting', and in four years he won fifteen British amateur championships and competitions and broke 192 world and British weightlifting records. He was now working as a picture framer and had turned part of his workshop at Camberwell in south London into a training room where, as well as the British, he also welcomed the teams from Australia, South Africa and New Zealand. Following the Olympics, he wrote:

You have to be a psychologist for my work. You aren't dealing only with muscles but with the power that *drives* those muscles. Each man is an individual problem. You plumb his capacity and estimate his temperament just as a producer does with actors or a trainer with racehorses. All of them have to learn self control, some must be stimulated, others restrained. Those who are too heavy must lose weight without reducing their strength in the process. Just imagine it for yourself. There on the ground lies a barbell weighing 240 pounds. Yet in less than a second, that dead weight has to be raised above a man's head. The secret is to exploit human emotion.

The competition featured thirty nations, which could enter up to two men at each weight. Each man had three attempts at three different types of lift—the Press, the Snatch and the Clean & Jerk. Wally Holland, himself a keen weightlifter, was in the audience at the Empress Hall:

Soon after I was bombed out of London and moved to Oxford I set up in my garage and called it the Warren Weightlifting Club. There were clubs in most cities, but weightlifting in Britain was only a minor sport. Women only came to watch if they were related to a competitor. Diet was difficult, there was never enough food. A weightlifter needs a huge amount. Belts to protect the back muscles and stomach muscles were not worn either. Drugs weren't used, but many of the men still smoked—it wasn't up to their coaches to stop them. But getting to bed early *was* something they always insisted on.

Holland went on: 'When we saw the Americans

we could see they meant business. They thought they knew everything. Bob Hoffman owned the York Barbell Club in Pennsylvania and brought over his best men.' The heavyweight John Davis proved to be a phenomenon; the first African-American to become a weightlifter, he was dubbed 'the strongest man in the world' when he lifted more than four times his own weight.

Weightlifting could lead to fame: the light-heavyweight Harold Sakata from Hawaii won silver at London and later moved to Hollywood, where he appeared in over twenty films. His most famous role was that of Odd-Job, the bowler-hatted hit man who fought James Bond in *Goldfinger*.

Another US light-heavyweight called 'Smiling' Stan Stanczyk brought the crowd to its feet when he broke the world record with a seemingly nonchalant lift. But he knew that his rear knee had touched the platform, so lightly that neither of the judges had noticed, and he would not accept his victory. 'The roar that greeted this wonderful sporting gesture was louder than any that he had received for his former success,' wrote Oscar State. Young Whan Lee of Korea also won the hearts of the audience with his good manners. Three times he failed to jerk up 1,245kg and at each attempt he carefully replaced the bar, stood up straight and bowed first to the referee and then to the audience with punctilious courtesy, before trying again.

The appearance of Khadr Sayed El Touni of Egypt in the middleweight class was a surprise. He had won gold in Berlin and was now thirty-three years old. He managed to beat his own world record in the Press, but this was only good enough for fourth place. The bronze was won by Kim Sing-jip for Korea's first Olympic medal, and this left the Americans Pete George and Frank Spellman fighting for the gold. George had already set a new Olympic record for the Jerk, and Spellman too had lifted a record 390kg, the only competitor without a single failure. Oscar State described the final stage:

It was clear that George had decided to go all-out for first place when he demanded 10kg over his own record. We in the audience were silenced by this. The only sound came from Spellman, his team mate and closest competitor, who urged him on. George paced up and down for what felt like hours, getting his nerves up. The atmosphere was getting more and more tense and we sat on the edge of our seats. George continued to stride up and down, rubbing his hands together on the block of chalk. Suddenly he turned, crushed the chalk between his palms and stood staring at the barbell. Thousands of spectators waited in electric anticipation. No-one dared to move. He took one step forward over the bar. You could feel the electricity flashing round the huge Empress Hall. George stooped down and gripped the bar with a fierce determination. He bent his knees and rose the bar up with a great moan. When he got the bar to his shoulders, he was still squatted underneath it. Slowly, carefully, he rose up to standing straight. The spectators roared with him until he was upright. Then there was silence again. Would he be able to get it up above his head in

295

one smooth movement? A quick jerk and it was there. All he had to do was get his legs straight. We all breathed in to applaud. But then his hand slipped, and the great bar crashed down onto the platform. Our applause turned into a groan, which echoed round the Hall. He may have been American, but we all so much wanted him to raise the record even further. Young George gazed sadly down at the weight. He was beaten.

The bantamweight class was new to the Games. 'But the little men soon showed that they were as stylish as the bigger fellows' wrote Oscar State. 'And indeed achieved more world records.' Maurice Crow from New Zealand was a pay clerk at a refrigeration plant, and nicknamed Pom because he was like a tiny Pomeranian dog. 'My mother was short but Dad was part Maori, tall and very strong. We came through the slump years and maybe that didn't help me.' At the age of fifteen he weighed a mere 3 stone 12 pounds and was only four foot tall. 'My elder brothers felt I was too young to die and decided that I needed building up if this was to be avoided. At sixteen I could not even lift a twenty-pound bar over my head but with training I became an excellent tumbler and hand balancer.' From 1943 to 1946 he was stationed in the Pacific with the New Zealand air force and did no weight training at all. During the five-week sea journey from New Zealand to England for the Games, Crow put on so much weight that on arrival he nearly had to compete as a featherweight. Harold Nelson, his captain, wrote in his diary: 'I blamed the manager for this. He did

296

not supervise training at all. The frantic attempt Crow made to bring his weight down at the last minute by starving himself only weakened him.' Crow himself was more sanguine. 'I had no trouble with my weight on the food ration we were getting and generally felt a bit hungry. Anytime I was near Soho, the boxer Freddie Mills gave us free meals in his night-club restaurant.' He also enjoyed an outing to the 'Miss Lyons Corner House' beauty competition, which was judged by Margaret Lockwood.

Maurice Crow was coached by Pullum together with Keith Caples, Australia's bantamweight. 'This entailed a lot of travel and expense,' said Crow. 'Our free travel passes only covered the fortnight of the actual Games. Prior to that, I was travelling across London four days a week, about three hours each way—walking, train, bus and underground, bus and walking, arriving back late in the evening. However, it gave me a chance to view the massive bomb damage in London. We were shown tremendous hospitality, a lot of which we were obliged to decline.' Crow had one special supporter in the audience:

During the war I had flown in the Pacific with an RAF squadron leader, Trevor Gallagher. Based near Oxford, he came to see me compete and one loud voice rang out in the stadium, 'Come on, Taranaki' (my home province). That was great. A couple of days later Mr Oscar State arrived with an Iranian lifter called Mahmoud Namdjou, who would be competing against me. He asked me to take him under my wing. He had been competing in weightlifting competitions all over Europe, hence his early arrival. His English vocabulary was very limited. We called him 'Squeak' as that's what he did when he lifted a weight. I took Mahmoud Namdjou into London one day to his Embassy to get some funds. We were teaching him to tell the time in English. We purchased a dirty great alarm clock which he took everywhere. The best he could do was, 'Half past twenty to four,' for everything. We gave up on him!

We were resting on our bunks one afternoon, doing our best to improve Mahmoud's English, when he leapt into the air shouting, 'Shah Persista,' and pointed out of the window at the parade ground. Sure enough, within a few minutes we were shaking hands with the young Shah of Iran.

Shah Mohammad Reza Pahlavi was a good-looking young man who had been brought up wearing a military uniform and educated in Switzerland. In 1941, the British had helped to depose his father, Reza Shah, suspecting his support for the Germans, and the king had abdicated in favour of his son. The young Shah rode, played tennis and was a good footballer, and he was visiting the Iranian Olympic team which he had financed out of his private fortune. On his arrival at Buckingham Palace he was treated to the first Guard of Honour mounted since the war, and this was followed by a visit to the Royal Tank Museum and an outing to the musical *Annie Get Your Gun*. 'From what we could make out, every top athlete in Iran was under Royal Patronage,' said Crow.

Perhaps more than any other Olympic sport, weightlifting attracted men who had overcome adversity. The bantamweight Abe Greenhalgh of London had spent eleven years of his childhood lying flat on his back with a deformed and twisted spine. But he still came second in the Press, and although he didn't win, he lifted a total of 267.5kg. Height didn't matter either. 'Mighty little' Joe de Pietro from the USA was only four foot eight inches tall. His arms were so short that even by fully extending them he could not lift the bar very high. To ensure that the referee could see a clear gap between head and barbell, he had a crew-cut. In the Two Hands Jerk he lifted 112kg, a new Olympic record and more than double his own weight. De Pietro won the bantamweight gold medal, the smallest ever Olympic champion.

Every Olympic record, including that for sheer bravery, was broken that year in the lightweight class. 'I reckon,' said Maurice Crow, 'that Jim Halliday produced the most remarkable performance of the whole 1948 Olympics.' Halliday, the British weightlifting captain, was incredibly strong, despite past difficulties that would have overwhelmed most people. As a schoolboy he had enjoyed boxing, wrestling and gymnastics, but it was weightlifting that had won him the Lancashire title in 1936. In 1939 he was called up and in 1940 his regiment was involved in the rearguard action to defend Dunkirk. Returning to London after being evacuated from Boulogne, he went straight to Pullum's gym for a bath and shave. In 1941 his regiment was sent to Singapore and when his ship was bombed in harbour, he escaped by jumping on to a ship berthed alongside. In 1942 he was captured by the Japanese and spent the next three and a half years as a prisoner of war, working on the notorious Burma Siam Railway where 15,000 men died of starvation and cholera. Halliday's strength got everyone into trouble on one occasion. A group of prisoners had carved a primitive barbell out of a tree trunk and he was the only one who could lift it. The camp commandant saw him do it and immediately reduced food rations, claiming they were all getting too strong.

When Halliday was released in August 1945, he weighed just 4½ stone (28.5kg). He immediately started weightlifting again and ate whole eggs, shell and all, to build up his calcium and restore his strength. To everyone's amazement, he was soon back in competition. 'I competed in Sheffield with Jim in 1946,' recalled the light-heavyweight lifter Ernie Roe. 'And I remember the state of his skin. Terrible it was.' By 1947 he had won the British lightweight championship. 'Far from being satisfied with this success,' he wrote, 'I *knew* I could do more and was determined to do so.' He shovelled coal all day at Kearsley Power Station and trained at night. 'I could only train at home. Unfortunately the bar was 6 foot 11 inches long and the widest part of the room was 7 foot 1 inch, so there wasn't much space. Unless you had perfect balance, it was very difficult. The bar had to go straight up and straight down. If you dropped it, it wasn't good for the bar, but even worse for the walls.'

'Every so often,' wrote Pullum, 'the crack performer arises who has "everything", not only

300

pronounced physical attributers but mental ones as well. An outstanding and extraordinary ability to stimulate that "super pitch" when circumstances demand. A man who enjoys popularity not merely by reason of being a champion, but also because he possesses an engaging personality. Halliday was such an individual.' Halliday believed in winning, but not at the expense of sportsmanship. In 1950 he wrote:

It has always been the Englishman's boast, almost his privilege, that he is a good loser. He is noted for his hail-fellow-well-met attitude, especially when he has just 'missed the boat'. We *apologise* for beating a foreign rival. Yes, it is just as easy—and in equally good taste—to be a *good sportsman, and win!*

On the morning of the Olympics I was filled with eagerness to be in action against the pick of the world's best! It was the fulfilment of my desire to be taking part in the most wonderful of all sporting events. After the trial weigh-in, I was resting in an endeavour to curb my impatience and quiet my fears and worries. I was anxious to enter the arena in the most suitable mental state possible.

I now stood on the stage with eighteen other athletes, and it is remarkable how calm and matter-of-fact I felt. I knew that each of these men was as determined as myself; that all had trained just as hard as I had, and that the slightest mistake on my part would be taken advantage of by them. Yet, here we were, talking, joking as if it were a cinema queue instead of the preliminary to a struggle long-awaited, long prepared for, and staged to decide both individual and national strength supremacy.

The fight for the lightweight bronze medal was between Halliday and an American, John Terpak. 'Who can realise my disappointment at only making one Press?' Halliday wrote. 'Or my anguish when my second Snatch was ruled out? Only I knew the inward determination with which I made my third Snatch and how I was all keyed-up inside for the final Jerk that gave me third place.' Having started from sixteenth place, Halliday won bronze with his very last lift and leapt high over the bell, earning himself the nickname 'Jumping Jim Halliday'. He went on to become British and Commonwealth lightweight champion and broke four weightlifting records. With the help of 'Dad' Pullum, he wrote a best-selling book called *Olympic Weight-lifting and Body-building For All*, which inspired a whole generation of young men. 'I look at my trophies and realise that I do not regret a second of my life' he wrote. 'Maybe I could have used up the time in a more lucrative sphere. I only know that if I had the option of reliving my life again, I should say: "Bring on the barbell." '

Two Egyptians, Attia Hamouda and Ibrahim Shams, competed for the lightweight gold and silver medals. Oscar State wrote:

Hamouda equalled the previous record in faultless style. Shams was left with one attempt in hand in order to win. The big arena was deadly quiet as Shams approached the barbell.

302

He crouched over it in his own peculiar style and summoned his nerves for the great effort. Suddenly he turned away and a great sigh came from the pent-up spectators. He turned back and again crouched to lift. He stopped and then as soon as he grasped the bar, he dropped it again and once more drew back. For a third time he concentrated, then swooped on the bar and with a terrific effort pulled it to his shoulders; another fierce movement from this tigerish lifter and there was the weight triumphantly over-head. It was a superb effort and deservedly earned him the premier position. Both he and Hamouda set up the same record total, 360kg, but Shams took gold as he was the lighter man.

The Games acted as a stimulus to the weightlifting fraternity. As soon as they were over, the inaugural British Empire Weightlifting Championships took place, joining forces at the Scala Theatre in London with the second ever 'Mr Universe' contest. The contestants included 'Mr Burma', 'Mr Middle East' and 'Mr Persia', who was none other than Mahmoud Namdjou, who had come fourth in the bantam class. There was no colour bar and Ron Eland competed as 'Mr South Africa', though 'Mr America' won. The New Zealander Maurice Crow broke the Australasian lifting record. 'I was placed second in my weight to a French Canadian,' he remembered. 'We were short of money and tried to sell my silver medal for funds but I was only offered ten shillings, so I kept it.'

Over at the Empire Pool, the swimming and diving contest had come to an end on the evening of Saturday 7 August. Within an hour, builders had moved in to prepare the arena for the boxing events. They had less than two days to construct a bridge over the water on which to mount the ring. Steel girders were required for the task and a Control of Iron and Steel Order had to be obtained from the Board of Trade. Only one manufacturer was found—in Sheffield—who had the twenty-five joists in stock. But the company would only part with them once it had been agreed that the joists, weighing a ton each, would be delivered to Wembley at a cost of £20 7s 6d, and sold back to Sheffield two weeks later for £14 10s.

Boxing proved to be as popular with the public as swimming, and tickets for the 230 fights were sold out a month before the Games began. The visible presence of water beneath the ring added a strange lustre to the scene. 'In the evening the bright lights and many coloured flags presented a kaleidoscopic reflection in the water around the ring, and without doubt enhanced the splendour of the scene,' wrote Sir Eugen Millington-Drake of the Organising Committee.

Despite the splendid scene, the boxing competition, in contrast to the weightlifting, was a fractious affair. 'The South African fans threatened to push the officials into the water underneath them,' wrote Denzil Batchelor. 'One young lightweight was so enraged at the judges' decision that he took off his gloves and hurled them at the referee. Several others burst into tears.' There were so many entries that there had been a serious problem finding enough qualified judges and referees. Visiting judges were closely observed by the Jury of Appeal and, as the Games progressed, the better ones were identified to preside over the semi-finals and final.

Even so, there were difficulties. 'Many of the participating countries took few precautions in the choosing of the boxing judges,' wrote George Whiting in *World Sports*. 'Their standards at home must be ludicrously low.' Understandably this led to outbreaks of anger that tested the Games' reputation for sportsmanship. *The Times* reported:

The boxing provided a partial exception to the blessed rule of good temper and good sense. There was the rather absurd scene in which the supporters of one country insisted on carrying their men round and round the arena in protest against an adverse decision. There was the resignation of the judges from another. Some hold that the Games would be the friendlier and more tranquil if there were no boxing. But boxing is a fine, manly sport and today a universal one, and the storms never raged far outside the tea cup.

The Times also reported problems over language:

In all sports the problem of referees and judges is troublesome because of the same difficulties that beset the builders of the Tower of Babel. When the referee's knowledge of either tongue is, as it sometimes appeared, extremely rudimentary, so that he must take refuge in pointings and gesticulations, life is not easy and understanding incomplete. Still it would be a mistake to exaggerate this eternal difficulty. It produced, for the most part, only smiles and the shrugging of shoulders.

'One Argie boxer got over-excited and assaulted a Wembley photographer for trying to take a photo from the wrong angle,' wrote Denzil Batchelor. 'The Argentineans plastered each other in kisses in a way never seen before in Britain. They exchanged more kisses than were ever crammed into the most sumptuous Hollywood musical epic.'

The flyweight gold medal was won by Pascual Pérez of Argentina, who stood 4 foot 11 inches tall. 'Argentina's new Olympic champion Pérez,' wrote Whiting in *World Sports*, 'a 22-year-old clerk in the Chamber of Deputies in Buenos Aires, had his anxious moments in the final against the 23-year-old Italian Spartaco Bandinelli. But his boxing was a model of how a right-foot-forward boxer may be kidded onto a right-hand punch.' Pérez went on to defend the world flyweight championship nine times.

The British flyweight entry was Henry Carpenter, not to be confused with the famous BBC boxing commentator of that surname, who was serving in the Navy at the time. 'At 22 Carpenter is much more capable of absorbing a punch than some of the youths of 18 or so,' wrote Whiting, this time in *Health and Strength*. 'Blessed with a natural left hand, he has shown a tendency to sling his right instead of directing it.' Carpenter was a maker of ivory-backed hairbrushes in

Peckham, and a champion of the New Bradfield Club. With only six defeats in forty previous bouts, he was thought to stand a good chance, but went out on points after three rounds. 'The neatness and crisp punching of Su Ann Han, a bonny little boxer from Korea, was considered the best in the flyweight division,' wrote Denzil Batchelor. 'But he was a victim of some strange judging. Maybe the RAF Band had bribed the judges. They had been given the sheet music for 57 of the national anthems, but the only musicians in Britain reputed to know the Korean one had failed to turn up. The band lapsed into *God Save the King* after a few bars of promising weirdness.'

At the weigh-in for the bantamweight class, Arnoldo Pares of Argentina found he was just a little too heavy to qualify, so he shaved his head, scrubbed his feet and even cried hot tears in a desperate bid to lose the necessary grams. He was still over until it occurred to somebody to check the scales, which were found to be faulty. Pares then beat Victor Toweel of South Africa but went out in the following round. He was joined by Aghassi of Iran, for whom the bright lights of London proved an attraction. 'One night Aghassi did not come to the camp and was reprimanded by the *chef de mission*,' said Mahmoud Namdjou, the weightlifter. 'He only had one fight, against Vicente Demenech of Spain, which he lost and so was eliminated. Aghassi later moved to Chicago to work as a waiter. You may have heard of his son Andre, who is now a tennis player.'

The British featherweight star was Peter Brander, aged twenty-one, an electrical engineer from Southampton. Encouraged by three elder

307

brothers who were all boxers, he took up the sport at fourteen and won the Amateur Boxing Association junior championship, thrilling a packed Albert Hall with his sparkling performance and fast footwork. 'I think we can call Brander the fastest amateur boxer in the country,' wrote George Whiting. 'And if his right hand is in punching order, the featherweights of the world can look out for trouble.'

'Once I was picked, I trained six days a week,' remembered Brander. 'We didn't do any sparring in case of injury. We didn't like wearing headgear.' Unfortunately, he was picked to fight in the first round against the Italian Ernesto Formenti and was knocked out. Formenti went on to win gold.

Bob Gosling, who had been the New Zealand bantam hope, found that he had put on so much weight on the boat journey that he was now a featherweight. 'He found training conditions extremely frustrating on the way over,' said his compatriot Maurice Crow. 'There was no one to even talk boxing with, let alone spar. Finally, Dutch Holland, our hurdler, gamely donned a pair of gloves and did his best to keep Gosling busy.' Arriving in London, Gosling was taken under the wing of the world light-heavyweight boxing champion Freddie Mills, who not only introduced him to Joe Bloom's gym but also invited the New Zealand team to eat at his restaurant in Soho. 'Our first meal there was a steak,' said Crow. 'But we had a shock when we ate it: it tasted like turpentine! We all emptied out in the toilet and were told it was whale steak. From then on we settled for fish.' At the Empire Pool, Gosling found himself on the receiving end of a battering from a talented American called Edward Johnson, but he won credit for the plucky way he stayed with it until the contest was stopped in the third round. Johnson's second bout ended in sensational fashion when he was declared the winner over his 33-year-old opponent Basilio Alvez of Uruguay. Alvez's supporters were incensed at the decision. They booed and stormed the jury table and hoisted Alvez high on their shoulders in a victory parade. The jury was unmoved, and the Uruguayan referee who had joined in the protest was banned from further officiating. Johnson was subsequently beaten in the quarter-final by the South African, Dennis Shepherd.

'These young lads conducted themselves like good sportsmen in conditions that would have shattered men of lesser calibre,' wrote George Whiting in *World Sports*. 'They also showed amazing pluck. In few other fields of endeavour do they breed the spirit exemplified by Dennis Shepherd, the South African featherweight.' Shepherd sustained a cut eye in his first match and during five tough bouts it had to be restitched several times. None of the boxers wore headgear but four doctors were in constant attendance. The Olympic organisers had also arranged for two beds to be set aside at the Atkinson-Morley Hospital in Wimbledon. 'These are for psychiatric disturbances resulting from head injury,' wrote Professor Alexander Kennedy. 'It is of course understood that if a competitor became dangerously insane then he could not be accommodated at this most respectable hospital.' After Shepherd won his semi-final, his opponent, the Argentinean Francisco Nunez, refused to leave the ring and his fans once more stormed the jury's table, again to no avail. Shepherd entered the final with a heavily stitched right eye and, like Brander, was beaten by Ernesto Formenti of Italy.

'Ron Cooper is easily the most distinguished of our lightweights,' reported *Popular Olympics*. 'Strong as a horse and with the heart of a lion, Cooper has his eye set on winning.' Cooper was a nineteen-year-old engineer from West Ham and a distant cousin of Henry Cooper, then only fourteen, but a future heavyweight boxing champion. Ron Cooper had himself left school at fourteen to become an engineering apprentice on the Isle of Dogs. 'One day I was sitting on a wall with my mate outside the works, eating our sandwiches. We looked up, and in broad daylight a Messerschmidt was coming down the Thames. It saw us and started to machine gun us. We dived down behind the wall and then it went for the works and got a direct hit. Anti-aircraft guns got it over the river. We saw it explode and crash into the water. It was a close thing.'

Ron Cooper began boxing as a featherweight at seventeen, and a year later was called up to the Navy. 'Ron descended on us as an unknown sailor in the 1947 Imperial Service Championships,' wrote George Whiting. 'Since when he has cleaned up everything in the way of international honours and the championships of the Royal Navy. A keen student of the finer points of the game, Cooper has the happy knack of learning something from every bout and is now reaching his peak.' He had recently won the Amateur Boxing Association title, and remembered:

As I came out of the ring they said, 'Right, now you're in the Olympics, mate.' I was gobsmacked. I couldn't believe they'd chosen me of all people. My father had just died and I was the youngest of eight and the only breadwinner left at home to support mother. There was no way I could afford to take time off for three weeks of training. But when my boss at the General Iron Foundry heard I'd been selected, he insisted I was given three weeks' pay in advance, so off we all went to Piggott Secondary Modern School in Wargrave, Berkshire, which had been emptied for training us boxers. At nine stone nine pounds, I was six pounds below the limit for lightweights and they said, 'We've got to build him up, he's so thin.' I'd once had steak before, but we weren't given anything like that, not with the food rationing. They gave me plenty of custard and jelly. Luckily I adore custard, but it's not exactly steak and pie, is it?

On the second day of the Games I was sitting there all ready to fight and I asked my trainer, 'When am I on?' He said to me, 'You've already been on. You were knocked out. But you won on points.' I didn't remember a thing about it.

Cooper had won the first round against Holland's Jan Remie but was then beaten on points by Ireland's Michael McCullagh. He watched Gerald Dreyer, a nineteen-year-old clerk from the Transvaal, win the gold medal for South Africa. Standing next to Cooper was a US boxer who said, 'I'll swap your Olympic beret for a pair of nylon stockings.' Cooper recalled: 'I was walking out with Bessie by then and so I accepted the offer with alacrity. After that, whenever anyone asked to see my beret I always said that someone had pinched it.'

'They were good-quality stockings,' his wife Bessie added. 'I wore them for at least a year.'

'Our middleweight is a rosy cheeked sailor from Potters Bar called Johnny Wright,' wrote George Whiting. 'A former Sea Cadet champion, nineteen-year-old Johnny left the welterweight ranks mid-way through the last season and shot immediately to the top via the Navy.' At the Games, Wright performed wonders to beat a Swiss, an Argentinean, a Dutchman and a Canadian, before putting up a great fight with repeated counter-attacks against the murderous left hooks of László Papp of Hungary. A skilful, hard-punching southpaw, Papp won the middle - weight class with several hotly argued decisions. In his exuberance at a Hungarian victory, one of Papp's fans hurled himself fully clothed into the Empire Pool.

The light-heavyweights sustained perhaps the most damage of any of the boxers. Guilberto Maurio Cia of Argentina broke his hand during an early bout but fought on after it had been injected with cocaine. His third opponent, Suares of Uruguay, was disqualified for the poor behaviour of his compatriots. His fourth was the plucky Australian Adrian Holmes, who had knocked out an Egyptian in the third round. Cia knocked Holmes down with his broken hand, in such a way that Holmes fell awkwardly, breaking his ankle and leaving the arena in a wheelchair. Cia won the bronze medal. The silver was won by Donald Scott, a lanky nineteen-year-old military policeman from Derby, whose nose had been broken during training. In the final, he was beaten by George Hunter of South Africa.

'The best boxers won by sheer style,' wrote Denzil Batchelor. 'Hunter relied upon footwork, light as a buoy bobbing on a high tide; on a straight left, like a piston, and on defence, including ducking and side-stepping, and skill at blocking the hooked punch.' Hunter boxed impeccably and in addition to winning the gold medal, he was awarded the Vel Barca trophy for the most stylish display of classical boxing.

Although Britain was the birthplace of boxing, and had strong entries in each of the classes, the team managed only two medallists, both silver— Johnny Wright coming second in the middleweight and Donald Scott in the light-heavyweight. South Africa topped the medal table with five medals, including two golds. For once, the USA won only a silver, at welterweight.

The press described the competition in a positive light. 'The boxing may have been scrappy but at least it was full-blooded and packed with endeavour, with every competitor giving of his utmost according to the style of his nation,' wrote George Whiting. As soon as the competition was completed, the management of the Empire Pool brought in the workmen again, the steel was returned to Sheffield and the Empire Pool reopened shortly afterwards as an ice rink.

19

HENLEY-ON-THAMES

Twenty-five miles west of Wembley, at Henley-on-Thames, the rowing, sculling and canoeing events began on Thursday 5 August. The beautiful weather had broken and a strong head wind blew on the backs of the rowers, accompanied by blustery rainstorms. Though it wasn't as bad as in the north of England, where whole villages were under six foot of water, railway bridges and tracks had been swept away, and mills inundated. Despite this, Richard Burnell, the *Times* rowing correspondent, commented:

> Finally, and perhaps best of all, there was Henley, where the sun played up nobly and gave to the scene all its traditional beauty. And the cheering thing was that it was the charming, domestic Henley as we know it. By some happy knack, the crews and the visitors from abroad had absorbed the family atmosphere that prevails there, so that we saw international sport, sometimes thought to be so dangerous, at its very best and friendliest.

Henley attracted a different class of sportsmen from the wrestlers, boxers and weightlifters. Half the British rowing team belonged to the exclusive Leander Club whose members have to demonstrate 'proficiency in good oarsmanship and good fellowship'. Most of the men had won prestigious events such as the University Boat Race or a race at Henley Royal Regatta and were from Oxford or Cambridge University. Situated on the Berkshire bank of the Thames close to the finish line, the club provided a well-appointed base for the British rowing team. When the Olympic regatta took place here in 1908, Britain was represented by eights from both Cambridge University and Leander Club. The latter won the gold medal by beating Hungary and Canada.

Despite protests from seven of the local parishes, the District Council raised an extra levy from the rates for the entertainment of Olympians. The Mayor of Henley gave a tea party in the town hall, whose exterior was floodlit for the first time since the wartime blackout. He was joined by the mayors from the surrounding towns—High Wycombe, Maidenhead, Reading, Wallingford and Wokingham—to welcome the Olympic oarsmen and canoeists. Extra trains from Paddington were laid on and the riverbanks were packed with men in boaters and blazers, and women dressed in flowery hats and smart summer frocks. Salter's river steamers were chartered to take competitors on river trips and a dance band played in the Market Place. The Henley charities—Freemasons, Oddfellows, Druids, Royal Antediluvian Order of Buffaloes and Nettlebed Farming Club—all laid on hospitality. 'Henley town was decked out with a colourful array of flags and bunting,' remembered Michael Lapage, one of the Olympic team. 'There were maypoles in red and white down both sides of Hart Street and all the foreign crews were accommodated around the town.'

'The Olympic Committee paid for our lodgings

on the Nettlebed Road towards Oxford,' said Robert Collins, another team member. 'We had to take our ration books. Salutation House was run by Miss Gem, the daughter of a bishop and a retired housemistress at Cheltenham Ladies College, and her friend Miss Wiggins. They normally took in children whose parents worked overseas in the colonies. They were sour, tough, old women.'

The marquees and landing stages erected for the annual regatta in July had been left in place on the riverbank and a special grandstand was erected for 4,000 spectators. Twenty-six countries had entered, though only Britain and Argentina took part in all seven of the rowing events. There were 86 crews and altogether 300 oarsmen. The course ran from Temple Island upstream towards the town and ended where the river begins to narrow at Phyllis Court. In order to accommodate three boats abreast, rather than the usual two, the course was 200 metres short of the Olympic norm but it was agreed that rowing against the stream would compensate for the shorter distance.

The British coxless pair, William George Ranald Mundell Laurie and John Hyme Tucker Wilson, had been rowing together since before the war when they were both at Cambridge and won three Varsity Races. But they were now out of practice, having spent the last ten years in the Sudan Political Service, where any rowing was impossible, and Wilson had been injured by a spear. Both aged thirty-three, they were home from the Sudan on leave and thought it would be fun to try for the Olympics. Their rusty form became apparent when they hit both banks of the Thames in the selection race. However, they were chosen and the youthful Robert Collins was full of enthusiasm: 'Ran Laurie and Jack Wilson, known as the "Desert Rats", were streaks ahead of everybody. They were a dead cert for a medal.'

On the night before the first race Laurie was up with a stomach upset, but they still managed to beat the Italians to the semi-final and eventually reached the final. The perfectly matched pair rowed on a wet day with the river flowing hard. Laurie described it as 'A thoroughly satisfactory race. It was the best row we ever had.' The official report had a little more detail: 'Switzerland led, with Italy and Britain racing level. At 1,000 metres Switzerland had an advantage of a third of a length. Then the British pair challenged the leaders and gradually forged ahead of the tiring Italians. Britain won by a bare length from the Swiss.' At last Britain had won a gold medal on home territory.

'Weary shoulders were braced,' wrote Richard Burnell of the victory ceremony:

Tired legs straightened as those lithe figures stood to attention in honour of their country. The poignant simplicity of the brief ceremony was enhanced by the colours which surrounded it. The brilliant green of the grass, the white flag staffs, the blazers of the men and the frocks of the women, the white canvas of the grandstand, and the scarlet, blue, green, yellow and white of the ensigns of the nations, outlined against the green of the hillside, made an unforgettable picture.

Four days later, Laurie's wife gave birth to a daughter and the family then returned to the Sudan. In 1954 Laurie became a doctor in Oxford and five years later his son Hugh was born, growing up to row for the University of Cambridge before becoming a well-known actor.

Robert Collins, at twenty-four, was reading Modern History at Trinity College, Oxford, having fought with the 12th Lancers in Italy and Palestine. He remembered:

I was invited to be in the Oxford Coxed Four at Henley regatta and to my amazement, I caught the eye of an Olympic selector. We were very amateur. There were no indoor rowing machines, only bank-tubbers which are static box boats that we sat in to practise. Although sliding seats had been fitted to shells since the nineteenth century, we trained on fixed seats.

Before the Olympics, we were normally clothed for rowing from the elbows down to the knees, so when we were issued with white singlets with a tiny Union Jack, we felt very naked. It was odd, really, because we were also issued with hand-knitted woollen Olympic scarves. The Olympic tie was unfortunately very short, more like a schoolboy's tie, narrow and unlined. It was black with thin stripes and nobody recognised it as something rather special.

'We had to make our own shorts,' his team mate Tony Butcher added. 'My mother made mine from some terry towelling she got hold of. They were better than most shorts, as they didn't slip. There

318

was a great argument over the caps and berets. We didn't like the caps at all, so we wore the berets.'

'Although popular in the provinces,' wrote the *Times* rowing correspondent, 'coxed fours look strange on the Henley course. This form of rowing presented considerable difficulty to some of the oarsmen who have been trying it out.'

'We only had one month before the Olympics to train properly,' said Collins. 'Then we were interrupted by the Opening Ceremony which thoroughly upset some people because it was a waste of time when we should have been training.'

Collins was joined in the coxed four by Tony Purssell, who had just taken his finals at Oxford. 'We had never rowed together before and I had only rowed in an eight,' Purssell remembered. 'We trained half of each day. I got so very hungry that I went to British Restaurants and ate two separate lunches for a shilling each.' 'British Restaurants' were set up during the war and until the end of food rationing served cheap, nutritional meals provided by local authorities.

'We didn't win our race,' Collins said, 'but it didn't matter. After the Olympics, I went back to Oxford where I rowed a bit and got a third-class degree, for trying. Brains, breeding or brawn were the three reasons to be at Oxford. I suppose I had the latter.'

Tony Butcher, who was in the Cox*less* Four, was twenty-two and a medical student at Guy's Hospital, London. He recalled:

They reckoned the coxless four was the best bet for a British medal. We trained all through the winter and spring of 1948 but once we had won all the races at Henley regatta I think we lost our spark for the Olympics. A lot of people felt that their performances were affected by the Opening Ceremony, with all that sitting around in the hot sun. We had a coach, but he didn't really know what to do. He believed that too much training could make you go stale. Two days before the race we all got gastroenteritis and he prescribed champagne, sulphonamide—an antibiotic— and port. We felt much better, but it didn't cure us. We only made it to the semi-finals.

The Eights had last been won by a British crew at Stockholm in 1912, though it had been something of a foregone conclusion given that 'Britain (Leander Club)' was racing against 'Britain (New College, Oxford)'. Ever since then the event had belonged to the USA. In selecting the British crew, the historic rivalry between Oxford and Cambridge was further complicated by a split within Cambridge. Michael Lapage explained:

The stroke Chris Barton was asked by the Olympic Committee to form a crew. He began by selecting those who followed his own style of rowing. But it was not a smooth-running boat and eventually several of us formed our own crew. Both our boat and Chris Barton's were beaten at the Henley regatta, so the best of the two combined to make up the Olympic Eight. The Americans and the Italians were favourites. Though one angry Italian, when reprimanded, jumped out of the boat and went

320

home along the towpath! Argentina also had a fast crew, when they were not arguing with their coach. By the semi-final the weather had turned wet and windy and we had a shaky start, but we won by over a length, which put us in the final with Norway and the Americans.

On the third day of rowing, weather conditions were at their worst, and spectators sheltered from the hard rain underneath their folded deckchairs. But on the Monday, the afternoon of the finals, the sun came out, with a wind blowing across the river. 'It was a tough race,' said Lapage. 'We started in the lead, but then the US drew level.'
'The machine-like precision and superior strength of the United States gradually wore down the young British crew of undergraduates,' reported *The Times*. 'The Americans were rhythmic and powerful, and won handsomely.' Sigfrid Edström presented silver medals to Lapage and his colleagues as they drew breath in their boat. The winning Eight, from California, stood on the jetty in their socks before picking up Ralph Purchase, their cox, and hurling him into the river.

*　　　*　　　*

While a rower handles one oar, a sculler has two. Britain had some good single scullers, but none with a chance of beating Jack Kelly of the USA, brother of the film star Grace. Their father had won gold medals in 1920 for single and double sculls and Jack had won the diamond sculls at Henley in 1947. Equally fast was an Australian policeman called Mervyn Wood, who was so handsome that he was known as the Cary Grant of Scullers. The British decided that their best chance of a medal was to put two of their best together in a double boat.

Richard Burnell's father had rowed in the 1908 Olympics and Burnell himself had been a keen rower while at Oxford before the war. 'A good rower needs the normal three years at university followed by a further three in which to develop a strong style,' he wrote in 1952. 'During the war there was no chance of this and the general standard fell considerably.' He was pleasantly surprised to find that the enforced absence had done his own style little harm. Burnell had ended the war in Germany, where he had rowed for the Hamburg Club. Despite heavy war damage in the city, the club and its boats had survived intact and regattas were held at weekends. 'I had visited this club in 1937 as a member of an Oxford rowing eight, and it was odd to find myself back there as a member of the Occupying Forces.' Burnell had come out of the Army in 1946 and a year later had decided to compete in the Olympic single sculls. 'But to do this, I needed two afternoons a week training from October to March and three months training at Henley. This was not going to be easy. In addition, the only decent coach, Eric Phelps, was in South America.' Burnell, by now rowing correspondent for *The Times*, had reached the age of thirty and he knew that these Games would be his last chance:

If I was to double up for sculls, it would have to be with someone younger than myself, someone who might benefit from my strength and experience, and in return contribute youthful exuberance and zest. The problem which ultimately presented itself was how to find two people who could scull fairly well together, who lived within reach of the same bit of the river, who could get off work at the same time, and finally who could bear the sight of each other's faces for ten months.

Burnell tried various partners but none suited his style until he met Bert Bushnell. The result was a pairing of starkly contrasted social backgrounds. Bushnell was a local lad, then aged twenty-six. 'I was brought up on the river. My family made boats at Wargrave for the Royal Navy, mainly assault landing-craft. My hobby was single sculling and my father bought me a sculling boat. It cost £40. I had one pair of sculls and I looked after them very carefully.' In 1928 one Harry Pearce had been refused permission to scull at Henley because he was a carpenter. Bushnell's father realised that his son had talent and in order to ensure that he did not lose amateur status, Bert was apprenticed as a marine engineer at Thorneycrofts in Southampton when he left school at fourteen. 'We worked a 52-hour week for £3.50. Thorneycrofts made destroyers and tank equipment. As an engine tester for torpedo boats, mine was a reserved occupation during the war. The boats were built in Hampton-on-Thames and then delivered to Woolwich. We had to navigate them round to Portsmouth where we ran trials before they were handed over to the Royal Navy.'
Burnell and Bushnell started training together three weeks before the Olympics. Both were

already tired after competing separately in the Henley regatta. 'We were an odd couple, all right,' recalled Bushnell:

Dickie Burnell was a rowing blue blood, 6 foot 4½ inches, 14½ stone, moulded at Eton and Oxford and decorated for valour as an army captain. I was just 5 foot 9 inches tall, 10½ stone, a local grammar school boy who felt he'd missed out on the war building boat engines. Dicky thought he was the tops and I thought I was. There was class tension there, and it came from me being bloody awkward.

Burnell was more sanguine about their partnership. He wrote in 1952:

Our respective weak points seemed to cancel themselves out, and our strong points were complementary. Bushnell was inclined to over-reach. I was on the short side in my forward swing and the result was we reached naturally to about the same place. Our sculling was soon the most enjoyable I had ever experienced. Bushnell's liveliness enabled me to get going fast and settle into a comfortable gait, while my weight helped us to keep it going. It was remarkable for Bushnell to fit in so quickly with the vagaries of a stroke behind whom he had never sculled before.

They met obstacles in training, including cross winds, rough water, the wake from steamers and launches, fevers, strained muscles, and, in the final week, a heatwave. 'There wasn't much to eat either, what with rationing,' Bushnell said. 'But Jack Kelly had his food flown in from America and Merve Wood got boxes of food from Australia House. I'd invite them to supper, and they'd bring the steaks!' He went on:

We only had a month, so I went training barmy. I lived in Wargrave with my parents and I didn't see my girl, Margaret, for six weeks. I stopped work and we sculled three times a day. We had no machines, we had to be on the water doing it. Before Dickie arrived from London, I'd run up White Hill, three miles up and three miles down. I used to needle him. If he'd say before training, 'We'll row 500 metres today,' I'd say, 'That's no bloody good, let's make it 750.' Though we were so different, we finished up with great respect for each other.

Burnell and Bushnell made it to the finals of the double sculls against Uruguay and Denmark. It was to be the last race of the competition. 'I went for a lie down back in Wargrave,' Bushnell recalled. 'But when I got back to the Leander Club, they wouldn't let me in to park. They said it was full. You see I wasn't a member—not posh enough.'

Bertie Bushnell turned out for the final with a knotted hankie on his head. 'The Olympics didn't feel a big deal. It was like Henley regatta with a few more foreigners thrown in. The fastest crew were the Danes, whom we hadn't met 'til the final.' He rowed at bow and the taller Dickie Burnell at stroke. Enthusiastic crowds lined the towpath and cheered them loudly as they paddled up to the starting line.

'At last,' Burnell wrote, 'we got the *Êtes-vous prêts? . . . Partez*, and the waiting was over. We went out like a shot from a gun and I didn't allow myself to glance out of the boat until a minute was gone.'

'There was very little in it,' said Bushnell. 'We all went off at forty strokes a minute, then slowed down to thirty-eight. After three minutes we were dead level and we decided we'd whack in some extra strokes. Dickie and I sculled for our lives. We pinched two lengths in that extra minute and the Uruguayans were left five lengths back.' It was all over in under seven minutes. Britain had won their second gold medal, by four seconds. Bushnell remembered:

I was rowed out and just plunged my feet in the water. Then we sculled the boat to where the bigwigs were congregated. I could hardly get out of the water, let alone stand to attention. The band played four bars of *God Save the King*. We just stood on the landing stage in our socks, there were no little blocks to stand on. Then we got back in the boat and sculled it to the Leander Club. We lifted it out of the water, pushed all those boys wanting autographs out of the way and sat in the shower. Then we went home. All my friends were stuck somewhere in the crowd. There was no fuss and my life wasn't changed. I went back to work as a marine engineer on the Monday. I didn't get paid to have days off and my employers considered I was a bloody nuisance. They didn't want to take any credit for it.

Six weeks later I got married to my girl,

326

Margaret. We went to Bournemouth for our honeymoon.

Bert Bushnell retired from sculling in 1951 and built up a successful cruiser hire business in Maidenhead. Richard Burnell believed it would have been vulgar to emphasise their triumph and simply noted in his article in *The Times* that 'In the double sculls, Bushnell and myself won safely from Parsner and Larsen (Denmark) with Uruguay third.' He remained the *Times* rowing correspondent for forty-four years.

*   *   *

Although the canoe is one of the very oldest forms of navigation, canoeing was only accepted as an Olympic sport in 1936, having previously been rejected as 'too young a sport', or 'not competitive'. Canada, the USA and fourteen European countries competed in seven classes for Canadian canoe and Kayak in conditions of heavy rain and strong currents. Women were still not permitted to row or scull. But women in Scandinavia were serious kayak racers, and Denmark led the call for their inclusion. For the first time in Olympic history, women were allowed to compete in canoeing and were allotted their own Single Kayak event. 'This one race proved fully justified, for ten nations sent entries and a very high standard was achieved,' conceded John Dudderidge of the British Canoe Union.

Frantisek Capek, a 33-year-old bank clerk from Czechoslovakia, arrived with a canoe he had designed and built himself. It was crooked like a

327

Venetian gondola, with a curved keel that made paddling only necessary on one side, thus maximising the strength and speed of his strokes. Although there were complaints, it was found not to violate the rule that said a Canadian canoe should have no rudder, and he won gold in the 10,000 metres Canadian Singles. However, the International Canoe Federation then banned the design from future competitions.

*   *   *

Britain won two gold medals and one silver at Henley-on-Thames, its highest achievement for any sport at those Olympics. 'When it was all over, we had a celebration dinner in a marquee in the Stewards' Enclosure,' said Tony Butcher. 'Nobody had had any alcohol for nine months, so everyone went berserk.' The British umpire Gully Nickalls had planned to make a speech in French, the language of rowing, but suddenly chaos took over. 'It was bloody awful food,' said Bert Bushnell. 'Then the Americans said, "These bread rolls are rubbish," and started hurling them around. It ended up with a first-class fight between the Americans, Argentineans, Canadians and everyone else. I was having a civil chat with one of them one minute and a punch-up with him the next. It was all taken in good part, though; it was called "letting your hair down".'

The press were busy downing pints in Henley's pubs that night. Much to the relief of the rowers, news of the fight never leaked out.

20

ARMED COMBAT

The first recorded international fencing match took place in 1190 BC in Luxor between swordsmen from Syria, Sudan and Egypt. In mediaeval and renaissance Europe, duels were fought over matters of honour, using weapons of increasing strength and finesse. Duelling was outlawed in Britain in 1819 and at the end of the nineteenth century the British army introduced fencing to their gymnastic training and the first rules of the modern sport were drafted. Fencing began as an upper-class sport, and members of the London Fencing Club held either army commissions or 'a recognised position in society': the banker Evelyn Baring, the actor Henry Irving, the composer Arthur Sullivan and the politicians Winston Churchill and Oswald Mosley were all past members. Many fencing instructors were killed in the First World War and the sport went into further decline during the Second, especially after the Belgian president of the Fédération Internationale d'Escrime was imprisoned by the Germans.

Despite this, the 1948 Olympiad saw the greatest number of countries entering the fencing events, in a competition lasting the full two weeks of the Games. The venue was the cavernous Palace of Engineering, part of the original 1924 exhibition site at Wembley. It was hung with the flags of the sixteen competing nations and echoed to the clashing steel of attacks and ripostes. 'There were many hard fought and brilliant bouts,' wrote fencer Charles de Beaumont. 'In the heat of battle, the packed rows of spectators sometimes showed displeasure with decisions by whistling, clapping hands and even booing, but they never failed to give the various winners a hearty reception.' For those who sought time out from the excitement, there was a lounge with Utility armchairs, and a canteen serving shepherd's pie and orange squash.

Fencers take many years to develop the required level of co-ordination of mind and body, quick thinking, poise, balance and muscular control. With practice, differences of height, reach, strength and age can be overcome. Most begin as teenagers and usually peak at about thirty, though many champions are much older. The average age of the Hungarian team in 1948 was thirty-five and Archibald Douglas Craig, aged sixty-one, was the oldest athlete in the British team—and the entire Games.

Both men and women competed in the fencing, but whereas the women were restricted to one competition—the individual foils—the men fenced in three classes: foil, épée and sabre, both as individuals and in teams. Most men could handle all three. Since 1904 the foil and épée had been dominated by France and Italy, while the Hungarians excelled at sabre. All fencing rules are still in French. Each bout required four judges— two on either side of the marked-out *piste* as well as one Président du Jury. As the *Daily Courier* noted, 'It is necessary for a judge to possess the eye of a hawk and the agility of a tiger in order to keep the lightning movements of both points well

330

under observation.' Competitors provided their own fencing equipment, which included three or four weapons with replaceable blades, a double-strength white canvas jacket, mask, glove, canvas breeches, stockings and plimsolls.

The foil has a light, flexible blade which evolved from the French court sword of the seventeenth century. The target is the torso between the collar and the hip, and bouts are for the best of nine hits within six minutes. At nineteen, Christian d'Oriola, competing with foils, was the youngest member of the French team, a brilliant fencer, tall and with a very long lunge. In 1947, he had amazed everyone by becoming the world champion and when he reached the semi-final of the individual foil at the London Games, he found himself in the same pool as the reigning French champion. Jehan Buhan, a wine merchant, was almost twice his age at thirty-six. Much to his disappointment, d'Oriola was told not to beat Buhan. 'Your time will come soon enough,' advised his team mates. Buhan duly used his skills to defeat the younger man, and when both men got through to the final Buhan won the gold and d'Oriola the silver.

During the semi-finals of the team foil, Rodriguez of Argentina was duelling with Yves of Belgium when a dispute arose. His team gave three cheers for their opponents and walked off in protest. 'Out went the protesting Argentines,' reported the *Daily Express,* 'after a claim for a hit against Belgium was disallowed. The decision was upheld by the Jury and the Argentina team refused to carry on.' The next day the Argentineans walked out again and Belgium was declared the winner. The Argentinean sports journalist Horacio Estol was once again on hand: 'The performance of the fencing team can only be called modest. Our representatives behaved admirably considering the opponents that they had to face.'

The 'automatic electric recorder' was demonstrated in 1896 but not introduced in épée championships until 1936. In 1948 the épée, which has a rigid blade, was still the only class to use electric scoring. Hits could be made anywhere on the body and a wire ran between the fencer's outfit and a scoring box which lit up to record a hit. The members of the British épée team were getting on in years. Ron Parfitt was the youngest at thirty-five, Bert Pelling was forty-three, Charles de Beaumont was forty-six and Terry Beddard forty-seven. De Beaumont ran an antiques shop in London. He had been épée champion three times before the war and once afterwards and he served on the Olympic jury. They had been training hard for a year and before the Games de Beaumont had recommended a break for three weeks. 'We are all verging on staleness,' he said. They did not make the final, which took nearly six hours and carried on late into the night. The gold was won by Luigi Cantone of Italy. 'The best épéeist of the day,' thought *The Sword* magazine: 'A left hander of medium height, he preserved an orthodox style throughout. He attacked with great speed and assurance mainly by *pris de fer* at the upper arm. Always well-covered, he demonstrated the efficacy of the cardinal rule of épée fencing, "to hit without oneself being hit".'

The British sabre team was knocked out by the USA. This was a disappointment for the British captain Roger Tredgold, who had been sabre champion twice before the war and four times afterwards. At thirty-seven, he had just qualified as an army psychiatrist and was the author of *The Textbook of Mental Deficiency*. 'The final of the sabre between Hungary and Italy,' wrote de Beaumont, 'was a magnificent display of sabre fencing. Aladar Gerevich of Hungary had won the world championship in 1935 and a bronze medal in Berlin. Despite a forceful tournament against his compatriot Kovacs, he won his bout with speed in attack, sureness in defence and choice of time.'

'Gerevich showed a speed even he had not reached before,' reported *The Sword*. 'He gave a dazzling display and his speed of hand and the splendid timing of his attacks beggared description.' Gerevich was a bank clerk who between 1932 and 1960 won seven gold, one silver and two bronze medals in six Olympics.

Inevitably the fencers sustained injuries, reported in the *Herald* under the headline: COUP DE PORRIDGE.

For 11 days with foil, épée and sabre, the best swordsmen of Europe and the Americas have been hot in attack, vicious in riposte. Medical attendants and doctors have been standing by and yesterday for the first time they had a patient. G. de Bourguignon, *beau sabreur* of Belgium, was taken off after a sabre duel, after he had a sharp rap on the chest. A doctor's examination showed there was no wound, and after being sponged down and wrapped in blankets, de Bourguignon felt much better and said: 'I think I have too much breakfast beginning with your porridge.' Back into the fray he went, to win the next fight. The only other casualty was the French swordsman Rommell. He was one of four judges who stand close to the contestants, and he took a loose sabre swipe between wind and water and was forced to retire.

Of the 4,000 active fencers in Britain in 1948, only 100 were women: their participation was somewhat frowned upon by the fraternity, though the 'Ladies London Fencing Club' had been established in 1901. In 1902 a public meeting had been held in Oxford town hall to encourage women to enter the sport; a special train had run from London and, alternating with musical interludes, Miss Esme Beringer, the well-known actress, had given a 'duelling duologue' with Mr Egerton Castle. The early costume for ladies consisted of white jackets and breeches worn under long black skirts. By 1948 the skirts had given way to 'wide breeches closed below the knee', with bare legs, ankle socks, and wire-mesh breast protectors.

Women's fencing had entered the Olympics in Paris in 1924, when Britain won a silver medal. In Los Angeles in 1932, Judy Guinness had demonstrated the British sense of fair play when she sacrificed her gold by acknowledging two hits which had gone unseen by the judges. Individual foil was the only class in which women could compete and they fought for the best of seven hits within five minutes as opposed to the men's nine within six minutes. Women from fifteen nations competed at Wembley and Britain's representatives, Miss Elizabeth Carnegie

Arbuthnott, a clerk at a child welfare clinic in Pimlico; Miss Guiter Minton; and hospital administrator Mary Glen Haig, were all fencing champions.

Glen Haig was thirty, the right age for an experienced fencer to hit top form:

My father, an army officer, fenced in the 1900 Olympics and I joined one of his classes at the age of ten. Before I was allowed to hold a foil I had to get my foot-work right and when I was eventually given one, the professor would conduct controlled bouts. I liked it immensely so I started to compete and gradually moved up to international level. The sport was very amateurish and nothing was laid on for you. When we went to a competition in France, my brother and I had to sit up all night on the ferry, get a train at the other end and then compete after that.

My training was walking round King's College Hospital all day. Any fencing practice had to fit around the men who were also preparing. If the men wanted to fence, all the women had to leave. We had to fight to get our training time in. The night before my event I was working until eight o'clock at the hospital.'

With her steely energy, Glen Haig beat all seven of the other competitors and reached the final. Then she made an unfortunate mistake. 'After the semi-final in the morning, when I had to fight five duels in which I won three, I was sent to lie down for a rest in a garden in Harrow, not far from Wembley,' she said. 'The ladies team manager,

335

Miss Puddlefoot, thought it would be helpful for me to have a rest. It was a lovely sunny day and I lay in a deckchair with my eyes closed. It was actually the worst thing to do—all my adrenalin drained away and when I returned in the afternoon for the final, against seven, I was far too relaxed and only beat one of them.' *The Sword* was sympathetic:

Mary Glen Haig's poor showing was hardly her fault. Of the many British officials present, it should have been someone's job to warn of the enormous nervous strain imposed by an Olympic final and get her mentally attuned. It would also have increased her chances if someone had seen that she did not go to sleep just before the final! As it was, it seemed as if she had never properly woken up, and she never looked like winning against Elek or Lachmann, both of whom she had beaten in previous rounds.

Mrs Ilona Scacherer Elek, aged forty-two, from Hungary, retained the gold medal she had won in Berlin. 'Her forcefulness and energy seem to have increased with the passing years,' wrote de Beaumont in *The Sword*:

Ilona Elek fought throughout the final with the dash and brio which the years have left undimmed. Unorthodox to the point of fantasy, her trump cards are great speed and the remarkable determination to hit her opponents by any method in the shortest possible time. Karen Lachmann of Denmark, the complete and orthodox foilest, was a delight to watch. She overcame the handicap of the severe back injury she sustained earlier this year with great courage but I have seen her fence better.

The staff at the Palace of Engineering had done their bit to lay on a successful competition. 'There was a happy and cheerful relationship established between personnel and all foreign team officials,' reported de Beaumont when the fencing was over. However, he had one grouse. 'Lavatory arrangements were *not* satisfactory. The additional chemical latrines were not emptied often enough. Furthermore, the staff never used the correct Elsan disinfectant and the use of ordinary Jeyes fluid was quite useless.' Two local heroes emerged to overcome these difficulties. 'Despite what might have discouraged the stoutest heart, Mrs Batmen, lady attendant and Sgt. Major Breakwell of the Corps of Commissionaires toiled with vigour and continual cheerfulness. Lavatory cleaning work is not the work of a commissionaire, therefore they deserve all the more credit for stepping in and tackling it for the good of the organisation.' Not one to dwell on such matters, de Beaumont concluded: 'The standard of the finals, except perhaps at sabre, was not quite up to that of fencing in the pre-war years. The extremely keen competition throughout, and the large entry, necessitated fencing for long hours on thirteen days of the meeting, but the outstanding feature was the atmosphere of good fellowship and good sportsmanship.'

The shooting events took place at Bisley Camp, the home of the National Rifle Association. Bisley is in Surrey and Southern Railways reopened a branch line from Waterloo especially for the Games. *The Times* found the location congenial. 'One day we could go to Bisley to watch the most illustrious pistol shots of the world in their almost secret hollow, delved out of sand and heather, a little world apart, quiet, almost intimate, and yet, like all the rest, intensely competitive.'

At the Paris Games in 1900 live pigeons had provided the targets, and duelling pistols were used until 1920. There were four events in 1948, the 300 metre free rifle, the 50 metre small bore rifle, the 50 metre pistol and the 25 metre rapid-fire pistol. Because of the dangers of shooting, spectators were banned and they would have seen little anyway because tarpaulins covered each firing point. Competitors from twenty-six nations assembled, including the entire Olympic teams of Lebanon and Monaco.

The 25 metre rapid-fire pistol featured a competition between Károly Takács of Hungary and the world record holder, Saenz Valiente of Argentina. Each man began with eight seconds in which to fire at five targets, then six seconds and then four. This was repeated four times. In 1938 Takács had been a sergeant in the Hungarian army and one of its finest marksmen, when a grenade had shattered his right hand. 'My right hand was completely destroyed and they gave me an artificial arm,' he said. While recovering in hospital, Takács had decided to teach himself to shoot with his left hand. Within a year he had won the Hungarian pistol shooting championship. Now aged thirty-eight, he had succeeded in qualifying for the Hungarian Olympic team. Valiente was surprised to see him in London and asked why he was there. Takács replied, 'I am here to learn.' He then proceeded to hit all the targets, won the gold and beat the world record. During the medal ceremony, Valiente, who took silver, turned to him and said, 'You have learned enough.' In Helsinki four years later, Takács won the gold again.

*   *   *

Fencing and shooting are two of the five sports in the modern pentathlon. One of the most gruelling of all Olympic events, it involves the longest competition for a single medal, and each of the five sports takes place on a separate day. 'What compels admiration about the pentathlon is that it calls for qualities normally to be found only in the heroes of adventurous romance,' wrote H.F. Ellis in *Punch*. 'To enter for the pentathlon, a man must be proficient at riding a 5,000 metres steeplechase, fencing with sabre, shooting with a pistol, swimming 300 metres and running 4,000 metres across country. To win, it is hardly necessary to add, he must be, on balance, more proficient at all these things than any of his competitors.'

Modern pentathlon had been introduced into the Games in 1912 by Baron de Coubertin, since when Sweden had won the gold medal on all but one occasion. Captain Willy Oscar Guernsey Grut, aged thirty-three, was one of three Swedish competitors in 1948. The Olympics were part of his family history, for his father Torben had been the architect of the Stockholm Olympic stadium in 1912. Willy was so jealous of guarding his health that he would not stand near a smoker, even out of doors. At fourteen he had won the Swedish schoolboys swimming championships and at nineteen had entered the army academy from which he passed out as best officer cadet. In 1936 he swam in the Olympics, and it was in Berlin that he decided to train for the modern pentathlon at the next Games. At the 1948 winter olympics in St Moritz he had won silver in the Winter Pentathlon, which featured fencing, shooting, horse-riding and downhill and cross-country skiing.

In preparing for the Summer Games, Grut's rigorous routine was as follows:

6.30 a.m. Riding
9.15 Work in army office
12.30 Running
1 p.m. Lunch with the Regiment
1.30 Shooting practice
2.15 Back to work
5.15 Fencing
6.30 Home for supper
8.30 Bed.

On Sundays he took his two sons to church and then sailed his dinghy.

The pentathlon events began on Friday 30 July and continued until Wednesday 4 August with cross-country running at Sandhurst, Camberley. Friday was dedicated to riding at Tweseldown, near Aldershot. The Organising Committee had purchased forty horses for use in the contest from the British Army in Germany. There was so little forage there that they arrived in extremely poor condition. For three months they were fed extra rations and then they were schooled at Aldershot by officers from the 7th Dragoon Guards Carabineers. The horses were then allocated to competitors by ballot. In the event, the steeplechase held at Tweseldown racecourse proved so difficult that only ten men completed within the required ten minutes. Grut won in the shortest time, with no faults.

On Saturday, over 300 fencing bouts were fought in the army gym at Aldershot. Most of the pentathlon competitors were soldiers, though Geoffrey Brooke, a lieutenant in the Royal Navy, fought back brilliantly to win his bouts after his nose was cut. Captain Karacson of Hungary had also sustained an injury, breaking his collarbone in the riding event the day before. Despite this, he managed to win no less than twenty-one bouts using his 'wrong' arm, his right arm bound to his side. Grut came first again with twenty-eight straight wins.

In pistol shooting on Monday 2 August at Bisley, Karacson hit nineteen targets, again using his left arm. Grut hit all twenty. On Tuesday in cold rain, Grut again triumphed in the 300 metres freestyle in an outdoor swimming pool belonging to Aldershot Borough Council. On Wednesday, he did less well, coming only eighth in the cross country run. In *Punch*, H.F. Ellis wrote:

Of all the names that have chimed like a bell on our wireless sets these last two weeks, the Zátopeks and the Blankers-Koens, none

341

stands higher than that of Captain Grut. Even the formidable four from Turkey, the mighty wrestlers Ake and Bilge, Stik and Dogu, whose country's national anthem crashed out four times running (in itself an Olympic record) cannot divert my attention for an instant from this astonishing Swedish soldier.

The measure of Captain Grut's achievement is that he emerged with 16 points against the next man's 47. He would be a useful man to have in a tight corner. If I were beset in a castle by armed desperadoes I should pick out Captain Grut without hesitation as the man to send off for help. 'Grut,' I should say, 'I depend on you.' He would then swim the moat with contemptuous ease, pistol his way through the beleaguering lines, and after dispatching some well-aimed thrusts at any hulking fellows ill-advised enough to try to bar his progress, would leap onto a handy horse and ride till the gallant beast dropped dead beneath him. There would be nothing for it but to cover the last 4000 metres to the police station on foot, which he would do in 15 minutes 28.9 seconds.

Grut had achieved the best score in Olympic history. He was awarded his gold medal in front of a large crowd of Swedish supporters at Wembley Stadium. 'They sang their national anthem with pride and sincerity,' *Punch* noted. 'It was the most fascinating auditory sensation of the Olympiad.'

Grut himself was not a man to soak up adulation. 'I shall be glad to be finished with it all,' he said at the time. 'In Sweden, an engineer or an agriculturalist only gets a paragraph in the papers, while a man who kicks a ball gets himself splashed over six columns. I don't approve of that. So many people now want only the gay life. That is why I am retiring. I set out to do a thing and I did it. Now I shall start on a new phase of my life.' This new phase included becoming a colonel in the Swedish army, captain of the Swedish Olympic team until 1960 and the secretary-general of the International Union of modern pentathlon.

21

GYMNASTICS

Gymnastics, now such a popular feature of the Olympics, was still considered an odd hobby sport in 1948, one enjoyed mainly by muscle-bound devotees in cold halls.

The Greek word 'gymnos' from which 'gymnastics' is derived means 'naked' but in 1948 officials were keen to maintain decency and male contestants were warned not 'to reveal their armpits or indicate their masculinity'. Men wore long trousers, singlets and plimsolls and, some - times, spectacles. The gymnasts were strong, agile, highly motivated and perfectionist, and the judges were amazed by the excellent physique on display from countries ravaged by war and famine. The eight men in each national team had to be all-rounders, performing twice on each piece of apparatus—parallel bars, pommel horse, wooden rings (nine feet above the coconut mat), long horse, and floor exercises without music. Rope climbing, club swinging and tumbling, all features of earlier Olympics, had been discontinued. Scores went towards both individual and team medals, and for the first time in the Olympics the judges had to demonstrate impartiality by holding up their score cards simultaneously.

The International Gymnastic Federation insisted that the competition should take place in the open air at Wembley Stadium, even though this meant all the equipment had to be removed by four o'clock in time for the evening football matches. They had clearly forgotten that when twenty-four British gymnasts had carried out 'synchronised drill exercises' at Antwerp in 1920, the heavy rain and extreme cold had led to their withdrawal before they could finish their routine. The three days of gymnastics were programmed for the second week of the Games, by which time the first few days of glorious weather had given way to severe storms. On Sunday 8 August, over an inch of rain fell in less than twenty-four hours. 'They were caught on the hop by the rain,' said George Wheedon, one of the British team. 'The stadium was more or less under water. The officials were all running around like headless chickens.' The equipment had already been set up at Wembley when the decision was taken to dismantle it, postpone the competition by three days, and move to the Empress Hall at Earl's Court where Ted Simmonds, the arena manager, had always wanted to stage the gymnastics. He pointed out: 'Indoors, spectators were able to follow more closely the beautiful work done by the teams, which provided such a feast of poetry in motion that the audience found it difficult to decide what to watch. The chaos that followed the rain storm at Wembley, and the last minute panic as venues were changed, was just one of many burdens which we had to bear.'

There were sixteen men's teams and eleven women's, which meant that many of the events had to take place simultaneously. Some spectators felt cross-eyed trying to watch everything at once. The British competitor Frank Turner was not pleased: 'It was very off-putting having the music from the women's floor exercise playing while you were trying to concentrate on the bar or the rings. There were too many things going on at once.'

For selection to the Olympic team, all the best British gymnasts had been summoned to show off their moves on a Sunday morning in early 1948. 'We had to compete on a stage, with coconut mats to land on,' remembered George Wheedon. 'My club, Regent Street Poly, wasn't interested in competitions. I was allowed to train twice a week, on condition that I did not inconvenience anyone else. There was no heating in the gyms—you just had to warm yourself up with exercise.'

At the outbreak of war, Wheedon had trained as an army PT instructor but in 1942 he had developed tuberculosis, then relatively common and treatable only with surgery. His infected kidney was removed. Then he broke a vertebra, which went undiagnosed and led to osteomyelitis, inflammation of the bone. Determined to overcome these obstacles, he was British gymnastics champion from 1946 to 1948. 'As far as I know, I was the only Olympic competitor with only one kidney,' he said.

'We didn't have machines to get fit, we just did

345

somersaults, hand balancing, that sort of thing. Floor exercises were on a bare wooden floor, with no mats. On a high bar I had a friend to catch me. It could be very frightening, but that fear element pushed you.' At five foot eight inches he was too tall for the parallel bars. 'My feet swept the ground when I swung up and down.' However, his long body helped him to achieve a good swing on the rings. To improve his gymnastic skills, Wheedon also learnt springboard diving, ballroom dancing, ballet, fencing and pole vaulting. 'I was the first gymnast to do the splits in a competition. I could do a one-arm handstand on top of a step ladder.' Tubby Atkins, the London weightlifting champion, helped him at Battersea running track. 'We had to get in what practice we could around our jobs.'

Wheedon was selected for the gymnastics team, together with Frank Turner, aged twenty-six, who was appointed captain. 'As a junior clerk in the Co-operative Bank,' Turner recalled, 'I had to go cap in hand and ask the seniors if they were prepared to move their holidays so that I could have mine in August. Frank Wilson of the *Daily Mirror* heard about this and contacted my boss, saying that if they didn't give me time off, he would write an article about it. I didn't get any extra leave, just my usual holiday.'

Like Wheedon, Turner had not had an easy career. He had first encountered gymnastics at the Broad Street Boys' Club in the East End of London. 'I first competed at ten and came second. My prize was a singlet and a pair of plimsolls. If I'd come first I'd have got a pair of shorts too. I won a scholarship to grammar school but my dad was a motor mechanic and we couldn't afford the

346

uniform.' At thirteen he had competed for Britain against Belgium, and at sixteen had left school to work in the bank:

When I was called up in 1940 I was asked what I'd like to do. 'Well,' I said, 'as I'm only five foot three inches tall and good at gym, I'd like to be in the army physical training corps.' But they sent me into anti-aircraft artillery, manning Bofors guns—until my leg was smashed up in Italy. Once it was mended, they let me join the PT corps.

The rings has always been my favourite, though I had to be lifted up to them. We had two coaches, Jim Wright who toughed us up and Bill Downing who improved our technique. There was no financial support for gymnastics, we had to train on home-made apparatus, complete with splinters and rust. No gloves, not even chalk on our hands. The trouble was, there was no British engineering firm able to make gymnastic apparatus and no money to import it.

Learning new and risky manoeuvres involved courage, skill, and enough friends to hold a blanket to catch you. 'Home-made equipment of incorrect width and insecurely constructed was used in make-shift training places,' recalled Jim Prestidge of the Amateur Gymnastics Association. 'The London squad trained in the cellar of a brewery because it had a beam. One end was fixed to a wall, while the other rested on a beer barrel. The compulsory vault was learned on a school vaulting box with no thought about the correct height.' The ceiling of the Crown and Manor Boys Club was so low that anyone attempting a giant swing on the horizontal bar had to bend their legs as they went over the top. On sunny days the team practised outdoors in Hyde Park, coaching each other as best they could.

Help was at hand, however, from an unexpected quarter. Early in 1948 Frank Turner was competing at the British championships in Leicester when the official Olympic coach, Arthur Whitford, called him over.

'Arthur said to me, "Frank, I've got a wonderful secret to help us win the Olympics. Go and talk to that man over there." So I went up to this man who was dressed like a convict and I said, "I understand you do gym." By way of an answer, he took his jacket off, tucked his trousers into his socks, leapt up onto the high bar, and went through the Olympic routine. We were flabbergasted and said "How did you do that?" "I have beaten Schwarzmann," he said.'

Alfred Schwarzmann, a baker from Nuremberg, had won two golds and a bronze at Berlin in 1936. The man Turner met was Helmut Bantz, a Luftwaffe pilot who had been shot down and now worked on a farm near Leicester, still retained as a prisoner of war. Bantz was an optimist who had not let these experiences get in the way of gymnastics:

We did a lot of sport in the camp, especially football and athletics. We organised a sports festival, like our old gymnastic mountain festivals. It was so good that even our English guards took part. All 80 prisoners of war had

348

to take part in each competition. No-one had to be particularly talented. Football was played, one barrack against another. Four ropes were attached to an oak tree to see who could move the fastest hand over hand. We did high jump and long jump and we ran the 100 metre race barefoot across the fields. It was great fun and ended with a big celebratory party when we put on a play and I went on as a girl. We had saved our beer rations for weeks.

Shovelling dung and digging had kept Bantz fit. 'In the bitter cold winter of 1947 we harvested savoy cabbages in forty centimetres of snow. An incredible price was paid for them at Covent Garden Market because there was no other vegetable in England.'

Bantz improved on his school English by reading Shakespeare and talking to officials from the Ministry of Food. To his delight he was given permission to attend the gymnastic championships.

Overjoyed, I travelled to Leicester. They asked me to show them something on a horizontal bar. I took off my jacket and shoes, undid my tie, and went to it without any protection on my hands. My heart had never beaten as fast before important exercises during world championships as it did then, when I was not a well-known gymnast but simply had to prove myself in seconds. Fortunately from working on the farm my hands had become so hard that they did not become raw. I had not been on an apparatus in years. But I soon recovered and the expressions on the faces of my audience visibly brightened. I asked about the Olympic compulsory exercises for the horizontal bar. I felt an inner joy—this exercise consisted almost entirely of pieces I had done before. The English, usually described as reserved, were clearly amazed. And even though I saw stars during each new movement, I was taken on as one of them. I was officially invited to come again the following day. The English gymnasts made bad mistakes, above all on the vaulting horse and on the rings. With my experience it was easy for me to explain the cause of the mistakes to them and give them good advice.

Frank Turner remembered:

Helmut turned out to be a popular and successful German gymnast and European champion, twice world champion and several times German champion. He became part of the British team as our secret coach. As a PoW he couldn't officially be acknowledged. But it didn't matter because he was so good.

I was very strong for one so small and Helmut said to me, 'Do what I tell you, and we'll be in the medal class. We'll alter your exercise on the rings.' Helmut taught me new manoeuvres and gave us all the correct interpretation of the set moves for Olympic gymnasts. We did a lot better than we would have, thanks to Helmut.

Bantz concluded:

Finally, I received an Olympic uniform and was treated like any other Olympic contestant. I lived with the British team in the Olympic village, ate with them and even took part in practice competitions. Everyone knew that I was a prisoner of war but even so, I was asked if I wanted to march in with the British team into the stadium. I would have been the only German participant at the 1948 Olympic Games! I declined but I had the great pleasure of seeing again many good, old friends in Olympic teams from better days. During the Olympics, from which Germany was still excluded, the war and dung shovelling were long behind me.

Because of the shortage of gymnastics equipment in Britain, visiting teams had been asked to bring beams, springboards and pommel horses with them. Switzerland was especially generous, arriving with three full sets of apparatus which they then left behind; some of it is still in use sixty years later at Frank Turner's home. However, the plethora of equipment suddenly available created problems of standardisation. 'One team's pommel horse,' wrote Jim Prestidge, 'was so unorthodox that the judges considered it gave an unfair advantage. So off they went to rummage through an odd assortment of horses until one was found to satisfy the head judge.' Mr Gander, President of the International Federation of Gymnastics, reported: 'The waste of time and confusion caused considerable chaos.' The hurried move to Empress Hall made it impossible to provide a large scoreboard, so a loudspeaker was used, but this was so unpopular with competitors that it was soon stopped.

The average age of the British team was nearly twenty-eight and hopes of a British medal were never seriously considered, despite Bantz's encouragement. 'Britain only came twelfth out of sixteen countries,' said Turner. 'But I was pretty chuffed to come second after George in our own team, and when it was over, Pavel Benetka of Czechoslovakia and I swapped shorts as a souvenir.'

Finland and Switzerland won almost all the medals between them. Although the average age of the Finnish team was thirty-three, they demonstrated perfect timing and controlled movement. The last of nine Olympic medals was won by Heikki Savolainen, aged forty-four, for his performance on the pommel horse. One of the Finns missed his grasp on the horizontal bar, but simply swung right round it on one arm as if he had meant to. The crowd roared their approval while the judges docked him half a point.

*   *   *

Although women had been admitted to Olympic gymnastics in teams since 1928, their inclusion was still controversial and the IOC only decided they could compete in May 1948. Many people felt that it caused unladylike perspiration and revealed rather too much body. According to Prestidge, the medical profession went further and claimed that 'contorting their bodies in ways that God had not intended' would ruin women's chances of motherhood.

Most of the women wore short-sleeved tops and shorts, though 17-year-old Laura Micheli from Italy, the youngest competitor, wore an all-in-one playsuit. Each female competitor in a team of eight performed six compulsory and six voluntary exercises on the beam, horse and rings, during which points were awarded for the 'physiological value of the exercise, beauty and composition, and correctness of execution'. One judge got so carried away that he awarded a score of 13 out of 10 possible points. The beam was the most popular for sheer expertise and daring, and Laura Micheli endeared herself to everyone with her flying pigtails and kisses blown to her team mates. Each team of eight also did a synchronised floor exercise, accompanied by a pianist. Leida Idla played not only for Sweden, but also for any other country who had omitted to bring their own pianist.

The British top scorer was Cissie Davies from Swansea, who was strong, supple and very well co-ordinated. She astounded onlookers with her elephant lift, a move which few gymnasts were able to perform, in which she stood with her hands placed in front of her on the floor, and then lifted her legs slowly up into a handstand. Had individual medals been awarded to women, Joan Airey, a canteen clerk at the National Coal Board, would have received a silver for her stylish vaulting. George Wheedon had coached her and she practised for the beam by standing on the edge of the bath at home. On the beam she could do cartwheels, a back-walk-over, a forward roll, high leaps, and a somersault off. Jim Prestidge wrote that her performance on the vault 'typified the spirit of the British team'. He explained how Karin Lindberg from Sweden had just received a high score, after spending a long time adjusting her special springboard; the American Clara Schroth followed, 'and great care was made to set up her American spring-board, which was entirely different from any other. Then came Joan Airey and the steward asked "Which board, Miss Airey?" "Anything will do. The one that's already there," replied Airey. She had spent six months training on a shaky beam in a brewery, she wasn't about to worry about which springboard.' However, the British women fared no better than the men, coming ninth out of eleven; only France and Belgium did worse.

The best overall female gymnast was Zdenka Honsova of Czechoslovakia, who would have won three golds had there been individual medals. Shortly after the Czechoslovak team arrived in London, one of its members, Eliska Misakova, fell ill with poliomyelitis and was rushed to an isolation hospital in Uxbridge. Czechoslovakia was suffering from an epidemic of polio, then treatable with only bed rest. As the paralysis spread, she was put in an iron lung to keep her breathing. But on the morning that her team was due to appear in Earl's Court, she died. The team, which included her elder sister Miloslava, decided to honour her by competing. They duly won the gold medal and the Czech flag was bordered in black at the victory ceremony. In 1960 Czechoslovakia became the first country in the world to eradicate polio, just five years after the first safe vaccines were used.

As the Czech Olympic team was preparing to return home, their captain Marie Provaznikova announced that she would be staying in London. In contrast to the British attitude towards women gymnasts, there had been a tradition of women's clubs in Czechoslovakia since the 'Sokol' (Falcon) movement in the late nineteenth century. These clubs encouraged social equality and political democracy through gymnastic festivals, and the new Communist regime in Czechoslovakia viewed them as hives of anti-Communism. Provaznikova, who was fifty-five, had been a member of Sokol since she was a child, and said she could not accept the displacing of Sokol gymnastic festivals by 'Spartakiads'—the Communist sports festivals set up in opposition to 'Western capitalist' Olympics. 'There is no freedom of speech, of the press, or of the parliament,' she added, and thus became the first political defector in Olympic history, setting a trend that would continue for the next thirty years.

22

THE VELODROME AND FURTHER AFIELD

The cycling contest, in which Britain had been successful at every Games but one and had won five golds in 1908, had always offered the best hope of Britain garnering some medals. The four track events took place at the Herne Hill Velodrome in south-east London. The home of track cycling since 1892, it had become a storage site for barrage balloons during the war. The

355

cracked and weed-covered track was now given a new bitumen surface and a small grandstand was built, all for £1,000. Despite the ban elsewhere on advertising at the Games, 'DUNLOP' was painted in huge letters on the track, but nobody seemed to mind.

The rain was falling steadily when the cycle racing began on Saturday 7 August. Many spectators preferred the shelter of the café, which over the four days of the competition served 13,400 cups of tea, 16,150 sandwiches and buns, and 12,200 ice creams. Virginia Graham, daughter of the comic poet Harry Graham, wrote a poem about it called 'Teas served here'.

> On the green green grass they have set a table
> From out whose bosom stems an iron pole
> Upon which, spread like a distended mushroom
> There flaunts a giant orange parasol.
>
> But here we need no shade. Beneath this fungus
> There shelters one young man holding a cup.
> The rain drips gently off the orange fringes,
> He turns the collar of his raincoat up.

Eddie Wingrave, a maintenance engineer in a paper mill and a keen tandem racer, took his annual week's holiday in order to be a cycling 'whip' at Herne Hill:

Bob Haynes of the British Cycling Federation gave every cycling official a job, so we could all go to the Olympics. We had to buy our own uniform—blazer, trousers and special tie. This cost more than if we'd bought grandstand tickets but we also got a London Transport travel pass. My job was to call up the riders for each event. I was also a holder. After the rider has strapped his feet on the pedals, you have to hold him upright and still until the race starts. Everything was okay except for a Frenchman, Dupont, who made two false starts.

All five Wingrave brothers were cyclists and the eldest Frederick attended to the results board.

Tom Godwin, six foot one and weighing over twelve stone (76kg), was one of the first of the power cyclists and competed in the 1,000 metre time trial. Before the race, the Belgian coach Louis Gerlash gave him a massage and asked if he wanted 'something to help him win the gold'. Godwin was furious. 'If I can't win it on my own, then I wouldn't deserve to win,' he told him and went on to take two bronze medals. Amphetamines were available, at a price, and there were no blood tests for drugs—but there is no documented evidence of drug-taking at the 1948 Games.

In the 4,000 metre team pursuit, the cyclists chased each other round the track for eight and three-quarter laps. Alan Geldard, Tom Godwin, David Ricketts and Wilf Walters represented Britain. Geldard, twenty-one and from Oldham, was an amateur cyclist working in Manchester as a commercial artist. During the war he had been a Bevin Boy, one of the thousands of men who worked in the coal mines in a scheme named after the Minister of Labour and National Service. Then in 1945 he had been conscripted into the armed forces and had only just finished that three-year

357

conscription a couple of months before the Games.

We owned our own bikes. They were good-quality steel tubing, made specially for us with drop handles and no gears, brakes or mudguards. Punctures were rare because the tyres were made of thick rubber with no inner tube. The frame cost two weeks' wages. The only contribution we got was Dunlop lent us tyres and then after the Games they were taken back. If Dunlop had used our names in their advertisements, it would have compromised our amateur status. We didn't get any sponsorship or expenses at all. We had no coaching whatsoever. You just worked at it hard and if you were any good you continued up the ladder to selection.

Geldard had never ridden in a team before, but every Sunday morning he cycled twice the Olympic distance:

We were still being trialled in the last fortnight. They couldn't decide until four days before the race who should be in the team, so there was no time to try out properly. We had never raced against France, and Uruguay, who came fourth, were an unknown quantity too. The team everyone feared was Italy but they had one super rider and the others couldn't keep up. You need a blend of four equal riders. If we had got our act together we might have won the gold but our officials didn't know what team pursuit was, so we were still learning as we competed. You go in a long line at pre-arranged intervals. Each team is separated by half a lap. Pace judgement is an important technique, not to run ahead at the beginning.

Coming after the war, the Olympics was like something out of the blue. Even with the rationing and equipment shortages, it was still a momentous occasion. There was a large attendance at the cycling track and the atmosphere was very exciting. Cycling was a buoyant sport, there were always lots of competitions, sometimes on grass or cinders. Athletics and cycling competitions were often combined but at the Olympics we never saw any other sportsmen. Even so, being at Herne Hill was the thrill of a lifetime. I was given permission to take three weeks off for the Olympics but when I went back with my medal, I was sacked for taking time off. There was no company pride in having a medal winner; I was just inconvenient. After that, I became self-employed and then the national champion.

Geldard's team came third, behind the French and the Italians.

In the 2,000 metre tandem race, British hopes were pinned on the reigning world sprint champion and war hero, Reg Harris. Eight years earlier he had been seriously injured while serving as a tank driver in North Africa, and after a whole year in hospital he had been discharged from the forces as medically unfit. He had regained his strength by returning to his pre-war love-affair with cycling and to everyone's amazement he had been selected for the Olympics. Always a tricky character, he was expelled from the team when he refused to leave Manchester to train in London with the others. But his friends protested on his behalf and he was reinstated after a ride-off against his tandem partner, Alan Bannister.

The event involved eighteen heats, each between two tandems, and these took so long to complete that the final between Italy and Britain began after dark. There were no floodlights at Herne Hill and cars were brought in to shine their headlights on the track. Even so, it was only possible to see the British riders, in their white singlets, rushing past—Ferdinando Teruzzi and Renato Perona, who were wearing navy blue, were almost invisible.

Harris and Bannister had a puncture in their front tyre but Harris managed to hold on and win the first race. Although a photo-finish machine had been installed, it was too dark to use the camera, but everyone agreed that the Italians won the next two races, and so Britain gained a silver medal. The telephone booths at the velodrome had no lights either, and the journalists used matches and torches to phone in their reports.

After the Olympics, Harris turned professional and won the world sprint championship four times. A hero to all small boys with bicycles, he nonetheless kept trying to give it up. In later life he managed not to stay the course as a journalist, a painter, and an Anglican priest. After a fourteen-year retirement he returned to cycling and, at the age of fifty-four, won the British sprint championship again. One day, when he was in his sixties, a policeman stopped him after he had jumped a red traffic light. 'Who do you think you are?' asked the officer, 'Reg Harris?'

Whereas the track riders had to be sprinters, those who raced on the road needed stamina. Great Britain had done well in this event ever since 1896, when Edward Battell, a servant at the British Embassy, had won the bronze medal. Despite the appalling weather, 15,000 people turned up to watch the 120-mile road race in King George's back garden at Windsor Great Park on Friday 13 August. The King's new son-in-law, the Duke of Edinburgh, wearing a large mackintosh against the downpour, officiated with the starting pistol. A serving naval officer at the time, he remembered the heavy rain that day as he started the race on Smith's Lawn, not far from the Royal Lodge, the weekend retreat of his parents-in-law.

The riders from twenty-nine countries set off to cycle seventeen laps round the park, followed by officials in a Rolls-Royce. The race was both an individual and a team event: each nation could enter four riders and team placings were determined by the fastest three. No team could be placed if fewer than three of its riders finished. The riders could exchange tyres, pumps and spanners (an efficient cyclist could change a tyre in under three minutes) but a wheel could only be changed if the Station Controller decided the damage was great enough. Riders could receive food or drink only after laps eight and fourteen and the public was forbidden from assisting riders 'in any way whatsoever'.

'Despite being swept three times before the race, the course remained a hazardous one,' wrote Harold Nelson. 'The surface was rough and it was impossible to pick up all the fine flints. Our Nick Carter punctured once on the first lap and twice

361

on the second. The course was a seven-mile circuit and by the fourth he was lapped by the leaders and had to retire. He was terribly disappointed with the result.'

The British team included 24-year-old Robert Maitland. He had been a toolmaker during the war.

My intention was to be a professional when racing started again and in 1946 I won the first international race in Switzerland. Going there was like a fairytale of plenty. All the other cyclists had the best; I had a 1930s sports bike. By 1947 I was working for BSA [Birmingham Small Arms, manufacturers of cars and motorbikes], and they helped me with a new bike. It was made from high-quality steel with a three-speed derailleur and, as a toolmaker, I gave it four gears. BSA bought me six of the best tyres they could find from Italy, so I had no punctures. The Italians had wonderful bikes. We trained after work in the dark and at weekends. Our team manager knew nothing about road racing and he left us to do what we wanted, so we rode three or four hundred miles a week through the London streets. We were too busy training to go to the Opening Ceremony. We were there to race, not walk round in the sunshine.

Belgium and Italy had the leading cyclists then and the Scandinavians were beginning; Britain was way behind. During the Olympics there was no fraternisation with the other nations. The Americans were laughably naive about training and had no clue about road racing. One of them, Ted Smith, came with us to train and we worked him hard. But before the event started he came to us in tears: he had been disqualified by his coach for training with us.

'The bicycling race in Windsor Great Park was a carnival sadly impaired by cold and rain,' reported *The Times*. 'But a most engaging spectacle for all that, with the variegated colours of the riders against the dark green background of the trees.'
Each lap took about eighteen minutes, up and down hills and round tight corners, over loose grit and through muddy puddles. The first time the field encountered the sharp corner at Blacknest Gate, two riders fell. A few laps later, an Argentinean and a Mexican skidded at the same spot and their bicycles became entangled. As the others sailed past, they argued passionately and hit each other a few times until the official car arrived. One rider then stomped off still remonstrating, while the other plonked himself down on the grass under a tree.
Gordon Thomas, a dogged Yorkshireman, was leading on the fourteenth lap. José Beyaert, a 22-year-old shoemaker from France, then sprinted ahead and won by eight lengths. It had taken him just over five hours, at an average of twenty-three miles per hour. He was carried round the field on his friends' shoulders and blew kisses to the spectators. Out of ninety-one cyclists who started, fifty-two suffered punctures and only twenty-eight finished. Kris Andersen of Denmark came in last, with a tyre hanging off its wheel. The three Argentineans who did not fall over all made it

home and their team came seventh. Horacio Estol tried to put on a brave face. 'With the results of the long-distance event at Windsor, the Argentinean cycling team saw the last hope of an honourable place in the Olympics vanish. Three members of the team managed to finish, though they arrived too late to come in the top twenty. We can now admit that there was no great hope of winning, and thus we can only call the performance poor.'

Only seven national teams completed, and Britain won silver while Belgium took gold. Maitland remembered:

After the race I was cold, wet and muddy. I had a cold shower in a tin shed and then they said, 'The Duke wants you.'

'Which Duke?' I asked.

'Edinburgh. Hurry up.' We met the Duke of Edinburgh and he said, 'How did you get on?'

Scott, the third man of our team, said, 'Oh, okay. I got a medal despite your dirty old park.'

'Jolly good show,' said the Duke.

There was no podium, nor lining up or national anthems. When we went back to Uxbridge, there was no greeting from the other competitors. It was a shame really.

Cycling was the only sport in which Britain won a medal in every event, taking three silver and two bronze.

*   *   *

'Basketball is a thrilling game, not yet appreciated here,' wrote *The Times*. 'Heavens knows who erroneously attributed it merely to girls' schools.' Arthur Elvin had certainly not anticipated it: 'Athletics, swimming, boxing and the Art competitions are the essentials, being universal to the ordinary people of all countries,' he wrote. 'One might possibly add football and cycling.' He did not mention basketball, which had been invented in 1891 by a YMCA instructor in the United States. It became popular in Britain after a visit by a team composed of Latter Day Saints' missionaries, and first appeared in the Olympics in 1936, when the USA won.

On the opening day on Friday 6 August, only 200 spectators turned up at Harringay Arena in north London, an octagonal building constructed in 1936 in the same style as the Empire Pool, over the Piccadilly tube line. But word got round that basketball was worth watching, and by the fourth day there were 2,500 spectators, enthralled by the speed and skill of the players. The twenty-three national basketball teams played a total of eighty-five matches.

'If basketball is the Cinderella of British games,' wrote the *Manchester Guardian*, 'then a great opportunity was lost at Harringay yesterday afternoon. When reservations were known to be slight, this was an occasion for some far-sighted Olympians to step in and offer free seats to, say, a thousand schoolboys. Young minds would have been rid of the conception of basketball as "a girls' game". Husky young men raced about the arena with such vigour that when one collided with a referee the official had to be carried off.'

Norman Charles, on holiday from Holloway Grammar School, was fourteen and often travelled around London on his own. 'I could just about afford a child's Underground fare, but not a ticket to get into the Olympics. So I'd stand outside the gate wearing my short trousers and a hang-dog look and hope for the best. Somebody would eventually offer me a ticket. At Harringay I'd never seen such sport before—the basketball was very fast and furious, rather unique and different.'

In both of Iraq's games, against Korea and China, they lost by 100 points. The British team contained not one, but three, sets of brothers: the Leggs, the McMeekans and the Westons. They were not very good and Uruguay knocked them out in the first round.

Ireland did no better. Before their first match, the bus taking them from Willesden College to the arena got so lost that the team had to change into their kit on the way. 'This incident had a very upsetting effect, from which the team never fully recovered,' said the Irish report. They were beaten in all their matches.

'Our basketball team showed us that we had reason to trust in our boys,' wrote Horacio Estol, the Argentinean journalist. 'We gained huge satisfaction in having played as an equal against the strongest team, the United States.' Argentina was beaten by only two points. 'However, our team later paid for this tremendous effort. The commendable desire to beat the best team demanded a lot of energy, since after this game the team did not perform as expected.' Unsurprisingly, the Americans dominated the competition after a shaky start. Several of their players were six foot six inches tall and one was seven foot. 'The idea is of course that the taller the man, the easier it is for him to pop the ball into the basket,' reported *World Sports*. 'If this process goes on, the basket will eventually have to be raised, and then still taller men will be bred up for future Games, unless they make a rule forbidding anyone over 6 feet 6 inches to take part.'

'Normally men of 6 foot 9 inches to 7 feet tall are not fast, but these players had all the agility of bantams!' wrote the sports journalist W. Browning. 'When height is combined with superb ball control and intelligence there is no answer. As soon as these giants entered the arena, the opposing teams seemed to wilt and fade away. Though some of the most scintillating ball play was that of Korea and the Philippines. Though small of stature, their speed and ball manipulation were an education. How the crowd loved them, and how well they earned the admiration and respect of all basketball enthusiasts!'

Despite the love of the crowd, the Koreans came eighth and the Philippines twelfth. The gold, silver and bronze medals were won by the United States, France and Brazil.

*   *   *

If basketball was a new sport, hockey in various forms had been played in the British Isles for several hundred years. When it was introduced to the Olympics at the London Games in 1908, for men only, the home nations entered separate teams, England coming out on top. Since then, either Great Britain or India had won every

Olympic tournament, but neither team had played the other before. In 1936 the Indians had beaten Germany 8–0 in front of 30,000 spectators. They were well known for their extraordinary control and nimble footwork, their players calmly collecting the ball and juggling with it while looking round for the next pass.

There were striking contrasts in the style of the thirteen teams in the 1948 competition, which started on Saturday 31 July. Argentina was playing Olympic hockey for the first time and though they also lost to India by eight goals, they were not downhearted. 'We have been invited to play in India,' wrote Horacio Estol. 'This in itself is a great triumph and we should not complain about the fact that our team did not get placed.'

The British played a direct game and were at home on wet grass pitches. 'Our hockey was entirely amateur,' recalled John Peake, who was in the Royal Corps of Naval Instructors at Greenwich College. 'Our players were all-round sportsmen from the professional classes, three schoolmasters, one doctor, two army and one naval instructor. At nearly twenty-four, I was several years younger than most of them.' The team was made up of five Englishmen, five Scotsmen and one Welshman. Players from Northern Ireland had been invited but did not wish to play separately from the rest of Ireland. Norman Borrett, aged thirty-one, captained England from 1939 to 1948, and also played rugby, golf, tennis and cricket for Devon. A scheming inside left, he scored ten goals, six of them against the United States. The right half, Micky Walford, was an Oxford rugby blue and played cricket for Somerset. The inside right, Neil

White, had played rugby for Scottish public schools and Cambridge University, cricket for Cambridgeshire, and hockey for Cambridge University and Scotland. He was also a geography teacher. 'In April, when I received the news that I had been selected for the Olympic squad,' remembered White, 'the excitement was tinged with apprehension as to how we could keep fit for an enterprise which would not take place until August. Rationing was still tight and an old school friend sent me a side of beef from Kenya. But it must have been packed next to the lions aboard ship, as it was inedible.'

John Peake remembered:

Hockey was not a game normally played in the summer. Most hockey pitches were being used for cricket, so there was no regular match-play to keep us in practice and it wasn't until shortly before the Games that the whole British squad could get together. Thus we were more a group of individuals than a well-bonded side. We probably improved as we went along. Once we moved to the RAF Uxbridge camp we had more training but not much. Colonel George Grimston, the team manager, regimented us and we went to a field and bounced up and down for a few minutes. One man was running round and round there in a strange wobbling way. When we finished he was still running. We discovered later he was Emil Zátopek. We got no expenses, though the Navy paid my bus fares. We each received a small tin of Nivea cream but there were no strings attached.

369

The preliminary rounds were played at the Guinness grounds at Park Royal in west London. During one match, a man wearing a badge and an armlet claimed to be an Olympic official. He collected valuables such as watches and wallets from competitors 'for safe-keeping'—and was never seen again. 'We were concerned, if not too downcast, to draw with Switzerland in our first match,' said John Peake. 'Guinness laid on free drinks after the game. The first Guinness is delicious, the second is good; the third quite good, the fourth a bit bitter and the fifth you can't remember.'

Our 11–0 win in the next match against the USA was heartening, though somewhat of a hollow victory as the Americans considered hockey to be a girls' game of no importance. Our third match against Afghanistan posed no problem and we were thrilled to be in the semi-finals. India and Pakistan were used to playing with a small, button-hook type of stick. Our British sticks were much longer. In beating Pakistan in the semi-final, we may have taken too much heart from the thought that India in the semi-final would find the thick Wembley turf harder to play on than we did.

For the final, 25,000 spectators filed into Wembley Stadium on a damp evening. Never before had so many people attended a hockey match in England.

'The final was played on quite the wrong surface for hockey,' said Neil White. 'After all that rain, the grass was about three inches long. The pitch had been rolled but by the time the match ended, the grass was standing up again. Classy stick-work was out of the question and this certainly affected us. But it didn't seem to worry the Indians, who played the ball in the air most of the time.' Although the Indians were used to hard, dry, bare grounds, their constructive play in midfield was fast and sophisticated. With an average age of twenty, some played in bare feet with their long hair tied up on top. G. Singh and T. Singh scored two goals each and Britain failed to find a reply.

'The Indians beat us soundly to take gold,' said Peake. 'But we got silver medals and did very well gastronomically. I felt sorry for the BBC radio commentators. Hockey is a fast game and the Danish team consisted of two Hansens, two Neilsens and a Sorensen, a Thomsen, a Johansen, a Jorengsen and a Jensen. The Indians had three men called Singh, Pakistan had three Khans, and there were six Afghanis called Nuristani.'

*   *   *

Eighteen nations entered the water polo competition and fifty-four preliminary matches were played in open-air pools at Finchley and Uxbridge before the final at the Empire Pool on Saturday 7 August.

Water polo originated in England in the 1880s and championships began a few years later. In 1948 the British team was drawn from eight different clubs and only met up the day before their first match. They knew they stood little chance of success and during their first three matches they managed only three goals. In the fourth match against Egypt, there was some doubtful refereeing and Tom Lewis sustained an ear injury. The brilliant Hungarians then beat them 11–2 and they were eliminated. Mr Fern of the Amateur Swimming Association was not pleased. 'Frankly the results were most disappointing. Almost too bad to be true, particularly having regard to the enterprising hard work of the water polo selection committee.'

Elsewhere in the competition, there was considerable criticism about the uneven standard of refereeing. Many underwater fouls went unchecked, including sinking opponents, kicking them and jumping on their shoulders. 'In many of the games the fouling was so persistent and continuous that referees had a well-nigh impossible task,' said the official report.

'I do not think,' wrote Mr Fern, 'we need unduly stress the lapses in sportsmanship evidenced in certain of the matches. Some of the newer devotees of the game are from the more excitable races. They have acquired a wonderful technical skill in a very short time and no doubt the finer points of sportsmanship will come to them after a longer apprenticeship.'

The final was between the Hungarians, winners in Berlin, and Italy, reigning champions of Europe. It too was not without incident. 'Six Players Ordered Out in Polo Shock', ran the headline in the London *Evening News*. 'Shortly after the start of the match, the referee stopped play and hauled a Hungarian out of the water so that grease could be rubbed off his back. The match finished with six men, three from each side, ordered out of the water for foul play.' Italy took the gold. 'There was an amazing demonstration of excitement by the Italian spectators at the end,' reported the *Evening News.* 'All the players were embraced by men and women, while two of the Hungarians burst into tears.'

23

TORBAY

The sailing competition at the Olympics requires a sheltered bay, large enough for three triangular courses and conditions that minimise the advantage of local knowledge about tidal flows or unusual winds. Torbay in south Devon has all these, as well as a decent harbour for both large and small yachts and plenty of hotels and guest houses. It is sheltered from the prevailing westerlies that blow in off the Atlantic, though the hills can cause light breezes to sigh across the water from surprising directions. A rough square of about three sea miles in each direction, it is small enough to be viewed from the towns of Torquay, Paignton and Brixham. In 1948 it was also free of the sunken vessels that made sailing hazardous in other places for some years after the war.

Lord Burghley had used his charm to persuade the Torquay Town Council not only to organise the sailing event but to pay for it as well. Needless to say, this was a major undertaking. However, the area had a lot to gain as tourism had collapsed during the war: coastal areas had been fortified, travel was difficult and food expensive. The Games were just what the area needed to trigger an economic revival.

The council was determined to overcome the prevailing austerity and resolved that 'All decorations, displays, and entertainments should be as lavish as circumstances permit, to make the occasion a memorable one.' Over £500 was spent redecorating Torquay Ballroom, which held nightly dances and concert parties with an extended liquor licence.

Before the war Torquay had been famous for its illuminations but with fuel shortages still a pressing issue, any decorative lighting was still 'absolutely prohibited': the council was hard pressed to find even enough bunting to hang up. Nonetheless, after two requests the Ministry of Fuel and Power gave permission for Torre Abbey and the Spa to be floodlit. 'Torquay had the privilege of being the first town in the country to resume illuminations since 1939,' commented Reginald Colwill, editor of the *Torquay Herald and Express*. 'This caused a considerable sensation.' The Parks Superintendent, meanwhile, had agreed with British Railways to decorate the station with flowers, though a few days later an unknown person was reported to the police for 'the attempted theft of two polyanthus plants'. Alderman Easterbrook strongly disapproved of the council's decision to charge for parking. 'This is the height of meanness and shows a lack of politeness,' he said. The majority of the council decided that visiting yachtsmen could not be given free parking when local residents had to pay.

'The Olympic Games brought all the towns

374

around the bay together to work in harmony for one common object,' wrote Colwill. The Chamber of Commerce made a concerted attempt to take advantage of the opportunity offered to conduct an export drive. Local tradesmen displayed motor cars, high-class clothing and luxury goods which were not available in British sterling, and took orders from visitors in foreign currency. Local rates were raised by a half-penny to cover the cost of advertising abroad and the production of a brochure in several languages.

With the national shortage of building materials, the Ministry of Supply had to issue reconstruction licences to the Torquay hotels before they could set about refurbishing their rooms. They agreed with the council to set their rates at only 15 shillings a day for both food and accommodation. 'Then difficulties began to arise,' wrote Colwill. 'The teams should have stated their requirements but some teams failed to communicate at all, and the first that was heard of others was when they were ready to race. Others selected their own hotels and refused to move to the hotels to which they had been assigned.' The hoteliers were livid— they had rooms lying empty while ordinary tourists were desperate for holiday accommodation. The Argentineans, who were first to arrive and spent several weeks practising in Torbay, failed to pay their hotel bills at all. Not all the competitors could afford even the reduced hotel rate. 'We stayed in a horrible boarding-house,' remembered Jean, the daughter of the British competitor Arthur MacDonald. 'It was all my parents could afford. This was our annual holiday. There was a long staircase and an awful smell of cabbage.'

Some of the officials, such as Charles Currey and his family, stayed in a converted bus on a farm.

To accommodate Olympic officials, the Marine Spa overlooking the harbour was allocated as their headquarters, and the resident staff of the 'Medical Baths Section' were instructed to take their annual holiday so that the BBC could use the bathrooms as their broadcasting studios. The Sun Lounge became both a Post Office and Information Bureau where foreign newspapers and twenty volunteer translators could be found. The Cooling Lounge became the Press Room equipped with desks, telephones and a bar for the sixty journalists.

Torquay Council was keen to include the Olympic torch relay in its pageantry but the Organising Committee decided it would be too expensive to take the torch any further than Wembley. Finally, in mid June, the organisers agreed that the torch could be carried the extra 200 miles from London to Torquay, on condition that Torquay Council paid. Another hundred torches at £1 15s each were purchased and Shell Mex charged £3 per day for the burner and bottled gas. The flame was carried by more than a hundred runners who took it from Wembley through five counties to Devon in just twenty-six hours. In the small Somerset town of Chard, the mayor, town band and 3,000 people turned out at 3 a.m. to cheer. In Newton Abbot there was chaos when several thousand people pushed and jostled the bearer, eighteen-year-old William Hibberd, so hard that he was knocked to the ground. He managed to keep the torch aloft and limped on until he could hand over. The 107th torch bearer,

Steven Francis, arrived at Torre Abbey in the afternoon of 2 August, bank holiday Monday. 'The whole Sea Front was a seething mass of humanity and in Torre Abbey meadows 30,000 people had congregated,' wrote Colwill. 'The pathway was lined with naval ratings, Boy Scouts and Sea Scouts, and through their ranks each of the 22 teams marched with its national flag. The Bay itself presented a picture of indescribable beauty with the amazing gathering of yachts and warships of many nations.'

Lying at anchor in the bay were the Royal Navy battleship HMS *George V* and the aircraft carrier HMS *Victorious*, along with Belgian and US destroyers. The French destroyer *Desaix*, captured from the Germans, had transported four yachts across the Channel. Two Swedish training schooners were dressed over-all with signal flags and the Oxford-educated Crown Prince Olaf of Norway, a grandson of Edward VII, had brought the royal yacht *Norge* on its maiden voyage and moored it below the Imperial Hotel.

On shore, outside Torre Abbey, the Olympic Hymn was sung and national flags hoisted. 'Suddenly there was a "whoosh!" and 600 pigeons, beating the start gun, were away on their mission, a full half-hour before their intended despatch,' reported the *Torquay Directory*. 'They flew to yachting centres all over the country. All that is, except for one who, disgruntled for some reason, resolutely refused to leave the battlement on which he had found a perch.'

The naturalist Peter Scott took a month away from the Severn Wildfowl Trust to chair the yachting committee and liaise with the local

377

authorities. The son of Captain Scott of the Antarctic, and now aged thirty-eight, he had won a bronze medal in a Finn dinghy in the 1936 Olympics, and narrowly missed inclusion in the 1948 team. In 1938 he and Charles Currey had invented the trapeze—a harness attached to the mast which enables the crew to stand out on the side of a dinghy. The device was so effective that it was banned from dinghy racing for the next twenty years. During the war, Scott had designed naval camouflage and helped to plan the D-Day landings.

The whole of Torbay harbour was reserved for the Olympic keel boats while the smaller dinghies were pulled out onto Beacon quay. The yachts and fishing boats normally moored there were given free berths across the bay in Brixham. Preparation for the racing involved the careful measurement of the boats' hulls to establish water-line length. The council had paid £693 for a huge brick tank to be constructed on the quayside for this purpose and a crane capable of lifting five-ton yachts. One yacht, a Dragon, was disqualified for having the wrong-shaped hull and another in the Six-metre class had to remove extra lead from her keel. There was a panic after two days when the crane broke down. Two Boy Scouts were sent by train to Southampton to collect a new part, and thirty men then worked for three days and nights to get all the boats back in the water in time for the first race.

'Torquay made an ideal venue,' wrote Ian Proctor, the dinghy designer, in *The Yachtsman's Annual*. 'The town is used to making people welcome; flags and fireworks come as second nature to her. She even provided a car park

378

attendant who could direct operations in several languages. But she could not do much about the weather. We got rained on hard and we got rained on soft and we got a really man-sized gale.' The ever-alert Torquay Council mobilised bricklayers to build a windbreak around the Olympic flame and the Brixham lifeboat stood by in case any ships were driven ashore. HMS *Anson* was anchored in the centre of the bay to transmit wireless-telephone messages from the small boats following each race to HMS *Tremadoc Bay* moored in the harbour. 'If the mast of an American yacht was blown away off Berry Head,' wrote Colwill, 'the fact was known in the newspaper offices in New York within ten minutes.'

This was the largest international event in 175 years of yacht-racing history. Twenty-three nations were taking part and over 60,000 people had bought tickets to walk along the Princess Pier which curves around the harbour. 'The scene at the quayside was at all times animated and interesting,' reported Colwill. 'Locals were delighted with the foreign lady visitors' bathing dresses and sun suits. Patterns, style and the briefness are quite new to the English crowds and approval is tinged with good-natured envy.'

At noon on the first day, Tuesday 3 August, the assembled warships fired a 21-gun salute in honour of the birthday of King Haakon of Norway and the racing began. Coloured smoke was released from a Royal Navy motor launch positioned at each mark, to show the wind direction. 'A more glorious sport can never have gladdened the heart of man,' reported *The Times*. 'One had an area of wonderful beauty, whose waters, if not wine-dark, were foam-flecked and sunlit and sparkling with all shades of blue and green. On this shining expanse were five clusters of sail, each the centre of a struggle of inexpressible intensity.'

To the seaward side of Torbay, the Six-metre and Dragon yacht classes raced over a course of fourteen miles; in mid-bay, the Star and Swallow yachts raced over ten miles; and in-shore the Firefly dinghies had a course of 5.6 miles. A triangular course is always chosen so that each race can start with a beat to windward, no matter which direction the wind is blowing that day. Boats raced on seven allotted days, and the crews had to contend with difficult winds, varying in strength, sometimes dying away completely and often changing direction. Points were counted for the six best races. The new scoring system, which had been invented by an Austrian scientist and yachtsman, was of impressive complexity: '101 + 1000 log A minus 1000 log n. Where A equals total number of yachts entered in her class and N equals finishing position.' This revolutionary formula rewarded a consistently good performance over the whole series, rather than a single freak win.

One boat per nation could be entered in each of the five classes and Peter Scott felt that 'On the whole, Britain's chances are good, for the sailing of small boats in rough seas seems to be peculiarly suited to the ancient traditions of our race.' When Mr C. Potamianos was asked whether Greece would win a medal he replied, 'Win? I do not think so. Our boats were built in 1934. But after all, does it matter who wins as long as we all do our best?'

The smallest of the racing boats was the new

twelve-foot Firefly, which had been designed in 1946 by the top British sailboat designer, Uffa Fox. The Organising Committee had ordered twenty-two new ones, at a cost of £150 each, from the boatbuilders Fairey Marine, near Southampton. The Firefly was the first dinghy to be built using layers of birch plywood shaped on hot moulds. A technique of great lightness and strength first used in wartime aircraft, it removed the need for bulkheads and ribs. With wide side decks and built-in buoyancy tanks, the Firefly performed consistently well in all conditions. To prove the hull's durability, Fairey had embedded an unvarnished hull in tidal mud and left it exposed to the elements for six years, after which they cleaned and rigged it and it came second in a race. Materials were still in short supply, so plywood for the hull was taken from wartime gliders and hardwood packing cases; and the foredeck and masts were made from aluminium.

The Firefly was designed by Fox as a two-man boat and when the French discovered that in the Olympics it was to be sailed single-handed, they were aghast. They maintained that this placed too much emphasis on technique, and not enough on racing tactics: 'Toujours le technique, pas de tactique.' Their objections were ignored and their man Jean Herbulot won one race but came seventh overall.

The British competitor was Air Commodore Arthur McDonald, the commandant of the RAF Staff College at Bulstrode and a man with an interesting service record. In 1937, he had helped to develop the all-important radar system to intercept incoming aircraft, which helped to win

381

the Battle of Britain in 1940. He had also designed the war rooms seen in many films of that battle, in which uniformed servicewomen push symbols of attacking and defending aircraft across a map; and he invented the pilot's radio code which is now part of the English language, including terms such as 'scramble' to describe a fast-reaction take-off. McDonald was forty-five years old when he was invited to the Olympic Firefly trials at Hayling Island. 'It was absurd,' he said later. 'My mind wasn't on sailing at all and I never thought about the Olympics. I hadn't got a Firefly, I'd never had one, I'd never sailed one.' So he borrowed one. 'I put the sails up and started my first single-handed race, my first race in a Firefly. It was all very interesting, one learned as one went on, and I thoroughly enjoyed it. At the end of the week I took the Firefly back to the owner, and thought, "That's that." ' To his surprise, McDonald was asked to attend the final trials at Torquay. 'I hadn't much hope because amongst my competitors were the best helmsmen in the country, including Peter Scott. In one race Scott was ahead of me, but it was blowing hard and when we came down to the gybe mark he capsized. As I passed him swimming, he sportingly gave me advice, "Careful about the gybe! Careful about the gybe!" '

McDonald was selected. 'Then I made a stupid error. I took the view that running a Staff College was more important than competing in the Olympic Games. I went back to my office desk in the interval between the trial and the Olympics. I should have been sailing round Torbay in a Firefly every day, day after day, hour after hour, getting really used to it.'

Lots were drawn for the boats two days before the start. The twenty-one countries taking part retained the same sails and hull throughout the competition and were not allowed to modify the rigging. This was a disadvantage to McDonald who had a first-class honours degree in engineering and had won the National-12 championships in 1939 after making his own improvements to the dinghy's rigging. At Torquay, tillers and cleats could be modified for single-handed sailing but polishing the hull was forbidden, as was filing smooth the galvanised steel centre-plate.

The weather was fair for the first three days but changed on the fourth when McDonald got off to a flying start. 'His beautiful start warmed us with anticipation,' wrote Ian Proctor. 'And not even the rain driving down our necks could quench our enthusiasm. He rounded the weather mark with a slight lead and increased this on the next two reaching legs.'

In contention with McDonald was Paul Elvstrøm of Denmark, whose attitude to the Olympics could not have been more different. Aged twenty, he had been sailing dinghies from the age of ten and intended to win every race he entered. He practised for hours every day at sea and lifted weights and ran to get fit. He had being sailing a National-12 for only a month when he had won the Danish Olympic trials.

Elvstrøm revolutionised competitive sailing by using the strength of his legs and abdomen to hang over the side of his boat for far longer periods than his opponents; this meant he could maximise the power of the wind and gave him a considerable advantage. He was also a student of weather and relished the idea of going out on stormy days to learn more about handling his craft. 'Elvstrøm lived on the Baltic,' wrote McDonald. 'He used to sail every day, single-handed, and he'd got completely used to dealing with any kind of weather.'

'Practising to win just wasn't thought to be the right thing to do,' Elvstrøm wrote later. 'People would laugh at me if I prepared so that I had a better chance of winning.' He had never even seen a Firefly before and he studied photographs and worked out ways to improve the design of the cleats that enabled the single sailor to retain and release the sheets controlling the jib and the mainsail. Before setting off for Britain, he took a week off from his work as a builder to practise with his new cleat, gybing and tacking for eight hours a day. He had still never sailed a Firefly when he arrived in Torquay a few days before the event.

'When I came to Torquay I was so shy that I didn't know there was a practice race and I missed it,' Elvstrøm said. 'At the first race I had to tack to avoid Palmgreen of Finland. He was three boat lengths from me and had no chance to hit me, but I didn't want to get into trouble so I retired.' Before Elvstrøm had left Denmark everybody had told him that provided he didn't come last, they would be happy. 'This made me feeling very low inside me. Then I said, "OK, you shall not be last," and I started feeling the boat better.' Having failed to finish on the first day, he then began to climb steadily up the points table. 'After that it went quite well and then I realised my complex had

384

disappeared. I was a little anxious in the strong wind because others had the weight and were keeping their boats upright.'

Like rowing, sailing was predominantly an upper-class sport, and this was reflected in the entertainments. At the end of four days of competition, there was a three-day rest period over the weekend, which provided an opportunity for some serious partying. 'The number of parties that everyone wanted to hold was embarrassing,' said Colwill. 'Finally Mr Holt had to say that the main purpose was yachting, not to dispense international hospitality. It was agreed that Brixham, Paignton, the Royal Navy and the three yachting clubs could each have one party, on days when there was no racing.' The *Tatler & Bystander* reported the reception on board HMS *Anson* for 800 guests. It also reported the cocktail party at the Royal Corinthian Club, hosted by Commodore Waddington-Smyth, where mingling with the competitors was the exiled claimant to the Spanish throne, Don Juan de Borbón. After his family's flight from Spain in 1931 he had continued his navy training at Dartmouth College in Devon. A keen yachtsman, he had sailed his yacht *Saltillo* from France to join in the festivities at Torbay, with a few companions including his brother the Duke of Segovia.

While most of the Olympic helmsmen were well-off, the young men who maintained their boats were often penniless. However, they were not forgotten by Peter Scott, whose attitude reflected that of his famous father in the Antarctic. A boatyard hand, Tom Hodgson, remembered:

Our accommodation was awful. We were bedded down rather like horses in a dark, deserted, oily, former wartime factory. Straw mats on the floor and poor food and no money. We were young and broke. All the high life was going on around us. After about four or five days, all of a sudden the door flew open, and I mean flew, bang, crash, and there was Scott. He'd heard about the situation. I suppose we'd all grumbled. He was fully dressed for dinner: stiff white shirt, wing collar, the lot. We looked at him in amazement. He looked at us on our straw pallets, he turned to the people with him and bawled, 'Get these men food and beer and bedding—NOW!' And they did. Then he came and sat with us and talked. This was the first time we'd ever seen leadership like this. Our reception changed from that moment on. Next day I was even treated to champagne for the first time in my life.

When the racing started again on Tuesday, Elvstrøm was lying in eighth place. 'I worked out that if I should have any chance for a good place I should have to win the last two races. The race before last it was a very shifty wind and blew more strongly, with squalls of rain. But I had the best direction and I came to the first mark a minute before the second boat. After that I sailed carefully.' After winning the penultimate race, he realised that in order to gain the gold medal, not only must he come first again, but he also had to ensure that the American, Ralph Evans, came no better than fourth. 'It was blowing hard and I had never sailed a dinghy in so strong a wind.' Elvstrøm was a lithe young man who weighed a mere 72kg and in that gale only the heavier sailors could manage unreefed mainsails. 'I couldn't keep the boat upright. So I lowered the jib and started with only a reefed mainsail. I had much better tactics than the others. They were faster, but I could tack faster in the wind shifts.'

The strong north-westerly winds proved too much for many of the helmsmen. Rooney of Ireland, in his red tarboosh hat, bright green shirt and striped football stockings was easy to spot when he capsized. McDonald too capsized, righted his boat and then went over again. His family was on the quay and his wife held up their two-year-old son Peter to a telescope. 'Look,' she said, 'there is your father capsized.'

At the first mark Elvstrøm was second to Herbulot of France who then capsized as well. Then Elvstrøm himself was overtaken. 'I hoisted the jib and put out the whisker pole and found I was gaining because I kept the boat straight and I had better balance than the others. Then I eased the mainsheet and then was *very* careful. I was not even hanging out completely in case the toe straps could break. The gold medal was now mine, but de Jong of Holland had to finish so that the American was lower than third.' Fifty yards from the finishing line, de Jong's dinghy became waterlogged and almost sank but he bailed out sufficiently to make it across the line, relegating Evans to second place overall. McDonald came third, and ninth overall in the competition. Elvstrøm won his gold, and when asked by a journalist to what he attributed his victory, he replied, 'The others—they were too slow.'

After 1948 the Firefly was replaced in the Olympics by a truly single-handed dinghy, the Finn, in which Elvstrøm won gold in 1952, 1956 and 1960. He was a reserve in the Danish team of 1964 and competed again in 1968, 1972 and 1984, becoming one of only four athletes to compete in eight or more Games. In the 1988 Olympics his daughter Trine crewed for him, the only father and daughter team ever to have competed. Elvstrøm also won eleven World Championships in seven different classes, wrote several books and started a company, Elvstrøm Sails, with branches throughout the world. He was voted Denmark's Sportsman of the Century in 1996.

In 1955, Arthur McDonald was appointed the last British Commander of the Royal Pakistan Air Force. In his eighties he developed a system of coloured lights for dinghy racing, based on his wartime work landing fighter planes at night. He won his last dinghy race when he was ninety years old.

*   *   *

The Star and the Swallow classes are both 6.9 metres in length, with a crew of two. On the first three days there was little wind and the boats moved slowly on a slight swell. On the last, the strong north-westerly favoured Britain's Stewart Morris and David Bond who had learnt to master sudden gusts on the Norfolk Broads. Exploiting the conditions, they won gold in their Swallow.

The Star had a mast that proved to be too

slender and the boats of France, Italy, Britain and Switzerland all lost theirs. 'There is a deal of difference between Torbay and Lake Geneva,' commented the Swiss team.

The elegant, high-performing Dragon was a racing thoroughbred—the sailing man's Bugatti. It was designed in 1929 as an entry in a Swedish competition to find an affordable weekend cruising boat for the Scandinavian lakes and fjords, by the Norwegian Johan Anker, himself a champion helmsman. The design won and the Dragon quickly became popular beyond Scandinavia. By 1940, over one hundred Dragons had been built on the Clyde and in recognition of Britain's aid to Norway during the war Anker insisted that no designer's royalty need be paid. The craft were beautifully constructed in pine carvel planking on a mahogany frame, and one was given to Princess Elizabeth and the Duke of Edinburgh as a wedding present.

The Dragon races were an exciting battle between the British boat *Ceres II* and the Scandinavians, who were quicker at hoisting and lowering their spinnakers when rounding a marker buoy. On the final day the Norwegians lay almost out of their boat in an endeavour to keep it upright and won the gold by three seconds.

The largest class was the Six-metre, which had a crew of five. Designed in 1906, they were first raced in the Olympics of 1908 off the Isle of Wight, where Britain won the gold. Six-metre yachts were valuable and often changed both ownership and nationality. In 1948 the Belgians were sailing *Lalage* which in 1936 had won gold for Britain. The Swedes won bronze in *Ali Baba II* which was renamed *Ralia* in 1952 and won bronze for Finland. The Argentineans were in *Djinn* which had been built in New York in 1938, and for once Horacio Estol had reason to be proud: 'The most outstanding performance came from our excellent helmsmen Enrique Sieburger, his son of the same name, his brother Julio, and his two friends Homps and Vivademás. In the last heat the Argentinean yacht came in first, with an advantage of nineteen seconds on her most immediate rival— the US yacht *Llanoria*.' *Llanoria*, built in New York at the renowned yard of Sparkman & Stephens, also had a crack crew. The helmsman was Herman 'Swede' Whiton, who had sailed in the 1928 Games near Amsterdam and twice won the Scandinavian Gold Cup. He had been the favourite for the 1936 Olympics too until he won the solid gold 'Adolf Hitler Cup' in a German regatta. After he refused either to salute Hitler or to dine with him, he was sent home before the Olympics.

On the final day there was a thrilling struggle between *Djinn*, *Llanoria* and the Norwegians in *Apache* and it was unclear who would win in the fourteen miles of rough sea and rising wind. The prize went to the USA with Whiton in *Llanoria*, and Argentina took the silver.

*   *   *

'This has been a great task and an epoch-making event,' said T.J. Reeves Taylor, the deputy mayor of Torquay. 'A complicated effort, fraught with difficulty, which has proved an astounding success and of very great and enduring benefit to the whole of the Torbay area, due almost entirely to the splendid team work on all sides.'

'Great Britain acquitted herself reasonably well,' commented the *Yachting Monthly*. 'But our yachtsmen have not the time, money and possibly the temperament to turn themselves into crack racing crews. The spirit of the racing throughout was of the best and it is satisfactory that the fifteen Olympic medals were distributed amongst ten nations.'

'Friendliness and kindliness pervaded the whole gathering,' agreed Ian Proctor. 'There were many protests, which the general public tended to misinterpret as squabbling, but when points were so vital at all stages, protests were inevitable, and friendship certainly did not suffer.'

The awarding of the medals and the closing ceremony were combined on a glorious evening. 'It was singularly beautiful, in the sylvan setting of Torre Abbey,' wrote Colwill. 'Greatly daring, the last memory was of a gigantic crowd all holding hands, swinging arms, and singing very lustily "For Auld Lang Syne". There had been some apprehension as to whether the many overseas visitors would understand the traditional British way of ending a happy party. But they need not have feared, as there was an immediate response. Even the Mayor left the terrace to join hands with the international gathering below.' As he climbed back into the first-class sleeper train to London, Sigfrid Edström declared, 'I find Torquay much nicer than Nice.'

One old sailor said afterwards, 'I have been a-yachting, man and boy, these forty years. Now, having seen "Torbay 1948", I could cheerfully prepare to chant my *Nunc Dimittis*, not presuming to hope to see again an occasion to match it in completeness and perfection.'

24

THE FOOTBALL COMPETITION

'The Olympic Games provided the most colourful and exotic football competition ever seen in England,' reported Bernard Joy, who had played centre half for Arsenal. 'Added spice came from the barefoot Indians; the deceptively lazy Mexicans; the close passing of the Chinese and Koreans; and the ball jugglery of the Egyptians.'

So many nations said they were entering football teams, that it was supposed at first that the tournament would have to begin early. However, Czechoslovakia, Iceland, Malta and Switzerland decided that they could not afford the expense of eleven men or more for the sake of a single medal, and withdrew. So only two preliminary matches were required, in one of which Afghanistan were beaten 6–0 by Luxembourg in Brighton. The Afghanis, whose other hopes rested solely on hockey, were out of the competition before the Games had even opened. Luxembourg fared little better, losing 6–1 to Yugoslavia in the next round. 'Luxembourg played attractive football but without the stamina or punch to trouble the better opposition,' wrote Joy. Luxembourg was one of several teams who brought no substitutes. Yugoslavia, on the other hand, had four.

First-round matches were played at the grounds of Tottenham, Greenford, Crystal Palace, Fulham, Walthamstow, Arsenal and Ilford. Many of the teams were short of match practice on their arrival in London. The football season had ended in May and no club teams were available for friendlies, though the Metropolitan Police made their squad available and warm-up matches were played between the nations. Poorly prepared and hampered by their Atlantic crossing, the US players had not played competitively for three months and they duly lost to Italy 9–0 at Brentford.

Of all the Olympic sports, the rules on amateurism probably affected football the most. Following the introduction of the World Cup in 1930, international soccer was played by professionals, but the Olympic football competition was still resolutely amateur. Though British professional footballers' wages were only £5 a week, this still made them ineligible. Late in 1947, members of the British Olympics Football Committee watched amateur matches all over Britain. They asked selected players to keep themselves fit at the end of the season, and to arrange their annual two-week holiday to coincide with the Games.

The Yugoslavs bent the rules by conscripting their best players into the army or civil service so that they could train while under government pay, and the 1948 Olympics saw the beginning of the domination of 'shamateur' teams from Eastern Europe. Austria were considered the favourite team, mainly because they turned a blind eye to the amateur rule and fielded such players as Ernst

Ocwirk, a Viennese garage mechanic who had been paid to play at Wembley before. Though they played some attractive football, they were eliminated by Sweden in the first round.

As the contest neared the end of its first week, the contrasting tactics of play attracted much interest. Those not at the Games benefited from the expert commentary of the Lancashire-born Kenneth Wolstenholme. A former bomber pilot, he had never watched a television before his first commentary for the BBC in 1946, but with his trained eye for detail he soon established himself as their authoritative voice of football. For the two weeks of the Olympics, he made his way from one football ground to the next, commentating for both radio and television. Television screens were small and black-and-white so that the detail of commentary required was very similar to the radio.

Each nation played football with a different style. The British preferred a cautious safety-first approach with three across the back. The 'Viennese School', favoured by Austria, Yugoslavia and Mexico, consisted of a short passing game with an aggressive centre half. With varied temperaments and different ideas on body checking, occasional flare-ups were inevitable, but these were easily outweighed by the sporting way in which the eighteen matches were played at clubs around the South East of England. Burma were thrashed by India in Worthing. Like their national hockey team, the Indian footballers, nine of whom played barefoot, were extremely light and nimble in playing on grass instead of their accustomed hard ground. They did not shirk tackles but their finishing was atrocious and they even managed to miss a penalty.

The Egyptians' ball control was outstanding but they too were accustomed to hard dry ground and were disadvantaged in playing the Danes on a wet evening when the grass was slippery. They were coached by Eric Keen who had played wing half for Derby County and England, and had two brilliant inside forwards in Mohammed Guindy and Kerim el Sakr. 'Guindy was a massive fellow, as black and as tough as ebony, yet with a delicate touch with the ball,' wrote Bernard Joy, 'while Sakr was a ball-juggler, able to run from one end of the field to the other with the ball balanced on head or shoulder.'

China was in the grip of civil war between the Nationalists and Communists and Chiang Kai-Shek, the Nationalist leader, declared any man of Chinese origin could represent the country. Their football managers had looked for players in Saigon, Manila and Singapore, which was still a British colony. The inside forward, 23-year-old administrator Chia Boon Leong, was among four from Singapore competing in London. 'We were all very excited because we had never been to Europe before. To see Hyde Park was so thrilling,' he remembered. 'We had already toured as a team to the Philippines, Indonesia and Bangkok so we were used to playing together.' The Chinese were drawn against Turkey at Walthamstow in east London. 'Turkey were a tough side, mostly picked from the army, some had no shoes. We were only one down at half time but then our centre forward was injured and we had no substitutes. We lost four-nil. But we were not downhearted.'

The Korean team, who had spent three months

travelling to London, were smaller than most other players and used to playing shorter matches. Their coach had played for Japan in 1936 and now, in middle age, he was at inside left. Everyone was amazed that they beat Mexico, but not surprised when Sweden then beat them 12–0 at Crystal Palace.

On the last Thursday and Friday, the final four matches were played at Wembley Stadium to sell-out crowds, bringing ticket sales for football up to nearly half a million. Prices ranged from 1/6d for the stands to a guinea for the best seats.

Denmark were coached by another Englishman, Reg Mountford. The draw had pitted them against the Italians in the second round. 'The contrast between the way the Danes obviously enjoyed their football and physical contact and the Italians' studied artistry made it the best match in the tournament,' wrote Joy, 'But it was lack of ruthlessness which probably lost them the semi-final against Sweden after twenty minutes of superb football had put them well on top. Adopting the English open and direct game, the Danes threw everything into attack, and in consequence left holes in the defence.'

Denmark's storming, breathtaking start in the semi-finals rocked their opponents, Sweden, back on their heels. A brilliant goal by outside left Holger Seebach, who ended a fifty-yard run with a fierce angled shot, put the Danes in front. Sweden maintained their methodical style and equalised after seventeen minutes with an extraordinary goal. Gunnar, the centre forward, who had stayed up-field as the Danes made an attack, realised that he was going to be played offside as his team

396

counter-attacked. Showing quick wits, he leapt into the Danish goal to remove himself from the field, and, with the goalkeeper out of position, caught the scoring header off his team mate. Within a few minutes the Swedes rattled in three more goals.

The Irish too were handicapped by the loss of their cream of talent to professional football and were beaten by Holland in the first round. The result came just as their organisers were once again threatening to pull out over their name. They nearly didn't make it to their match, as the bus taking them to the railway station got lost, and the train to Portsmouth was ready to move out as they leapt on to it.

The manager of the French delegation was predictably frustrated by the poor arrangements for his team's food, and also because although instructed to bring studded boots, goalkeeper's gloves and a change of kit, no mention had been made of bringing a football. This somewhat hampered their training, and their embarrassment got into the press. The unfortunate manager was enraged. 'The committee have without doubt decided that a football was a useless requirement.' It was not his fault, he said, it was the fault of the trainer, or if not him, then of the French Olympic Committee; and if not them, then the British Organising Committee were to blame.

Britain had won Olympic gold for football in 1900, 1908 and 1912, but had not been placed among the medals since then and few expected them to do well now. Players from England, Wales, Scotland and Northern Ireland who had never been together before had to be forged into a team.

397

This task was entrusted to Matt Busby, the Scottish manager of Manchester United. Of the twenty-two players in the squad, eleven were English, two Welsh, two Irish, and seven Scots from Queen's Park Football Club. Among them were a student, a doctor, a policeman and a soldier. 'As manager of the British Olympic team I did a job of work which I shall always regard as one of my best,' Busby recalled in 1957. 'Steering Manchester United to the championship of the Football League First Division was child's play beside the problems of sorting out a winning team from spare-time footballers from four different countries. Most of the players were strangers to each other, and all except one, Bob Hardisty from Bishop Auckland, who had played with me at Middlesbrough during the war, were unknown to me.'

Angus Carmichael, who had been a schoolboy fire-watcher in Glasgow, had joined Queen's Park soon after he had left school and begun studying at veterinary college. 'Queen's Park attracted young footballers who were too young for professional teams,' he said. 'The goalkeeper Ronnie Simpson was the youngest player ever to have made his debut for the club, a month before his fifteenth birthday. Many older players had returned after the war, but by 1946 half the team had turned professional. I had only been in the first eleven two years when I was picked for the Olympic team.'

Eric Lee from Chester at centre half and Eric Fright beside him at left half were the backbone of the team. Denis Kelleher, a stocky, Irish doctor from Barnet in north London, was a forward who had played for Northern Ireland and Middlesex Wanderers before the war. As a naval lieutenant he had been captured at Tobruk when his ship was sunk, and taken via Sicily to a prisoner-of-war camp in Germany. For three years he learnt German and then, posing as a Dutch Merchant Navy officer, walked to the Baltic coast where he boarded a neutral Swedish cargo ship going to Stockholm. Three weeks later he walked into his parents' home in London and three days after that he played for Barnet Football Club, scoring both goals in a 2–0 victory.

Busby wrote:

There were some fine characters in my squad. Hardisty's successes between 1947 and 1957 earned him the right to be classed as one of Britain's greatest-ever unpaid footballers. Tommy Hopper was one of the most courageous players with whom I have ever been associated. Harry McIlvenny and Eric Lee, the comedians of the party, were both excellent footballers. It was a pleasure to work with such men, though I wondered what I had taken on. This was a job presenting a real challenge, and I realised right from the start that many hectic weeks of hard graft lay ahead. The Manchester United players were wonderful, spending hours of their own closed-season break coaching and encouraging the amateurs in every possible way. They had just won the FA Cup, and might have been excused if they had chosen to emigrate rather than perspire at Old Trafford, but they all weighed in with the big job.

Present too was Tom Curry, the legendary trainer now in his forties, who had made over 200 appearances for Newcastle United in the 1920s.

'Staying at the Midland Hotel in Manchester was a stylish treat,' Carmichael remembered. 'Tom Curry would come round and tell us to go to bed at ten o'clock. Apparently his professional footballers always obeyed his bedtimes, but we ignored him. Many of the Olympic players were quite mature: they had already been through the war.' The seven Scots players naturally stuck together. Jimmy McColl remembered:

During my four years playing at Queen's Park, we were always in the First Division and even as amateurs we had already knocked Rangers off the top of the league. So we had a fair amount of confidence when facing up to top-class teams. What we lacked more than anything was familiarity with our new colleagues from England, Wales and Ireland. Matt Busby insisted the team met every weekend from May in Manchester and we played Manchester United in several friendly matches for practice. They looked down their noses at us 'amateurs' but I reckoned being premier league in Scotland we were just as good. Our ground in Scotland is the greatest in Europe.

There was still a large hole in the roof of the Old Trafford stand, left by an air raid.

'I handled them as I would professionals,' wrote Busby. 'I worked them like slaves and not once did

I hear a word of complaint. They deserved a lot of credit for the spirit and enthusiasm with which they tackled a strenuous routine, especially as they were not accustomed to concentrated training.'

Stanley Rous, the secretary of the Football Association, organised warm-up games in Switzerland, Holland and France. 'On the 7th of July I graduated as a veterinary surgeon,' Carmichael remembered. 'That evening I caught the night sleeper to London and flew to Basle to play against Switzerland.'

'The British team was beaten, well beaten, by the Dutchmen on their home ground,' wrote Busby. 'Although that match revealed certain encouraging signs to indicate that my task was not entirely hopeless.' Following this tour Busby summoned the players for two weeks at Grove Hall Hotel, on the Thames near Reading. Although it cost most of them lost wages, they all turned up. Training conditions were not ideal and they had to use the hotel lawns and a dilapidated tennis court. Difficulties continued when they moved to Uxbridge for the Games. 'The facilities were more for an RAF barracks than Olympic competitors,' recalled McColl, by profession a ship's draughtsman.

'We used to go down to the canteen at Uxbridge for a cup of Horlicks before bed and sit and listen to Matt Busby,' said the hockey player Neil White. 'He'd pull out a packet of cigarettes and pass them round, so no one paid much attention when I helped myself at the end of the line. Busby did not motivate in his evening talks, it was late-night prep planning. He had dozens of set moves and all the players knew what they had to do in different situations.'

The Football Association supplied a kit of white shirts with a Union Jack badge and black shorts, but players were expected to provide their own boots. The British Hosiery & Knitwear Export Group also donated sweaters, scarves and red stockings. 'Matt Busby told us we could treat the new tracksuits as walking out gear,' said Jimmy McColl. 'The English FA lent us second-hand tracksuits, which had been used by the English team, for our training. When the Games finished we had to hand in the new tracksuits or pay £5.'

'We were a cheerful confident crew,' wrote Busby, 'as we prepared to meet our first round opponents at Highbury Stadium.'

For their opening game at Highbury on 31 July they were drawn against Holland—the same team that had severely beaten them in the friendly only weeks earlier. The Dutch now took full advantage of the leniency of the Danish referee Vlad Laursen, to lead 1–0 and control play for most of the ninety minutes. But the British had improved by a surprising amount and, in the dying moment, a left-foot shot by their inside forward Weilkes took the match to extra time. The man of the match was their other inside forward, the Irishman Denis Kelleher, whose dribbling and passing brought the British increasingly into the match. It was not pretty. Tommy Hopper from Bromley left the field with concussion, his face covered in blood, though he insisted on returning. Gwyn Manning was another victim of the exceptionally robust Dutch tackling, but struggled on gallantly and the players made up for what they lacked in technical ability with team spirit and enthusiasm.

Both teams found goals easier to come by as the other team grew tired and the British eventually triumphed 4–3. Their unexpected triumph had taken two hours in tropical heat, and when Harry McIlvenny of Bradford scored the winning goal, Tommy Hopper collapsed unconscious.

This victory re-established much of the prestige that amateur football had lost since the war. Few had expected Britain to reach the second round but Busby had rubbed off the rough edges and welded the team together to make the best use of his talented individuals. 'Our next match was against France at Craven Cottage,' he wrote. 'Although the game was something of an anti-climax after the stirring events at Highbury, the British lads won again, the score being 1–0. We had reached the semi-final, and were drawn against Yugoslavia, all virtual professionals, at Wembley.'

'Yugoslavia's style was similar to Moscow Dynamo,' reported Bernard Joy, 'played with much progress across the field. Usually the Yugoslavs appeared to walk the ball into the net.' On this occasion they chose to breach the British defence by shooting from a distance and the goalkeeper Kevin McAlinden was kept busy turning shots round his post. Nonetheless, the visitors were too strong and Yugoslavia won 3–1. Jimmy McColl remembered:

By the time we reached the semi-finals we felt comfortable with our colleagues. We were disappointed at the result but Yugoslavia had been training together for four years and it showed in their performance. I noticed that

403

every player who received the ball always had two others to pass to. It sounds simple but it worked. There were no outstanding players in their team but they took up position immediately one of their colleagues received the ball.

The two losing teams still had to play for the bronze medal, and McColl recalled:

After the semi-finals, Matt Busby addressed the squad. His view was that as some of us had not been picked up to then, he would rather bring all the players in even at the risk of losing. We immediately all agreed that that was how we felt too.

In that last match, Britain played against one of the most talented international teams ever fielded by Denmark. In heavy rain, on a slippery pitch, the centre forward Harry McIlvenny put Britain in front and when the Danes went 2–1 up, the Reading policeman Bill Amor converted a penalty to equalise. However, the Danish centre forward Karl Praest scored a fine goal from the left wing and then headed a fifth and Denmark won by five goals to three.

Busby was disappointed not to have won the bronze but he could justifiably claim that Britain had done better than anyone had anticipated, particularly given that his team had been picked by Olympic selectors without his assistance. 'If only I had picked my own team, we would have done even better,' he said. 'It was not really encouraging to have twenty-two unknowns thrown at me in the hope that "Matt Busby will sort them out"! To give credit where it is due, once the players were in my charge, the officials gave me full freedom to select my team for each match. I got a great kick out of working with such a grand set of amateur footballers.' In February 1958, Tom Curry, together with eight Manchester United footballers and eight sports journalists, was killed in the Munich air disaster. Matt Busby was seriously injured.

The final, on the evening of Friday 13 August, pitted the Yugoslavs against Sweden. The Swedish were very strict on maintaining amateurism in their national World Cup team, and so could assemble an Olympic team who had been playing together for years. Their coach was an Englishman, the practical and energetic George Raynor. 'Sweden had power, control and polished teamwork, and modelled their play on the English professional teams,' wrote Bernard Joy:

Gunnar Nordahl was the best centre forward in the Olympics: big, strong and fast, he was the spearhead of their attack. On either side of him were first-class inside men—Gunnar Gren, an accurate shot, and the elusive Garvis Carlsson. The polished Knut Nordahl was right back while the third Nordahl brother, Bertil at centre half, never knew when he was beaten. No man allowed his individuality to shine at the expense of his teamwork.

The wet and heavy pitch at Wembley made for a tough final. The British referee William Ling wore tweed shorts and a matching jacket with his football boots. Sweden went ahead and Bobek equalised with a fierce shot. Gunnar Nordahl wrested back control with an inter-passing move that took him to the edge of the area and through to score a memorable goal. Bill Ling's refereeing was weak and Bertil Nordahl twice escaped punishment for fouls which rattled the Yugoslavs, who lost their rhythm. 'The Swedes were not put out of their stride by the intricate and often bewildering pattern-weaving of the Yugoslavs,' wrote Bernard Joy. 'They were the first to recover after one or two players on both sides had been carried away by the excitement of the moment.

Sweden were worthy winners of the gold by three goals to one. Gren, Gunnar Nordahl and Leidholm went on to play for Naples as 'The GreNoLe Trio' and Nordahl still holds the record score of any Olympic football tournament, with seven goals in 1948. Sweden was the last non-Communist football team to win Olympic gold until France won in 1984.

As the football fans filed out, the goal posts were removed and the stadium was prepared for the fourteenth and last day of the Olympics.

25

LET US BE GLAD!

The final competition at Wembley, and of the Games, was the equestrian event. After all the rain during the second week, a bright hot sun had returned on Saturday 14 August, and a capacity crowd was thrilled by the spectacle of the riders, whose military browns were enlivened by splashes of huntsman's pink, set against the green turf and colourful jumps. 'The arena looked most attractive and one cannot help feeling that the 84,000 spectators, many of whom were probably seeing high class jumping for the first time, must have realised how exciting a well organised jumping contest can be,' reported *The Times*.

Stables had been built behind the stadium and they proved a big draw to horse lovers. One visitor was Captain Xavier Bizard of France, a brilliant rider who had competed in the George V Cup in 1937 on a horse called Honduras. Bizard had last seen Honduras in 1940, in the stables of the National Cavalry School in Saumur in the Loire Valley. After the Germans captured the town, Bizard assumed his horse was dead. But now, lo and behold, here he was, in the US stable and renamed Nippy—he had been liberated in 1945. When Bizard, full of emotion, revealed how old he was, his rescuers withdrew Honduras/Nippy from the competition.

The contest had begun two days earlier at the army training grounds at Aldershot. There were six sets of Olympic medals on offer: individual and team dressage; individual and team three-day event, which included cross-country; and individual and team showjumping, also referred as the Prix des Nations. Requiring talent, stamina and split-second judgement, the equestrian event is the only Olympic contest featuring the human relationship with animals, and the horses' strength, courage and intelligence contribute to the result. Equestrian events originated in the army, where the skills acquired in hunting, polo and steeple-chasing were considered part of an officer's training. Although the cavalry no longer had a role in warfare, the ideal of the hussars and the cavaliers lived on. 'The authorities realised the virtue of horsemanship as a means to develop decision, dash, and an "eye for the country", an invaluable military gift,' wrote John Board in the *Royal Armoured Corps Journal*. Two captains actually named Chevalier took part in 1948 and one of them won a gold medal for France.

The equestrian event was still limited to male commissioned officers and there had been much discussion about whether military uniforms could be worn. Lord Burghley was against it but he was reminded that British soldiers had competed in the recent Winter Olympics in uniform and the King had appeared in naval uniform at the Opening Ceremony, so he was unable to insist. The British team included a brigadier, two lieutenant-colonels and three majors, and the Spanish team was led by a general and included three colonels. Midway through the team dressage an official noticed that Gehnall Persson of Sweden was wearing a sergeant's cap. The Swede continued and won

408

gold, only to be disqualified months later for not being a commissioned officer. The team's gold medals were returned and awarded to the French.

The dressage, which had taken place on the first day, consisted of a series of disciplined manoeuvres while cantering, trotting and walking. 'It called for an exceedingly high standard of horsemanship in which only a finely schooled horse, balanced, supple, light, free, bold and yet intelligently submissive, could hope to gain a place,' wrote R.A. Brown, Secretary of the British Horse Society. Designed to be well beyond the ability of ordinary good riders, the event attracted only nine entries, none of them from Britain. The French team, who were later awarded the gold, were led by Captain André Jousseaume, aged fifty-four, who had been in the team when they had won gold in 1932 and silver in 1936, and who also won silver for individual dressage. Hans Moser of Switzerland won the gold medal for individual dressage on his horse Hummer.

On the second day, the competitors had faced a gruelling endurance test on roads, tracks and across country, with thirty-four jumps which included a concrete wall and fences erected at awkward angles. R.A. Brown wrote:

Some of the competitors seemed disappointed with the character of the land over which they had to ride. It was obviously an army exercising ground, rather than the grassy velvet of the typical English hunting country of their dreams. They had not appreciated that most English meadows, so velvety in the damp of an English autumn, turn to concrete of an English

409

August; nor that one cannot gallop across an English county in the height of a farming season; nor, perhaps, that the best hunting counties are mostly far distant from the essential facilities needed for a competition on this scale.

The third day brought the competitors to Wembley Stadium for the showjumping event. There were nineteen difficult jumps, from over five foot high to a water jump nearly fifteen feet long. *The Times* reported:

> The course was formidable but well laid out, a thorough test for horse and rider. Though bright sunshine enhanced a vivid scene, owing to heavy rain and the activities of the footballers the previous evening, the going was terribly deep and some of the take-offs became really boggy. It is only a very bold horse under a superlative horseman who will jump consistently from an uncertain foothold. There was a remarkable number of refusals, which are the exception rather than the rule in this, the highest form of show jumping. But neither horses nor riders had ever jumped in this arena before and the occasion was one of very great nervous strain.

Only twenty-three out of the forty-four horsemen completed the course.

The British team consisted of Lieutenant-Colonel Harry Llewellyn in hunting pink and Lieutenant-Colonel Nicoll and Major Carr in uniform. Llewellyn owned two of the British horses—his own mount Foxhunter, and Kilgeddin ridden by Nicoll.

Llewellyn was thirty-seven, son of a Welsh colliery owner, and educated at Oundle School where he had learnt to shoe his own horses. A keen steeplechaser, in 1936 he had come second in the Grand National. In 1947, the family's coal mines had been nationalised and Llewellyn had decided to become the best showjumper in Britain. He studied the records of almost a thousand horses before buying the Norfolk-bred Foxhunter, an upstanding seven-year-old golden-bay gelding, for £1,500. For a year Llewellyn felt 'There is very little contact between my brain and his,' but with careful training, they built up an exceptional rapport. He wrote:

Foxhunter has always been a most courageous battler, especially as the fences have gone higher. He seems to realise that he has to make an extra effort, and he jumps big fences cleaner and in better style than small ones. Combined with this incredible courage goes a surprising calmness. He is invariably cooperative and even when the pace is furious, he checks willingly to a gentle pressure on the rein. I always felt that Foxhunter was a bit of a show-off. When he was being schooled in the big ring he would very quickly become bored— but not if he had a crowd of admirers.

At one prize-giving, Foxhunter munched the flowers decorating the hat worn by a Swiss general's wife. This time Llewellyn and Nicoll came joint seventh. Carr on Monty, named after

General Montgomery, had a disastrous round, which began with a refusal, and he came nineteenth. 'The performance of the British team was most gratifying for they had been able to train for a scant six months whereas all the other competitors had been two years or more in steady preparation,' wrote *The Times*.

The riders who surprised everyone that day were the Mexicans, Captains Uriza Castro and Valdez Ramos and Colonel Mariles Cortés. Their wiry horses would have looked at home on a polo ground but turned out to be bold and careful jumpers, beautifully schooled and ridden with great precision and elegance. *The Times* reported:

With a beautiful display of horsemanship, the very last competition had the most perfectly dramatic, exciting, and friendly ending. The last horseman, Colonel Mariles Cortes of Mexico, rode solitary into the stadium. Excitement among the spectators mounted steadily as it was soon obvious that here was an outstanding rider. Mariles showed a perfect combination of control and impulsion and, wisely, took no chances by impetuousness. There was a tense hush as Arete, a high jumper of great reputation, faced each succeeding obstacle. He made only one semblance of a mistake at the fifteenth jump and finished brilliantly. After he had landed safely over the final jump, there was an outburst of applause for his immaculate round. It was a magnificent performance and a thrilling climax to an intensely exciting event.

Cortés gave one of the finest ever performances

in showjumping history, securing the Prix des Nations event for the Mexican team and winning the individual gold for himself. Uriza won the individual silver on his small but beautifully formed liver-chestnut Hatvey. The Spanish, riding Irish horses, showed great quality and confidence and came second; and as no other full team completed the course, the British team won bronze.

'Throughout the afternoon a packed stadium had cheered with zest and full appreciation the feats of horsemanship necessary to survive the exacting test of the Prix des Nations,' reported *The Times*. 'It was rather surprising when one thought of the masses of motor vehicles parked outside. When the last victory ceremony had been performed, and the two successful Mexican cavalry men and one French chevalier in hunting attire had been cheered off the field, most of the impedimenta of equestrianism quickly disappeared.'

*   *   *

The Closing Ceremony, which began as soon as the equestrian events were over, was small and low-key compared to the opening one. 'I was reluctant at first to go to the Closing Ceremony,' said the New Zealand weightlifter Maurice Crow. 'The Opening, with its doves of peace and our nervous and stammering King had brought a lump to our throats.'

'They asked us to go to the closing ceremony at Wembley, but I was too tired,' boxer Ron Cooper said. 'Johnny Wright and I ate haddock and egg at home. That was our closing ceremony.'

'The music of the massed bands of the Brigade of Guards sounded the re-entry of the flags,' reported *The Times*. 'The wooden tablets, euphemistically described as shields, bearing the names of the countries were carried by Boy Scouts, in the sunlight which had kindly returned.'

Reg Allen was a Boy Scout from Brixton, on a camping holiday in Epping Forest:

Getting out of Brixton was the highlight of our year. The Scout leaders didn't want to come, so us boys were on our own. One day we were asked if we had our scout hats with us, and what condition they were in. We were needed to take part in the closing ceremony of the Olympic Games. We set about ironing our wide hat-brims flat. I used a tin mug filled with hot water. We were loaded on to a bus to Wembley, and watched the finals of the show jumping. We were quite excited as this was the first time any of us had been this far away from home. At the Closing Ceremony some of us carried flags and others placards with the name of the country. We went snake-like across the arena and waited for what seemed a long time in rows. That was a bit boring, just standing there.

All the competitors had been invited but many were already on their way home, and the organisers had wisely omitted plans for them to join the procession. The King and Queen had already departed for Balmoral in time for the start of grouse shooting on 12 August. The Royal Box was occupied by the Duke of Edinburgh, the US

414

ambassador, the Maharajah of Jaipur and various other dignitaries. When the time came, three flags were raised: the Greek flag representing the birthplace of the Olympics, the Union Flag and the flag of Finland which was to be the next host country in 1952.

Sigfrid Edström, chairman of the IOC, spoke from a platform made of white-painted corrugated iron.

The spirit of the Olympic Games, which has tarried here awhile, sets forth once more. May it prosper throughout the world, safe in the keeping of all those who have felt its noble impulse in this great festival of sport. They competed with the highest efforts they could muster, but in spite of the fight they remain friends. Ties of brotherhood and friendship have been formed, which will always remain. We exercise our sport not only for the joy we obtain and for the physical advantages it gives us, but also to improve the physical health of our nation. The Olympic Games cannot enforce peace, to which all humanity aspires, but it gives the opportunity to all the youth of the world to find out that all men on earth are brothers.

At six o'clock precisely, Edström handed the Olympic flag to the Mayor of London, the flame was extinguished, and a new anthem rang out. The tune of 'Let Us Be Glad' was the familiar 'Londonderry Air' ('Danny Boy'), with words by A.P. Herbert, chair of the Olympic Literature Committee. Conducted by Sir Malcolm Sargent, the choir led the packed stadium in singing:

415

Let Us Be Glad

The race is run, the winner wears the laurels,
But you and I not empty go away;
For we have seen the least unkind of quarrels,
The young men glowing in the friendly way.

Refrain:
Let us be glad—but not because of winning:
Let us go home one family today.
God make our Games a glorious beginning,
And hand in hand, together guide us on our way.

If all the lands could run with all the others,
And work as sweetly as the young men play,
Lose with a laugh, and battle as brothers,
Loving to win—but not win every day.

'Most of us kept our emotions in check until we all sang the closing song,' said Maurice Crow. 'It was about going home better people, because of what we had witnessed in the previous two weeks. Not a dry eye in the place after that.'

Nobody cared that, with the heatwave at the start, and the torrential rain after that, the weather had been the worst in Olympic history.

26

TIDYING UP

On Sunday 15 August the new editor of the *Observer*, David Astor, wrote:

> Enormous crowds, beating the 1936 Berlin record, have packed the stadium careless equally of scorching sun and drizzling rain; and with limited resources we have managed to offer a hospitable welcome to great numbers of competitors and visitors from abroad. We can take some credit also for having entered a team for every event, including basket-ball. All this we have done quietly, with none of the nationalistic ostentation which travestied the Olympic spirit in Berlin. We can feel modest pride that the London Games have been one of the most successful of these festivals of sport and quite the most harmonious on temper. May we not claim to be leading contenders for the honourable title, Enemies of Nonsense?

On the evening of the closing ceremony, the Organising Committee held a party for all the remaining competitors. 'We had had hardly any contact with other teams, even at Uxbridge,' said hockey player John Peake. 'But right at the end, we came across many of them, at the farewell gathering at the Hurlingham Club. That was a great party for indulgence, in such a happy atmosphere, tinged with relief and pride.'

'Macdonald Bailey had friends in the rag trade,' said the hurdler Mary Glen Haig. 'He got us women smart party frocks. None of us could have got frocks like that on our clothing coupons. That was really rather thrilling.' A budget of five shillings per person had been set to cover bridge rolls, cheese straws, trifles, jelly, lemonade, cider and fairy lighting. The competitors enjoyed dancing and fireworks, while the International Olympic Committee and the British organisers drank wine and spirits in a private room.

The IOC does not recognise the ranking of countries by the number of medals won, but the press has never been able to resist it. The USA came top with eighty-three medals, thirty-eight of them gold. 'American Athletes Sweep the Olympics', shouted a headline in *Life* magazine, above photographs of their medal winners. To everyone's surprise, Sweden came second, taking home forty-four medals, of which sixteen were gold. 'When looking at the Swedish success story in London,' a Swedish newspaper admitted, 'one has to keep in mind that Swedish sports have not suffered as much as some neighbouring countries. Many other countries had not yet recovered from the devastating Second World War.'

The home nation had won three gold medals, but none of them at Wembley. 'I learned the Swedish national anthem—they won so many medals, ' said tele-printer operator Eileen Mitchell. 'Maybe it was because they had not just fought a war. We yearned to hear our own British national anthem but the only time was when Arthur Wint won the hurdles for Jamaica, which as a colony of Britain still used "God Save the King".'

France, despite a very difficult war, came third with twenty-nine medals. Of the fifty-nine nations that took part, thirty-seven won at least one medal. Britain came twelfth with a haul of twenty-three medals. 'We didn't mind,' said the gymnast Frank Turner. 'We'd already won by putting the Olympics on. Anyway, it showed that Britain didn't cheat.' Great Britain had not done much better or worse in winning medals than in the previous four Olympics.

'The Games went on smoothly and splendidly to a majestic and moving end,' said Edström a few days later. 'When 85,000 spectators sang together "Let Us Be Glad", my eyes were filled with tears and I was not alone. I say a hearty Thank You to Britain.' Edström then announced that he would retire after the next Olympics.

The British Consul in Seoul wrote to the Foreign Office to report that 'Dr Chung Han Pum, head of the Korean team, was delighted with the King and enchanted by the beauty and charm of the Queen. Shop assistants were also kind and tea shop girls even lent the Korean athletes money to pay for their tea and buns.'

In a letter to *Picture Post*, Ingemar Garpe, a Swedish spectator, commented, 'It was a pity that the starts were not punctual but in no country could one have found such friendliness and politeness. Though one small but quite important point: it would all have been so much smoother if we could have had a teaspoon each when we had tea in a restaurant. No matter how many we were in a party, always one spoon. We laugh at it, of course, but it's just one of those tiny touches that make a visitor recoil.'

The general consensus was favourable. 'The success of the Games completely confounded those critics who had pessimistically forecast dire failure and international discord,' wrote John Macadam of the *Daily Express*. Viscount Portal wished all the competitors 'the hearty clasp of congratulations. For the Games fortnight brought together more different types of temperament than there are circles in the Olympic badge: Dutch phlegm, English sangfroid, Mediterranean volatility among them.'

'One thing about the British,' wrote Denzil Batchelor the following year, 'we may not win all the races, but we laugh loudest when we don't. Against all odds the English have done it again. They have done it too, on a shoe-string: on the smell of an oily rag.' Batchelor claimed to have met a South American journalist in the press bar who told him, 'I am laughing for you. Your weather was like a comedy on English weather—first too hot to breathe, and then so wet it was a waste of time to have an Olympic Pool. But in all fairness I am laughing because of your fantastic English runners and jumpers. God bless you English. Always you give the rest of the world something to laugh at.'

The Games had been so friendly that *The Times* thought it worthy of comment:

It is necessary to come to a delicate subject, namely, the absence of disputes. These, which had been hitherto regarded as inevitable, were few indeed and not to be taken too seriously.

One observer saw no single manifestation of discontent. When we recall how cross people can get and how rude they can be to one another over the most trifling points in purely domestic games, there is much cause for congratulation over the general good temper that prevailed. An obvious example was the disqualification of the American team in the 400 metres relay race owing to a venial error of a judge, and its subsequent rectification on photographic evidence. The verdict was received with decency and dignity and its reversal of our runners' victory, even though our only one, was in the circumstances far more bitter than sweet.

Considering the large numbers of athletes involved, the risks they took and the often slippery, wet conditions, the incidence of accident and injury at the Games was surprisingly low. There were three major fractures, two dislocations of the shoulder and one case of concussion. Most of the medical problems treated by the Games' medical director Sir Arthur Porritt and his team were not related to sport at all. Seventeen men and ten women had tonsillitis, twenty-three men had boils and nine had conjunctivitis.

Crime was also low. After a week, detectives in Torquay had made no progress in finding two Olympic flags, which had cost the council £6 each. One went missing from the railway station at about the time the night sleeper left for London. The other was taken from the Marine Spa a few days after a foreigner had offered an official £35 for a flag. However, the Torquay Borough Engineer reported that fifty ladies' hats and twelve gents' hats had been left behind, compared to none throughout the summer of 1947.

*   *   *

Tidying up had to be done quickly, especially at Wembley Stadium where they could ill afford to lose any more revenue from greyhound racing. The cinder running track was removed and relaid at Eaton Manor sports club in London and only two weeks later the greyhounds were tearing round the track again. Sir Arthur Elvin bought what was left of the wine stock that Viscount Portal had brought to the stadium, including 134 bottles of port at 19 shillings each. Surplus wood donated by Sweden and Finland for the floor of the Empress Hall was sold and the amount covered the Argentine Olympic Committee's cheque for £280, which had bounced.

Considerable expenditure was recouped by selling off other equipment, including equestrian jumps and wrestling mats. The Firefly dinghies, built at £150 each, were sold for £135, and a yachting trolley which had cost £20 was sold for £25. The Olympic flags flown at the housing centres were offered for £2 10s each; basketballs went for 35 shillings each. Wallingford Rowing Club won the ballot to buy the British Eight for £230 and raced it until 1960. The Amateur Swimming Association bought the springboards and Mr R. Hodgson bought eight water polo balls for £28. Weightlifting equipment was sold for £180 and the forty horses bought for the modern pentathlon, which were now in peak condition, were all auctioned off.

On 14 August the last Olympian left the Richmond Park camp, and it was returned to the War Office Signals Regiment. During the Suez Crisis of 1956 it served as a reception centre for evacuated families and when it was dismantled in 1965, one Olympic hut was re-erected at the New Malden Rifle and Air Pistol Club, where it remains in use today.

In December 1947 the Organising Committee had estimated the cost of mounting the Games at £743,000. When they sat down to calculate the actual expenditure, the figure came to £732,268. Wembley Stadium was compensated for the loss of £92,500 from the suspension of greyhound racing. Robert Hart & Sons, builders, waited until October to send in their invoices. The Ministry of Works and the Air Ministry knew they had to wait until the Games were over to be paid for their accommodation but when they heard rumours of a profit, they submitted inflated bills. In a classified Cabinet document, Attlee informed them that this was 'not on' and they would have to accept their original quotes.

The cost to the Ministry of Supply of transporting more than a hundred separate parties, over a total of 345,966 miles, was £28,000. The Finance Committee calculated that if teams had made their own arrangements the bill would have come to £75,000. The Boy Scouts Association was paid £50 for the whole event, while Army Training Corps cadets were given three shillings a day each. A Mr Beardsall of the postal department was compensated £20 for a pair of trousers, which had been damaged while on duty by a nail in a table, on condition that he forfeit the entire suit. The cost to the British Olympic Association of their team of 440 people came to £9,838, or £22 per head, double the amount in 1936.

After paying for the crane and settling up hotel bills, Torquay Town Council was left with a loss of £9,500. The Mayor and Corporation set off for London and met Viscount Portal, who agreed that the Organising Committee would settle it. Once all the bills had been paid, a handsome surplus of £29,420 was declared. Although tickets for the Games had been exempt from Entertainment Tax, the Inland Revenue now laid a claim on this profit. Months of argument followed and eventually the Committee were forced to pay £9,000 in tax. When the Committee was wound up in 1952, the remaining assets of £15,333 were donated to the IOC.

A portion of the profit had been used to publish a 600-page official report, relating to every practical detail of the Games from the design of the torch to the speed of every runner. It was intended as an aid for future Olympic planners but by the time it came out in 1951, priced at two guineas, the Helsinki Games were almost underway and sales were low.

One reader of the report was not happy. Mr Ellibank, a director of Wembley Stadium Ltd, was enraged to discover that the role of his organisation had been passed over in silence:

Where are any expressions of gratitude to Sir Arthur and Wembley, even of the faintest kind? The answer is 'nowhere'. There should be at least *some* expression of gratitude on the part of the Olympic Committee to Sir Arthur and the company for their ready assistance in making it possible for the Olympiad to be staged at Wembley. How extremely kind and gracious of them to 'invite' Sir Arthur to sit in such august company when it was Sir Arthur who was the presiding genius. Not a single hint of appreciation for the very generous financial assistance of nearly £100,000 free of interest and not payable until after the event. The omission in this report to pay the slightest tribute to Sir Arthur and his Wembley staff for the outstanding part they played is so *marked* that the obvious question must be asked 'What kind of people are they who directed all the credit for the success of the Olympiad to themselves?'

Sir Arthur himself remained upbeat about his achievements. 'The dismal Jimmies who prophesied a failure have been put to rout,' he said. 'The Games were devoid of any so-called international incidents. The attendance figures have been the highest-ever at any Olympics. At Wembley alone, well over a million people attended, in 33,000 cars and countless bicycles and buses.' His sentiments were shared by the sixth-formers writing in the magazine of Wembley County School:

The bright, cheerful hats of Scandinavians; the flowing, graceful robes of eastern women; the attractive national costumes of Europeans; the wide brimmed Texas Stetsons; Turkish Fezzes—all combined to make Wembley the most cosmopolitan of boroughs. Our sense of humour has been stirred by athletes lying on the ground furiously pedalling invisible aerial bicycles, or by news-film men wheeled about the field under green umbrellas. Whatever memory is especially ours, we will not forget the five linked rings and the athletes competing with one another in friendly rivalry.

Lord Burghley's claim that £1 million would be brought into the country was impossible to prove either way. Certainly the number of foreign visitors was not as large as had been hoped, mainly because their countries had their own foreign exchange problems. The Post Office did very well, selling over 240 million Olympic stamps, to a value of £3 million. But whatever the overall financial implications, the Olympics had raised morale in business and the leisure industry, and reminded the nation that they could do it, even in such dire circumstances.

AFTERWORD:
WHAT HAPPENED NEXT

'As the years roll by, what will stand out as the fadeless memories of the Games?' asked Denzil Batchelor. 'The hair-splitting victory of Mrs Blankers-Koen in the women's hurdles? Harrison Dillard, jet-propelling himself clear from that superhuman field in the hundred metres and McCorquodale hurling himself through to the finish? Zátopek running with knotted shoulders, strained face and almost camel-like gait to streak away on winged feet on that last marvellous lap that brought him to breathe hot on the neck of the staggering winner in the final dramatic strides to the tape?'

'These were the friendliest and least political of all Olympics,' said the high jumper Dorothy Tyler, who had competed in four of them. 'They were the start of the revival of athletics in Britain, the results of which we appreciate today. All sports took on a new glow after 1948.'

In 1950, Ernest Bevin unveiled a commemorative plaque on the wall of the Empire Stadium featuring the names of all those who had won gold within. It was carefully removed when the stadium was demolished in 2002 and will be remounted on the new Wembley Stadium, along with the renovated Olympic flame peristile. The new stadium seats 90,000 spectators, and its magnificent arch retains its position as a landmark of London. The water was drained from the Empire Pool and the building became the

Wembley Arena; the swimmers' changing rooms became artists' dressing rooms and the Beatles, The Who and the Rolling Stones performed there to packed and screaming audiences. In 2006 Wembley Arena had a complete refit but the pool is still beneath its floor.

Herne Hill Velodrome and Tweseldown Racecourse are still functioning, though the 1948 grandstands are no longer used. After the Olympics, Harringay Arena hosted the Horse of the Year show every year until it became a food warehouse in 1958 and was demolished twenty years later. The Palace of Engineering at Wembley and the Empress Hall in Earl's Court were also demolished in the 1970s. Torbay in Devon, Henley-on-Thames and Windsor Great Park have hardly changed since 1948.

In the New Year Honours of 1949, sport was recognised for the first time. Don Bradman, the rowing coach Harcourt Gold, who was chairman of the stewards of Henley regatta, and Stanley Rous, secretary of the Football Association, were all knighted. Viscount Portal, president of the London Olympic Games, was created a GCMG and Colonel Evan Hunter, chief administrator of the Organising Committee, a CBE. The men and women who had won Olympic medals received nothing and nor did Lord Burghley, who wondered if it was because he had recently divorced his wife.

Sir Arthur Porritt went on to preside over the Royal College of Surgeons and the British Medical Association. In 1967 he returned to New Zealand as his country's first native-born governor-general and was created Baron Porritt of Hampstead and Wanganui. Every year until Harold Abrahams' death in 1978, they dined together at exactly 7 p.m. on 7 July to commemorate the hour and day of the 100 metre final at Paris in 1924, when they had won gold and bronze.

As for Roger Bannister, watching the Olympic Games altered his whole outlook. 'Sport changed from being a jumbled striving of individual athletes and teams to a new unity, with a beauty that is evident in man's highest endeavour. The debt of loyalty that I had reserved for Oxford I now found I owed to a whole world.' He came only fourth in 1952 at the Helsinki Games but then in 1954 achieved fame by being the first to run the mile in under four minutes. He later became a consultant neurologist and Master of Pembroke College, Oxford.

The youthful hurdler Joe Birrell returned to the North West where a benefit cricket match was held in his honour and a new leather suitcase and a set of starting blocks were presented to him by Chief Constable Barnes, the chair of Barrow Athletic Club. 'Although I was out in the first heat,' he concluded, 'it was the highlight of my sporting career. The school bought me a silver watch; and the Methodist church bought me an inscribed gold one—I went from having none to two.' With no television signal yet available in Lancashire, few people knew what hurdling looked like and thousands turned up to watch his exhibition race at Barrow Rugby Ground. Birrell hoped to train as an army officer at Sandhurst but despite passing all the written examinations, he was not accepted. 'They didn't want officers with northern accents,' he said sixty years later. He did his national service as a radio mechanic in the Royal Signal Corps and then went to Kenya as a teacher where he also coached Olympic athletes.

Arthur Wint led Jamaica again to gold in the 4 x 400 metre relay at Helsinki. He later qualified as a doctor and became High Commissioner in London, a popular choice with both Jamaicans and the British public.

The Mexican rider Colonel Mariles Cortés had a sad demise. In 1964 he shot a man during a 'road rage' incident and was sent to prison. Some years later he was released under presidential pardon but in 1972 he was arrested again, this time for smuggling drugs, and he died in prison before the trial.

Harry Llewellyn and Foxhunter won Britain's only gold medal at Helsinki and together they helped to establish show jumping as a popular spectator sport. Foxhunter became such a beloved character that his autobiography was published and when he died in 1959, his skeleton was preserved by the Royal College of Veterinary Surgeons.

In 1949 Donald Finlay won the Amateur Athletics Association hurdles championship at the age of forty and set the Veteran's world record. Peter Elliot, the diver, did his national service in the RAF. He became a singer, performing regularly with the Beatles and Cliff Richard in the television series *Oh Boy*.

The US athlete Bob Mathias won the decathlon gold medal again at Helsinki in 1952, and ten years later he starred with Jayne Mansfield in a film about the first modern Olympics, called *It Happened in Athens*.

Emil Zátopek returned to Czechoslovakia with

his gold and silver medals and was promoted to First Lieutenant. He married Dana Ingrová, who went on to win a gold medal for javelin in 1952. At the same Games Zátopek's career reached its zenith when he won gold in the 5,000 metres, 10,000 metres and in the marathon—a distance he had never run before. In all, he broke eighteen world records and was the first man to run more than 20km in one hour, a record which he retained for twelve years. Ron Clarke was an Australian runner who had also broken eighteen world records but only ever won an Olympic bronze; when he visited Czechoslovakia in 1966, Zátopek acted as his host:

Emil looked after me wonderfully; nothing was too much trouble. He took me to Prague airport and, as he escorted me on to the plane, handed me a small packet with whispered instructions not to open it until I was out of Czech air space. All he added was 'Not out of friendship but because you deserve it.' I wondered whether I was smuggling something out for him. I retired to the privacy of the lavatory. When I unwrapped the box, there, inscribed with my name and that day's date, was Emil's Olympic 10,000 metre gold medal. I sat on that toilet seat and I wept.

Zátopek was a hero in his homeland, but like many others he fell from official favour in 1968 when he spoke out publicly against the presence of Soviet tanks in Prague. At the age of forty-five he was dismissed from the army and forced into a manual job. 'I ended up working 600 metres

431

underground in a uranium mine with a miner's helmet on my head,' he wrote. It was not until 1974 that he was transferred to a more congenial administrative post and when he died in 2000, at the age of seventy-eight, he was given a state funeral with full honours.

The row over the name of Ireland continued until April 1949 when the Republic of Ireland was declared, and the IOC finally agreed that the country was indeed called Ireland. Even so, a British commentator at the opening ceremony in Melbourne in 1956 referred to the team as coming from 'Eire'.

The German Olympic Committee was reconstituted in September 1949, and from 1952 to 1964 a single team represented Germany. In 1968 in Mexico City teams from the West and East competed against each other and continued to do so until they were reunited at the Games of 1992 in Barcelona.

After the Soviet Embassy officials had reported their findings on the London Games, the Soviet Union also decided to form an Olympic committee. In 1952 a huge team competed in Helsinki, bringing with them the Bolshoi ballet to entertain them and the training methods of the Imperial Ballet. The high standards they achieved were intended to demonstrate the superiority of Soviet citizens over their capitalist counterparts and thus Olympic propaganda became a weapon in the Cold War.

By early autumn 1948, Korea had been divided between a Communist-backed North and USA-backed South, a decision which led to war from 1950 to 1953. It has not competed as a single

Olympic team since then. In 1988 South Korea staged the Games at Seoul and Kee-chung Sohn, who had run the marathon in 1936 and been Korean team captain in 1948, carried the final torch into the opening ceremony at the age of seventy-six. Television pictures showed him leaping on to the podium with joy as the audience roared and wept.

The London Games left behind an important social legacy in which sport ceased to be the preserve of gentlemen amateurs. This trend was encouraged by popular culture. The fictional Alf Tupper appeared as 'Tough of the Track' in several British boys' comics between 1949 and 1969, including *Rover* and *Victor*. Alf was an eighteen-year-old working-class lad with a gift for running, who lived with his Aunt Meg and slept on a mattress on her kitchen floor. Though regarded as a 'guttersnipe' by the posh blokes from the Amateur Athletics Association, he frequently won championships on no sleep and a diet of fish and chips. Alf Tupper inspired many young people to overcome social obstacles and train as athletes.

In 1952 the International Stoke Mandeville Games attracted 130 competitors. Since 1960, the Paralympics have been held in the same year as the Olympic Games and since Seoul in 1988 they have taken place at the same venue.

At the meeting of the IOC in Helsinki in 1952, it was assumed that vice-president Avery Brundage would become the new president until Sir Arthur Porritt proposed Lord Burghley too. An election was held and Brundage won. Lord Burghley then stood as vice-president, and lost by two votes to Armand Massard of France. As president of the

IOC, Brundage continued to be controversial in his determination to ignore global politics. In 1968 he expelled sprinters Tommie Smith and John Carlos from the US Olympic team after they stood on the victory podium and raised their clenched fists in support of Black Power. Many people were surprised that after the Palestinian terrorist attack at the Olympics in Munich in 1972, in which eleven Israelis were killed, Brundage ordered the Games to continue. He opposed the exclusion of Rhodesia due to its racist policies and he did nothing to prevent the 'shamateurism' of Eastern bloc countries. He did not always get his way: he wanted to eliminate all team sports from the Summer Olympics, and abolish the Winter Games altogether. Brundage rescinded on the agreement to allow women to sail and it was not until after his retirement that women were admitted into yachting classes. Brundage died in Garmisch-Partenkirchen in Bavaria in 1975, aged eighty-seven, two years after marrying a German princess.

Great Britain ceased competing in Olympic football after 1972, hampered by professionalism and unable to resolve the problem of combining teams from the four home nations. The question of Olympic amateurism returned to the agenda in 1992 when professional footballers under twenty-three years old were permitted to play; since 1996, teams have been allowed up to three professionals and women's football has also been introduced.

Since Brundage died, women have been allowed to participate more. In 1976 they competed in basketball, sculling and rowing; in 1980 in hockey; in 1984 in the marathon, cycling road-race and pistol-shooting; and in 2000 they competed in the modern pentathlon, the triathlon, weightlifting and water polo.

Mary Glen Haig won the British women's fencing championship eleven times between 1949 and 1962. In November 1948 she was the first woman to become a member of the Amateur Fencing Association committee. She stopped fencing in her fifties and became Britain's first woman on the International Olympic Committee, only the third woman in the world to be elected.

Helen Gordon became the first Scottish woman to win a gold medal in any sport, at the Empire Games in 1950. At Helsinki in 1952, she was the only British swimmer to win a medal—the bronze in the 200 metre breaststroke. In 1994 she won three gold medals in the World Masters Games, a swimming contest for over-fifties.

The Scottish swimmer Cathy Gibson went on to own a pub, and in the 1980s she was walking one day on the beach in Ayreshire when she saw a boy in trouble about half a mile out to sea. She dived in and rescued him. 'I wasn't a spring chicken even then,' she said.

Ngaire Lane and the New Zealand team returned home on an even slower boat. 'The spirit of Olympism never leaves you,' she said sixty years later. 'Although there can only be a small percentage of the competitors who make it to the medal rostrum, the pride and the pleasure of those past memories never fades. I feel I was hugely blessed to have made the New Zealand team and had an opportunity to feel that intense pride. The friendship I made with Helen Yate, Britain's backstroke representative, has lasted ever since—

nearly sixty years so far.'

The Australian runner Shirley Strickland became a lecturer in mathematics. In 2001 she sold her Olympic medals to raise £150,000 to help save the world's forests. An outspoken campaigner, she stood for election for the Australian Democrats, whose aim was 'to keep the bastards honest'. She died in 2004.

Dorothy Tyler and Fanny Blankers-Koen, two mothers who defied all advice to give up on their ambitions, became life-long friends. When Tyler retired in 1956 after gaining her fourteenth world record, she commented, 'After that it wasn't really fair to carry on.' Sixty-five years after winning her first silver medal, she was awarded an MBE. 'What kept you so long?' asked Princess Anne. 'That's what I'd like to know,' she replied mischievously.

Fanny Blankers-Koen retired in 1955, after setting sixteen world records in eight different events and winning fifty-eight Dutch championships over a period of twenty years. Her success matched the record of four gold medals set by Alvin Kraenzlein of the USA in 1900, equalled by Jesse Owens at Berlin in 1936. In December 1999 she was voted 'Sportswoman of the Century' by the IOC and died five years later at the age of eighty-five.

The International Gym Congress agreed to standardise equipment in future competitions, and to hold them indoors. 'They realised it had all been a bit of a mess,' said George Wheedon, who soon afterwards married Joan Airey. The couple honeymooned in Winchelsea and competed together in the next three Olympics.

The gymnast Helmut Bantz met up again with

his British friends at Helsinki, though he was now competing for Germany; and at thirty-five he won the gold medal for gymnastics at Melbourne in 1956. 'We all admired Bantz, he was an excellent teacher,' Frank Turner recalled, 'and such a lovely man.' Bantz kept his British Olympic trousers all his life. 'My wife always threatens to give them to the rag man,' he said. 'But what can she know of how much the memories of captivity and its strange experience can mean to a man?'

Turner too competed in 1952 and 1956, acted as gymnastics coach in 1960 in Rome and was a judge at Barcelona in 1992. He presented a children's television series on gymnastics and worked as a stunt man in films starring Burt Lancaster and Roger Moore. Turner hopes to be chosen to bear the final torch that lights the cauldron at the London Olympics in 2012. 'The new Olympic stadium is in my manor, that's where I was born,' he said. 'I'll only be ninety years old. I hope it's me.'

APPENDIX 1: ACCOUNTS

Receipts

Revenue from tickets, etc.	£545,628
Housing, transport, feeding of competitors	
	£174,097
Miscellaneous income	£41,963
Total	**£761,688**

Expenditure

Staff wages and equipment	£121,741
Works at Wembley and other venues	£78,120
Wembley Stadium Ltd—compensation	£92,500
Government telephone and accommodation	
	£118,033
Housing and feeding of competitors	£164,644
Transport	£37,925
Insurance against cancellation (£337,000)	£7,821
Equipment of British team	£10,884
Administration	£90,557
Payment to IOC	£5,000
Entertainment & hospitality	£3,638
Permanent record at Wembley Stadium	£1,000
Office furniture (written off)	£405
Total	**£732,268**

Excess of income over expenditure, subject to income tax:	**£29,420**
Tax paid	**£9,000**

(From the *Official Report of the XIV Olympiad*, London Organising Committee, 1951)

Note: The cost of £732,268 is equivalent to about £20 million in 2008.

APPENDIX 2: UNOFFICIAL RECORDS SET IN 1948

A comprehensive list of world and Olympic records established at the Fourteenth Olympiad in 1948 can be found at www.olympic.org, the official website of the Olympic Movement.

Longest male name:
William George Ranald Mundell Laurie; British gold medal winner of coxless pairs, rowing.

Longest surname:
Araswna de Belaustegigoitia of Mexico; came last in the women's springboard diving.

Oldest athletics medal winner:
48-year-old Terence Lloyd-Johnson; British, won the bronze medal in the 50-kilometre walk.

Oldest sports competitor:
British fencer Archibald Douglas Craig, aged 61 years; was defeated in the first round.

Oldest Olympic medal winner:
John Copley; British, won a silver medal in the etchings class, at 73 years.

Youngest competitor:
Gunter Mund from Chile, aged 13 years; came last in the men's springboard diving.

Longest Olympic career:
Paul Elvstrøm from Denmark and Durwood Knowles from Britain; both sailed in the Olympics for 40 years, from 1948 until 1988.

Shortest medal winner:
Joe de Pietro from the USA; was four foot eight inches tall and won gold for bantam weightlifting.

Smallest national teams, one competitor each:
Panama (100 metres dash), Malta (100 metres dash), Singapore (high jump), Syria (swimming), Venezuela (cycling)

Largest national team:
USA: 302 competitors

Furthest distance travelled to the Games:
New Zealand: 11,801 miles, or 18,992 kilometres

Number of pairs of Y-front pants issued:
600

ACKNOWLEDGEMENTS

Thank you to the following people who gave me interviews and information about the Games:

Administration and History: Verily Anderson, Sir Roger Bannister, Michael Davison, Juliet Gardiner, John Gibbins, Pamela Hampton, Eileen Mitchell, Ian Payne, Brijesh Patel, Sonali Puri, Bryan Stokes, Sarah Waters, Gillian Wilson, Zoe Young

Athletics: Macdonald Bailey (Trinidad), Joseph Birrell, Mieke Blankers-Kasbergen (Netherlands), Stan Cox, Malcolm Dalrymple, Jack Holden, Kees Kooman (Netherlands), Lorna Lee-Price, Alistair McCorquodale, Bill Nankeville, Harold Nelson (New Zealand), John Newling, John Parlett, Tore Sjöstrand (Sweden), Dorothy Tyler MBE, Brigadier Richard Webster, Douglas Wilson

Boxing: Peter Brander, Ron Cooper

Boy Scouts and messengers: Reg Allen, Adrian Buckland, John Glenister, Peter Hammond, Tim Lowry, Donald Watson, Norman Watson

Broadcasting and newspapers: Arthur Prince, Harry Walker

Canoeing: Norman Dobson

Cycling: HRH the Duke of Edinburgh, Alan Geldard, Tom Godwin, Gordon Thomas, Robert Maitland, Paul West, Eddie and Anne Wingrave

Equestrian: Necmettin Ozcelik (Turkey)

Fencing: Dame Mary Glen Haig, Bobby Winton MBE

Football: Gary Bloom, Angus Carmichael, Chia Boon Leong (China), James McColl, Gordon D.M. McBain, Chu Chee Seng (China)

Gymnastics: Frank Turner, Meg Warren, George Wheedon

Hockey: John Peake

Rowing: Bert Bushnell MBE, Tony Butcher, Robert Collins, Rev. Michael Lapage, Anthony Purssell, Julie Summers

Spectators: Ian Adams, Joseph R. Bickley, Dick Booth, Gordon Broughton, Norman Charles, Cyril Cook, Freddie Dunkelman, A.J. Everson, Eric Ford, Sir Clement Freud, Maurice Graham, Dennis Hamley, Eric Hulse, John Lyne, George Mills, Dennis Newton, Jim Parry, Bruce Peppin, Julian Potter, Malcolm Tappit, Dick Tyler, Phebe Tyson, Norman Watson, Beryl Webster, Derek Wood

Swimming and diving: Don Bland, Peter Elliot, Ngaire Galloway née Lane (New Zealand), Cathy Gibson, Helen Gordon, Ray Legg

Weightlifting: Maurice Crow (New Zealand), Tony Flood, Wally Holland OBE, David Webster

Yachting: Peter Bruce, Charles, Bobby and Mimie Currey, Ann Dean, Paul Elvstrøm (Denmark), Lady Philippa Scott, Tim Street, Stuart Jardine, Robin McDonald, Jackie Reid, Jean Williams

Many documents were in foreign languages and I am grateful to the following for their translations: Alan Adler (Swedish), William Beinart (Afrikaans), Emma Hallencreutz (Swedish), Nickola Kakanskas (Spanish), Chloe Purcell (Spanish), Nicola Russell (French), Clare Savory

(German), Julio César González Tobaoda (Spanish), Harriet Waterston (French)

The following archivists and libraries have helped with information:
   Janet Adams, Bank of England
   Lucy Bailey, Education, Arts and Libraries, Brent Council, London
   Roger Billington, Butlins archive
   Bodleian Library, Oxford
   Wendy Coles, Amateur Swimming Association, Loughborough
   Cowley Public Library, Oxford
   Malcom Fare, National Fencing Museum, Malvern
   Ian Gawn, Royal Lymington Yacht Club
   Mark Holland, *The Times digital archives 1785–1985*, Thomson Learning
   Dr Robert Treharne Jones, Leander Club, Henley-on-Thames
   Josephine Ilagan, Sparkman & Stephens Inc., New York
   Leander Bookshop, Vasteras, Sweden
   Martin Leath and Robert Farley, Society of Olympic Collectors
   Carys Lewis, Victoria and Albert Museum
   Malcolm MacCullum and Peter Holme, National Football Museum, Preston
   Linne Matthews, *Best of British* magazine
   Tina Morton and Alex Sydney, Brent Archives, London
   Betty Moss, Alexander Turnbull Library, New Zealand
   The National Archives, Kew

445

Geoff Old, Torquay Library, Devon
Paul Owen, British Canoe Union, Nottingham
Anne Pond, Bartlett Library, Falmouth,
    Cornwall
Mark Pool, Torquay Museum, Devon
Marti Reddin, British Gymnastics Association,
    Shropshire
Jackie Reid and Peter Bartlett, Royal Yachting
    Association, Hampshire
Kelly Russell, Henley River & Rowing Museum,
    Oxfordshire
Kevin Smith, Wembley Stadium Archives,
    Plowden & Smith, London
Wesley Taylor, Wembley Stadium Ltd, London
Catherine Theakstone, Hulton-Getty Archive,
    London
Godfrey Waller, Cambridge University Library
Josephine Warburton, National Maritime
    Museum, Cornwall

The following representatives of national Olympic
associations involved in 1948 sent me their reports
and provided contacts:

Gabriel Bernsasconi, Comité National
    Olympique, France
Anthony Th. Bijkerk, Secretary-General of the
    International Society of Olympic Historians,
    Netherlands.
Chris Chan, Singapore National Olympic
    Committee
Björn Folin, Sveriges Olympiska Kommitté,
    Sweden

Press Office, Hellenic Olympic Committee
Nour Elhouda Karfoul, Syria Olympic
  Committee
Greta Larmer, New Zealand Olympic
  Committee
Linda, Liechtensteinischer Olympischer
  Sportverband, Liechtenstein
Eric Michalko, Canadian Olympic Committee
Fatolla Mosayebi and Esmail Kad, National
  Olympic Committee of Iran
Necmettin Ozcelik and Nese Gundogan,
  National Olympic Committee of Turkey
Joy Nash, Bermuda Olympic Association
Oscar Pandre, Biblioteca del Comité Olímpico,
  Argentina
Lewis Portelli, Olympic Committee of Malta
Dermot Sherlock, Olympic Council of Ireland
Amy Terriere, Ellie Shoesmith, British Olympic
  Association
DezsVad, Hungarian Olympic Committee

Sincere acknowledgements for the use of John Pudney's poem 'The Games' from The *Observer* (Copyright Guardian News & Media Ltd 1948); Souvenir Press Ltd for extracts from *My Story* by Matt Busby; and *Punch* Limited for quotations from articles by H. F. Ellis, Evoe and Neville Wallis.

I am especially grateful for the practical assistance given me by my husband Charles, my agent Simon Trewin and my editors Natasha Martin, Celia Hayley and Liz Hornby. Only they know how important their contributions have been.

447

BIBLIOGRAPHY

BOOKS

Abrahams, Harold, *Track & Field Olympic Records*, Playfair Books, 1948.

Abrahams, Harold, article in *The Olympics*, ed. J.E. Morpurgo, Penguin, 1948.

Alston, Rex, *Taking the Air*, Stanley Paul, 1951.

Aplin, N.G., et al., *Singapore Olympians: A Complete Who's Who from 1936 to 2004*, SNP International Ltd, 2005.

Bannister, Roger, *The First Four Minutes*, Putnam, 1955.

Batchelor, Denzil, *Days Without Sunset*, Eyre & Spottiswoode, 1949.

Batchelor, Denzil, and Abrahams, Harold, *World Review: The Olympic Games*, Hulton, 1948.

Beaumont, Charles L. de, *Modern British Fencing*, Hutchinson, 1949.

Bland, Ernest A. (ed.) *Olympic Story*, Rockliff, 1948.

Booth, Dick, *The Impossible Hero: A life of Gordon Pirie*, Corsica Press, 1999.

Briggs, Asa, *Sound & Vision, 1945–55* in the series *The History of Broadcasting in the United Kingdom,* Oxford University Press, 1979.

Brunnhage, Lennart, *Olympiaboken 1948*, Svenska Sportforlaget, Stockholm, 1948.

Buchanan, Ian, *British Olympians: A hundred years of gold medallists*, Guinness, 1991.

Burnell, R.D., *Swing Together: Thoughts on Rowing*, Oxford University Press, 1952.

Burnell, R.D., and Rickett, H.R.N., *A short history of the Leander Club, 1818–1968*, Leander Club, 1968.

Busby, Matt, and Jack, David, *Matt Busby: My Story*, Souvenir Press, 1957.

Commons Hansard, volumes 433–453, HMSO, 1947–49.

Coote, James, *History of the Olympics in Pictures*, Tom Stacey, 1972.

Dear, Ian, *The Royal Yacht Squadron, 1815–1985*, Stanley Paul, 1985.

Dorner, Jane, *Fashion in the Forties and Fifties*, Ian Allan, 1975.

Elvstrøm, Paul, *Elvstrøm speaks*, Nautical Publishing Company, 1969.

Fairley, Gordon, *Minute By Minute: The story of the Royal Yachting Association 1875–1982*, Royal Yachting Association, 1983.

Fare, Malcolm, *A Century of Fencing in Britain*, 2000.

Foster, Brendan, *Olympic Heroes*, Harrap, 1984.

Graham, Peter J., and Ueberhost, Horst, *The Modern Olympics*, Leisure Press, New York, 1976.

Halliday, Jim, *Olympic Weight-lifting and Body-building For All*, Pullum & Son, London, 1950.

Heerden, Ernst van, 'Die Sewe Vrese' in D.J. Opperman, *Groot Verseboek Nasionale Boekhandel*, Cape Town, 1967.

Huxley, Elspeth, *Peter Scott: Painter and naturalist*, Faber & Faber, 1993.

449

Joy, Bernard, 'Scandinavian Ascendant' in Fabian, A.H., and Green G. (eds), *Association Football*, Caxton, 1960.

Killanin, Lord, and Rodda, John, *The Olympic Games*, Barrie & Jenkins, 1976.

Knight, Donald, *The Lion Roars at Wembley*, Sabie, 1984.

Kozik, Frantisek, *Zátopek: The Marathon Victor*, Artia, 1954.

Kynaston, David, *Austerity Britain, 1945–51*, Bloomsbury, 2007.

Llewellyn, H.M., *Foxhunter*, Hodder & Stoughton, 1949.

Laing, Desmond, *XIV Olympiad: An illustrated record*, Laing, 1948.

Lyon, Lt.-Col. W.E. (ed.), *The Horseman's Year*, Collins, 1949.

Macadam, John, 'Sport in 1948', *The Butlins Holiday Book 1949–50*, Butlins, 1949.

Nankeville, Bill, *The Miracle of the Mile*, Stanley Paul, 1956.

Oaten, H.J., *Olympiad 1948* (foreword by Jack Crump), Findon, 1947.

Pilditch, James, *Can We Stay up and Watch the Bombs?*, Verulam, 1996.

Portelli, Lewis, *Malta Was There Too: Malta and the Olympics*, Lux Press, Hamrun, 1960.

Prestidge, Jim, *The History of British Gymnastics*, British Amateur Gymnastics Association, 1988.

Proctor, Ian, 'The Olympic Games', *The Yachtsman's Annual, 1948–49*, Adlard Coles, 1950.

Reid, Charles, *Malcom Sargent*, Hamish Hamilton, 1968.

Rivers, James (ed.), *The Sports Book No. 2: Britain's Prospects in the Olympic Games and in Sport Generally*, Macdonald, 1948.

Smith, Michael Llewellyn, *Olympics in Athens 1896*, Profile Books, 2004.

Thirkell, Angela, *Love Among the Ruins*, Hamish Hamilton, 1948.

Tomlin, Stan (ed.), *Olympic Odyssey*, Modern Athlete Publications, 1956.

Toohey, K. and Veal, A.J., *The Olympic Games: A social science perspective*, CABI Publishing, 1999.

Vesper, Hans Egon, *Canoeing: Fifty years in the Olympic Games*, International Canoe Federation, Yugoslavia, 1988.

Wallechinsky, David, *The Complete Book of the Olympics*, Aurum Press, 2004.

Wallis, A.J., *Olympic Who's Who, 1948*, Background Books, 1948.

Walters, Guy, *The Berlin Games: How Hitler stole the Olympic dream*, John Murray, 2006.

Webster, Lt.-Col. F.A.M., *Olympic Cavalcade*, Hutchinson, 1948.

Williamson, Margo, *The Olympic Games 1948–1972*, Paul Hamlyn, 1972.

Yogi Mayer, Paul, *Jews and the Olympic Games*, Valentine Mitchell, 2004.

NEWSPAPERS AND MAGAZINES

Barrow Evening Mail; *The Bermuda Olympian*; *Boxing News*; *The Calcutta Telegraph*; *Classic Boat*; *Children's Weekly*; *Crítica* (Argentina); *Daily Courier*; *Daily Dispatch*; *Daily Graphic*; *Daily Mirror*; *Dominion Sunday Times*; *Evening News*; *Evening Standard*; *Everybody's*; *The Horseman*; *Harrow and Wealdstone News*; *Health and Strength*; *Illustrated London News*; *Illustrated Magazine*; *John Bull Magazine*; *Kenya Weekly News*; *Life Magazine* (USA); *Liverpool Echo*; *London Calling*; *Manchester Guardian*; *Maribel* (Argentina); *Minneapolis Tribune* (USA); *La Nación* (Argentina); *New Zealand Sportsman*; *News of the World*; *North Western Evening Mail*; *The Observer*; *Ogonyok* (Moscow); *The Olympian*; *Olympic Newsletter*; *Picture Post*; *Punch*; *The Racing Pigeon*; *Radio Times*; *La Razón* (Argentina); *Reynolds News*; *Richmond Park Newsletter*; *Royal Armoured Corps Journal*; *Se* (Sweden); *Sports Historian*; *Strand Magazine*; *Sunday Chronicle*; *Sunday Dispatch*; *Sunday Empire News*; *Sunday Graphic*; *Sunday Times*; *Surrey Comet*; *The Sword*; *Tatler & Bystander*; *The Times*; *Torbay Herald and Express*; *Torquay Directory*; *Torquay Times*; *Track Stats*; *Town and Country*; *Transportation Magazine*; *Wembley County Grammar School Magazine*; *Wembley, Kingsbury and Kenton News*; *Western Morning News*; *Willesden Chronicle*; *World Sports*; *Yachting Monthly*; *Yachting World*.

PROGRAMMES AND REPORTS

XIV Olympiad 1948 Olympic Regatta and Canoe Races, 1948.

Church, R.F., Bland, E.A., and Jones, H.W., Daily programme and Information, XIV Olympiad, Press department of the Organising Committee, 1948.

The Daily Telegraph Guide to the Olympic Games and London, Geographia Ltd, 1948.

De Lotbinière, S.J. 'The BBC and the XIVth Olympiad', *London Calling: Overseas Journal of the BBC*, 24 June 1948.

Edström, S. Speech at Closing Ceremony of the London Games, IOC Bulletin, Lausanne, November 1948.

Guide to the Olympic Games and London, Daily Telegraph, 1948.

Henley-on-Thames Souvenir: Olympic Regatta, Henley Town Council, 1948.

Illustrations from the XIV Olympiad spirit in art exhibition, Victoria and Albert Museum, 1948.

Minutes of the 47th Session of the IOC, Helsinki, Bulletin du Comité International Olympique, 16 July 1952.

Municipal Entertainments, Borough of Wembley, 1948.

Official report of the XIV Olympiad, London Organising Committee for the XIV Olympiad, 1951.

Official report on Ireland's participation, XIVth Olympiad, Irish Olympic Council, 1948.

Olympic Games London 1948, Official Souvenir, 1948.

Olympic Games Via London Transport, London Transport Executive, 1948.

Olympic programmes for each day and event, McCorquodale & Son, 1948.

Opening Ceremony official programme, Olympic Committee, 1948.

The Post Office at Your Service: Olympics, GPO, 1948.

Preparations for the XII Olympic Games, Helsinki 1940, Helsinki Organising Committee, Helsinki, 1939.

Thomas, S. E. World's and British Records and Useful Visitors' Guide to London, 1948.

UNPUBLISHED DOCUMENTS

Charles Louis de Beaumont, fencing scrapbook, 'The Olympics 1948'.

British Olympic Football Committee, Minutes 1947–48, Wembley Stadium Ltd archive.

George Bushell & Sons, photographs of Henley Royal Regatta.

Comité national Olympique et sportif français, Report sur le séjour de la délégation française aux Jeux Olympiques de Londres, 1948.

Captain Charles Currey CBE RN, yachting scrapbook, 1936–1949.

Charles Currey RNVR, yachting scrapbook, 1947–1955.

Arthur McDonald, 'My life in the RAF', unpublished autobiography.

Medical Committee of the Organising Committee of 1948 Olympics, Minutes, British Olympic Association archive.

Harold Nelson, New Zealand team captain, diary July 1948.

Organising Committee. Letters 1948, Wembley Stadium Ltd archive.

Organising Committee, Report of the British organising committee for the XIV Olympiad to the IOC, September 1946, British Olympic Association archive.

Public Record Office files, Kew:
Home Office HO 45/22460.
Foreign Office: PRO/ FO 370/1629; FO 370/1592; FO 370/1595; FO 371/7876; FO

938/205.
  Cabinet file: PRO/ CAB 21/2256; CAB 124/767.
  Metropolitan Police file: PRO/ MEP 2/8026.
  Ministry of Food: PRO/ MAF 256/191.
Peter Scott, Press-cutting scrapbook, 1946–1952,
  Cambridge University Library.
Stitt-Dibden, W.G., 'The 1948 Olympics at
  Wembley' (stamps), 1959.
Torquay Borough Council, minutes, 1947–49.
Torquay Borough Council, Olympiad 1948
  yachting at Torquay, scrapbook, 1948.

WEBSITES

www.bbc.co.uk/making history

www.la84foundation.org   *Amateur Athletic Foundation of Los Angeles, Interviews by Dr Margaret Costa of Vicki Draves, 1999, and Mel Patton, 1991*

www.london2012.org

www.measuringworth.com/ukcompare/

www.news.bbc.co.uk/sport

www.olympic.org   *Official site of the Olympic Movement*

www.sporting-heroes.net

www.topfoto.co.uk/gallery/olympics/1948

www.wembleystadium.com

www.wordiq.com/definition/1948_Summer_Olympics